HUMANITIES
Self, Society & Culture

Claude Monet. *Impression, Sunrise*—1873 (dated 1872).
Courtesy of Musée de Marmottan, Paris.

HUMANITIES
Self, Society & Culture

Fourth Edition

General Editors:
William R. Hanna and Clive Cockerton

Contributors:
Hugh Armstrong, Michael Badyk, Bernadette Barber, Kathy Casey,
Melanie Chaparian, Wayson Choy, Clive Cockerton, R. Chris Coleman,
John Elias, Toby Fletcher, Jay Haddad, William R. Hanna, Don Holmes,
Jill Le Clair, Mitchell Lerner, John Maxwell, Wendy O'Brien-Ewara, Tom Olien,
Earl Reidy, Barbara Ritchie, Morton Ritts, Sarah Sheard, Antanas Sileika,
Linda Smithies, John Steckley

Editorial Committee:
Michael Badyk, Remo Brassolotto, Gary Berman, George Byrnes, Kathy Casey,
Melanie Chaparian, Wayson Choy, Clive Cockerton, R. Chris Coleman,
Brian Doyle, John Elias, Mo Farge, Jay Haddad, William R. Hanna, Don Holmes,
Michael Horwood, Joe Kertes, Mitchell Lerner, John Maxwell, Joey Noble,
Barbara Ritchie, Antanas Sileika, John Steckley, Herman Suligoj,
Maureen Wall, Donna Williamson

THOMPSON EDUCATIONAL PUBLISHING, INC.
Toronto

Requests for permission to make copies of parts of this work that are under the publisher's copyright should be directed to the publisher. Additional copies of this book may be ordered from the publisher:
Thompson Educational Publishing, Inc.
14 Ripley Avenue, Suite 105
Toronto, Ontario M6S 3N9
Tel. (416) 766-2763 Fax (416) 766-0398.

Canadian Cataloguing in Publication Data

Main entry under title:
Humanities : self, society & culture

4th ed.
Includes bibliographical references.
ISBN 1-55077-060-8

1. Humanities. I. Hanna, William R. II. Cockerton, Clive.
H85.H85   1993   001.3   C93-094698-7

Printed in Canada.
  2 3 4 5   96 95 94

Contents

~ UNIT 5 ~
ARTS AND CULTURE / 229

~ APPENDIX ~
THINKING AND WRITING SKILLS / 285

Introduction for the Student

Everyone, it seems, wants to be an individual, to be recognized as a unique and special person. Most people also relish the notion of freedom, the idea that they hold the reins, at least some of the time, in determining the course of their lives. Yet, as desirable as individuality and freedom are, very few of us want to live alone. Indeed, most of us need a community of others if we are to live well and flourish. However, the cost of living in a community is usually some sacrifice (in theory anyway) of our individuality and freedom.

Our family expects us to behave in certain ways, our friends demand a code of behaviour, and all the institutions of society, our schools, businesses, churches and government, influence and control our behaviour on many levels. So to live with others is to live with constraint, and yet if we submit to everyone's expectations of us, we run the danger of losing ourselves, our sense of who we are. A natural tension exists in every healthy life and this tension between individual and larger goals doesn't ever finally resolve itself. It is not something you grow out of; it doesn't go away. Just when you're being most dutiful, you can be haunted by the temptation to be wild. Just when you think that indulging your every whim is the answer, the heart responds to a larger call and responds to a need greater than the self.

What do you do with a tension that cannot be resolved, that resists easy answers? You can pretend it doesn't exist and be blown about by the forces of change in an unconscious way. Or you can seek to understand the great tensions and problems of our day and hopefully gain not only awareness but also some influence on how your life evolves.

This book attempts to grapple with some of the difficult problems that confront everyone, from questions of our basic human nature, to social change, to politics, to technology and to arts and culture. This is frequently a dark and complex world, and the modern student needs all the information, all the understanding, all the light he or she can get if they are to find their own way in this world. Grappling with these questions will most probably give your grey cells a good workout, and thinking skills can be developed that will be useful in all your courses at college and, even more importantly, in your place of work. The possibility of developing your high-level thinking skills through the study of this text is of real and obvious practical benefit. But along the way, not in every section or issue, but perhaps in some area, we hope you find some personal revelation and acquire some understanding that is unique to you.

UNIT 1
THE INDIVIDUAL

■ **ISSUE 1:**
Why Are We the Way We Are?

■ **ISSUE 2:**
Freedom and Constraint

ISSUE 1

Why Are We the Way We Are?

Give me a dozen healthy infants, well-formed and my own specified world to bring them up in and I'll guarantee to take any one at random and train him to become any type of specialist I might select—doctor, lawyer, artist, merchant, chief and, yes even beggarman and thief, regardless of the talents, penchants, tendencies, abilities, vocations, and race of his ancestors.

John B. Watson

We believe that civilization has been built up, *under the pressure of the struggle for existence*, by sacrifices in the gratification of the primitive impulses.

Sigmund Freud

One of the most revolutionary concepts to grow out of our clinical experience is the growing recognition that the innermost core of man's nature, the deepest layers of his personality, the base of his "animal nature" is positive in nature—is basically socialized, forward-moving, rational and realistic.

Carl Rogers

Personality

Jay Haddad

How much of our personality is learned and how much of our personality is part of our genetic endowment? How much of your personality is changeable and how much is not?

Think about yourself for a minute—would you consider yourself moody? Or shy?

If you feel that you are a moody person, from where does such a trait come? Could it have been genetically passed on to you in the DNA which you inherited from your parents? Is it perhaps an integral part of your body chemistry? Could your "moodiness" be caused by psychological tensions, by anxieties that are stored in your unconscious? Could "moodiness" be a stage you are going through? Or is it a permanent fact of your personality? Will it change? Can it change? You can ponder the same questions with regard to shyness, in fact, to any aggressive or passive behaviours you are aware of as being part of who you are.

As we begin Unit I, you will see that there are several schools of thought with respect to the nature and origin of personality; at times, the schools are not in conflict with one another but quite often there is a fundamental difference in the way in which the human personality is viewed.

A great deal of conflict often exists in the *basic assumptions* made by each school about the *nature of personality*. Your task, depending on the trait or situation you are attempting to examine, will be to evaluate critically the relative merits of each school's attempt to explain the root causes of human personality.

"You know, out of all the animal species, I reckon the human must be about the nearest to us in intelligence."

SCHOOLS OF THOUGHT

Traditional Biology

The assumption here is that humans have very little choice or free will because our biology determines personality. This "anatomy is destiny" view points to a strong causality between genetic programming and human personality. This view assumes that the 23 chromosomes you inherit from your father and the similar number you inherit from your mother will determine the person you will be. The assumption is a little like Charles Darwin's theory of "natural selection" where strong breeders, that is, people with "good genes," will have strong offspring. Perhaps "good genes" mean that particular gene combinations give some individuals a headstart on a successful life. In short, the biological view assumes humans are controlled by instincts and inborn physical capacities: you are born with your strong points and weak points and there's nothing you can really do about it.

Be aware that what one person may define as "good genes" may be totally offensive to another person. Because chromosomes may now be technically manipulated and altered by "gene engineers," many

THE TRADITIONAL BIOLOGICAL SCHOOL

The traditional biological view assumes humans are controlled by instincts and in-born physical capacities: you are born with your strong points and weak points and there's nothing you can really do about it.

SCHOOLS OF THOUGHT

SCHOOLS OF THOUGHT	MAJOR THINKERS	BASIC ASSUMPTIONS ABOUT THE NATURE OF HUMANITY
Traditional Biological	Biologists	*Human beings have no free will.* Humans are animals whose behaviours are controlled by inherited instincts, in-born physical capacities and individual physical handicaps. Humans are genetically "programmed" at birth.
Psychoanalytic	Freud	*Human beings have no free will.* Humans are not just physical beings, but complex psychological beings, controlled by powerful biological urges from within which are largely unconscious. Humans are in constant conflict between strong sexual and aggressive drives and the controls of conscience and the laws and morals of society.
Behavioural	Watson Skinner Pavlov	*Human beings have no free will.* Humans are infinitely flexible and their behaviours are controlled and shaped by the environment and the effects of its rewards and punishments.
Humanistic Existential	Rogers Maslow	*Human beings have free will.* Humans are humane and caring, motivated from within to grow and develop towards "self-actualization" or the fullest blossoming of their potential.

unspoken social, ethical, legal, political, racial and gender questions, etc., need to be raised and openly examined.

Some might argue that the biological view absolves the individual from taking any responsibility for behaviour because "I was born this way."

One could also assume that gifted or delinquent or athletic children are exempt from their parents' input because their genetic programming was with them at birth. The parents only carried the genes: the genetic inheritance caused the child's intelligence, delinquency or athletic abilities. This is referred to as the "nature" argument in the *nature vs. nurture* debate. The biological school would assume that personality is basically an inherited phenomenon, and that humans have genes which map out traits like moodiness, shyness, dominance, passivity, and so on.

Psychoanalytic School

Sigmund Freud (1856–1939) devised an interesting way to examine the dynamics of human personality. There are, he assumed, three distinct aspects of human personality:

First, there is the self we think we are, the self which attempts to deal with reality. This Freud called the *ego*. *Ego* is who we are; it's our awareness of self. It's the person we think we are and the person we display to the outside world. But *ego*, theorized Freud, is never in control of self; *id* comes first!

The *id* is our unconscious, the largest and most important part of personality. The *id* must contain the two biological instincts which govern, dominate and motivate *all* human behaviour—*eros* and *thanatos*. *Eros* is referred to as our "life" instinct, but is more generally thought of as the sex, lust, or "pleasure drive." *Thanatos* relates to our "death" instinct but more commonly it is viewed as the human drive toward aggression, hostility and destruction.

As children, the unconscious *(id)* instincts (sex and aggression) surface freely into *ego* or into behavioural action. Children can exhibit anger, rage, destruction and hatred as well as lust, pleasure, arousal and sensuality.

Soon, though, the third aspect of personality emerges: *superego*. *Superego* is, very simply, our conscience; *superego* is our *moral* sense of personality, the part of us that knows (or is supposed to know) right from wrong.

As a person grows up, psychoanalysis assumes, the biological, unconscious, real urges from the *id, eros* and *thanatos*, are no longer

Sigmund Freud

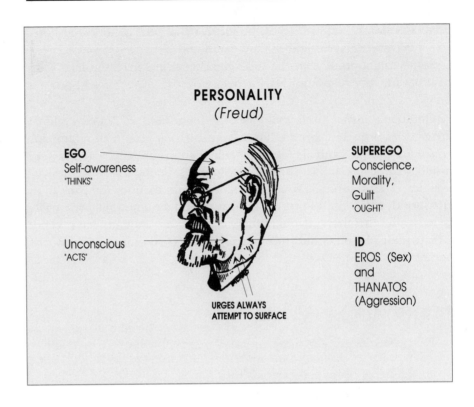

PERSONALITY
(Freud)

EGO
Self-awareness
"THINKS"

SUPEREGO
Conscience,
Morality,
Guilt
"OUGHT"

Unconscious
"ACTS"

ID
EROS (Sex)
and
THANATOS
(Aggression)

URGES ALWAYS
ATTEMPT TO SURFACE

freely displayed. This is called socialization or internalization which is really the *superego's* attempt to influence *ego* into becoming the personality you are "supposed" to be. As you mature, you also internalize the values and ideals of your society—certainly of your family, your surrounding culture, etc.

(Note that as Freud was developing his concepts, he himself was greatly influenced by his own family history and by the values and pressures of his own society. For this reason, many of his pioneering ideas are often challenged today as being sexist or culturally biased.)

On the next page is a graphic presentation of the psychoanalytic view of personality:

The urges or impulses from our unconscious put great pressure on *ego* because *ego* often cannot deal with them or will not deal with them. *Ego's* function is to "think" and *ego* must handle the conflicting demands of *id* and *superego*. *Id* is the primitive, unconscious, childish part of self, saying, "*Do it!* Go for it! I want it!" *Superego*, our moral arbitrator, jumps in and says, "*No!* Don't do it! It's not right! You know better than that!" *Ego* must weigh the nagging voice of parents and society (morality) against the urges of our unconscious (sex and aggression). Human personality emerges, Freud suggests, by the interactive func-

THE FREUDIAN SCHOOL

The assumptions of the Freudian school are simple: in order to gain insight into the causes of personality, one must delve into the world of *id*—the human unconscious which contains all hidden memories, childhood experiences, early life traumas and forbidden fantasies.

tions between *ego, superego,* and *id.* Too much *ego* repression or denial caused by anxiety or guilt (*superego*) could leave a personality in a disturbed, frustrated or highly dependant state. However, if there is too much *ego* expression, then the *id* surfaces freely, especially if there is insufficient internalization of values by the *superego.* If the *id* is allowed to dominate, one's aggression or delinquency will necessitate society's intervention.

The assumptions of the Freudian school are simple: in order to gain insight into the causes of personality, one must delve into the world of *id*—the human unconscious which contains all hidden memories, childhood experiences, early life traumas and forbidden fantasies. Freud and his followers initiated the "talking" cures, intended to give patients insight into their own unconscious minds. Imagine a patient lying on a couch, talking freely of his fears and fantasies, with the therapist sitting at his side, taking notes—and you have the stereotyped beginnings of psychoanalysis. From such talks, from both random and guided conversations, pioneering Freudian psychologists attempted to unlock the unconscious, go deeply into the *id,* and bring to the *ego* an awareness of the causes that may be troubling the patient.

With such knowledge, we can at least begin to understand the complexities of personality.

Behavioural School

Now we arrive at the "nurture" component of the nature-nurture debate. This school makes three assumptions: behaviour is learned; behaviour is reinforced, and that which is learned can be unlearned and relearned.

This view about personality places the emphasis on the environment and the manner in which you are raised. Your input from your genes is minimal; you can be anything in life, if you are nurtured (rewarded) toward achieving that goal. Star athletes, musicians and academicians, for example, have been nourished and reinforced in their personality development with increased and enriched opportunities. Deprived children, on the other hand, learn low self-esteem and may receive encouragement or a payoff for breaking the rules or breaking the law. Human personality is "shaped," according to behavioural theory.

The cause (*stimulus*) seems unimportant; people emit behaviours, that is, people just do things and don't concern themselves with the "why" (the *cause*) of the behaviour. We are interested in the *payoff!* If whatever you do (and let's not care about "why" you did it) is positively or negatively reinforced, the likelihood of you doing it again *increases.* Similarly, if whatever you do is punished or ignored (no reinforcement),

THE BEHAVIOURAL SCHOOL
The behavioural school views behaviours as learned phenomena. Our society merely exerts reinforcers on each individual to shape personality. The assumption here is that delinquent behaviours, addictive behaviours or anti-social behaviours are all *learned inappropriate responses.*

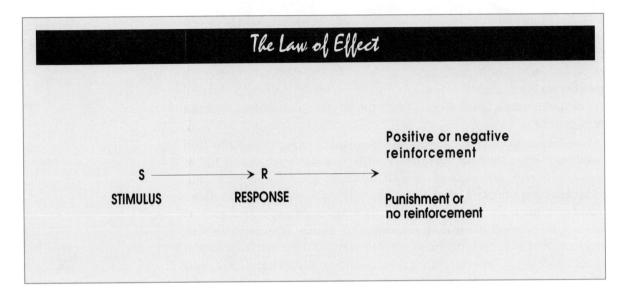

The Law of Effect

S ——————→ R ——————→ **Positive or negative reinforcement**

STIMULUS   **RESPONSE**   **Punishment or no reinforcement**

the likelihood of you doing it again *decreases.* This is the *Law of Effect,* the most important equation in all of behavioural science.

B.F. Skinner (1904–90) in his books and articles (*Walden Two, Beyond Freedom and Dignity,* etc.) attempts to explain the importance of "shaping" behaviours by their consequences. He discusses how personality is relatively neutral and becomes dominant only in the way behaviours are rewarded or not rewarded. For example, a three-year-old child, standing in a checkout line with her mother may ask for some candy two feet away from her. Mother says, "No." The child throws a tantrum, screams, cries and jumps up and down. Mother relents; the child gets the candy and stops crying. The Law of Effect explains what has happened from a behavioural point of view. The response of the child (the tantrum) led to a reward (positive consequences) in that the child received the candy (payoff). Is the tantrum behaviour, according to the Law of Effect, likely to *increase* or *decrease* in this child's personality repertoire?

The behavioural school views behaviours as learned phenomena. Our society merely exerts reinforcers on each individual to shape personality. The assumption here is that delinquent behaviours, addictive behaviours or anti-social behaviours are all *learned inappropriate responses.*

If you assume, as behaviourists do, that anything that is learned can be unlearned and relearned, there is great optimism for changing behaviour (through therapy or intervention techniques). Simply change the reinforcers so that tantrum behaviour (as in the 3-year-old) is no longer rewarded and the child will learn a new behaviour. (Hopefully,

B.F. Skinner

a more appropriate behaviour will take its place.) Therapeutically, this is called *behaviour modification*, with no references to "unconscious" impulses or to genetic predispositions at all! One may simply change the behaviour by changing the *consequences* which modify each response.

The important question to ask is not why any person does something inappropriate (Why are some men abusive? Why do some women drink all day? Why is crime increasing among 14-year-olds?)—but rather, in what way is the inappropriate behaviour leading to a payoff? That is, in what way is the behaviour of drinking or sexual abuse being rewarded or reinforced? In what way does crime (anti-social behaviour) lead to payoff in groups of young people today? The Law of Effect, in summary, allows us to examine personality based on behaviour and reinforcers.

Humanistic-Existential School

The previous three schools share one important dimension in common: they assume that the individual is *not* in control of self. Your personality, in other words, is motivated by genetic factors of which you are unaware (biological school), or by unconscious forces from the past of which you are unaware (psychoanalytic school), or, finally, by learned, inappropriate social responses of which you are unaware (behavioural school). All of these theories assume a lack of choice or *free will* on the part of the individual. Personality, they emphasize, is *determined* by forces outside of your control!

The humanists assume that we all are fundamentally *free* to make choices at each and every turning point in our lives. We have "free will" irrespective of our biology (genes), our past (unconscious), or our conditioning (Law of Effect). This is the newest of the schools of thought and, because of its emphasis on *choice* and *free will,* probably the most popular theory today.

There is an apparent optimism but a heavy responsibility in assuming that despite your biology, your past or your previous learning, you are free to be whatever you want to be—you are *limitless* in exercising the potential you have within yourself for growth or change! For example, if you were moody or shy as a teenager, you can enjoy the thrill and challenge and excitement of making new choices that will change you. If you were terribly repressed sexually or behaviourally (perhaps due to your parents' hangups), *you* don't have to be—you are free to change (if only you realize it)! If you learned delinquent patterns in your youth and were rewarded for anti-social behaviours, "today is the first day of

THE HUMANISTIC-EXISTENTIAL SCHOOL

The *humanists* assume that we all are fundamentally *free* to make choices at each and every turning point in our lives. We have "free will" irrespective of our biology (*genes*), our past (*unconscious*), or our conditioning (*Law of Effect*).

"I think if you let your hair down you'll be able to close your eyes."

the rest of your life." Change! Grow! Recognize your incredible potential! The choice is yours!

This tone of optimism for personal growth and change strongly inspired the "School of the '60s," giving rise to the Human Potential Movement. Walk into most bookstores in North America today and you will discover that the majority of modern books on psychology (at least 80% of them) have been influenced by the humanist-existential school. Authors from Rogers to Maslow, Dyer to Buscaglia, Harris to Gordon, clearly support the humanistic message: control is yours, no one else's!

Human personality is capable of changing; humans are motivated from within to grow and develop. This view holds that personality is not static but rather dynamic, always changing. If a person is moody, it is the individual's choice to be moody; the control or responsibility lies with the individual. Thus, "hope springs eternal," for one's past, one's biology and one's learning, are not as important as the present "now" for doing something about yourself, for making choices that will allow you to change and grow.

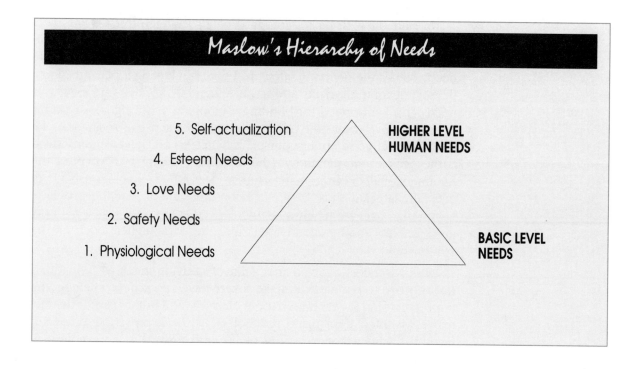

Maslow's Hierarchy of Needs

5. Self-actualization

4. Esteem Needs

3. Love Needs

2. Safety Needs

1. Physiological Needs

HIGHER LEVEL HUMAN NEEDS

BASIC LEVEL NEEDS

Abraham Maslow, one of the pioneers of the Human Potential Movement, wrote "the bible" for humanistic psychology (*Toward A Psychology Of Being*). Prior to Maslow, psychological theory was always oriented toward balance (equilibrium, homeostasis); that is, when human needs arise, the individual is in an "unbalanced" state (disequilibrium) and therefore seeks "balance" (homeostasis) by satisfying that need. For example, if your stomach is growling and you are preoccupied with satisfying your hunger needs, then you are in an "unbalanced" (disequilibrium) state. In order for your body to return to homeostasis (balance) you must satisfy your hunger needs by eating.

Maslow, however, rejected this quest for seeking balance in his new psychology (he actually called his humanism the "third force" in contrast to both psychoanalysis and behaviourism). Maslow stated that the "unbalanced" state is the *normal* state. According to Maslow, we are always in a state of "need" (i.e., unbalanced); we are always, therefore, "unbalanced"!

In attempting to seek equilibrium or balance we are not aware of the fact that the satisfaction of one need only leads to the creation of yet another need; it's our needs that are in a continual pattern of change. From this, Maslow developed his famous pyramid where he demonstrated the existence of our needs in a hierarchical manner:

Abraham Maslow

We start off with basic biological needs: hunger, thirst, sex, sleep, elimination. When our basic needs are met, new needs arise—but needs of a higher level. For example, following our basic PHYSIOLOGICAL needs comes the need for safety and security: having a place to sleep, the security of territoriality and so on. When SAFETY needs are met, LOVE needs arise—our need for bonding, belonging as strong social needs. Following love comes the need for ESTEEM, the sense of self-worth, the ability to feel good about yourself. Ultimately, our never-ending need is the peak of the hierarchy—the need for SELF-ACTUALIZATION or the fulfilment of all of our human potential. This lofty need obviously never gets fully satisfied; thus, we are in a constant state of evolving, growing, becoming ... yet we are always "unbalanced"! One need satisfied simply gives rise to another need—perhaps one of a higher level, as the pyramid shows.

Maslow's theory evolved after years of studying "healthy" individuals (as opposed to people who have severe psychological problems). The important thing to remember about Maslow (and humanism) is the fact that he wanted humanistic psychology to be a prescription toward health, toward a better quality of life and toward a more complete understanding of the "wholeness" of being human as we seek growth and fulfilment throughout our lifetime.

Conclusion

It must sound fairly confusing to lay down the assumptions made by personality theories and discover that they are quite opposite and contradictory!

If the humanists believe that we are essentially "free," while the behaviourists believe that we are essentially "controlled," which school is more correct? Carl Rogers says this is a unique paradox with which we all must live: both schools are correct; we are at the same time helpless souls conditioned and shaped by the reinforcers in our environment AND supreme masters of our own destiny, making free choices throughout every phase of our lives.

Can we understand this paradox? Søren Kierkegaard, a famous Danish philosopher, said: "The paradox is the source of the thinker's passion and the thinker without paradox is like a lover without feeling."

This paradox is uniquely human and allows us to discover the complexity of the human psyche. We *are* influenced, programmed, or controlled by forces totally external to us. Yet, we are also capable at any time of making spontaneous decisions, decisions for which we are wholly responsible.

Personality: Four Schools of Thought

This section discusses four reasoned approaches to the question, "Why are we the way we are?"

According to the biological model of human nature associated with 19th-century naturalist Charles Darwin, personality is inherited and cannot be altered through human choice or behaviour. We are determined by heredity, not environment. We must play the cards nature has dealt us because we will pick up no others along the way.

A late 19th- and early 20th-century Viennese doctor named Sigmund Freud revolutionized our perception of human personality by proposing an intricate psychoanalytic model involving components that he called the *ego*, *id*, and *superego*, which interact with each other to determine personality. The id, our unconscious, is comprised of our pleasure drives (*eros*) and our drives towards aggression, hostility and destruction (*thanatos*). The superego is our moral sense; the ego is our self-awareness or consciousness which negotiates between demands of the id and the expectations of the superego. According to Freud and the psychoanalytic school, the degree to which the ego and superego repress, alter, or fulfill biological drives determines personality.

The third school of thought is the behavioural school. Behaviourists minimize the role of heredity and heighten the role of environment in determining why we are the way we are. According to the behaviourists, behaviour is learned, is reinforced through positive or negative rewards, and can be changed through conditioning. B.F. Skinner is a major proponent of the behavioural school.

The biological, psychoanalytic, and behavioural schools maintain that we are shaped by outside forces and we do not possess free will. The fourth and most recent school of thought, known as the humanist-existential school, suggests that we possess free will and the power to change ourselves and the outside world. Humanists contend that we hold all the cards in the game of life and are free to deal them as we wish. The multitude of self-help books and personal growth manuals in bookstores suggests the prevalence of this view in contemporary western society.

These four schools of thought contain many differences, even contradictions. Which one is right? Or does each reflect some part of the whole make-up of personality? Collectively, these four schools of personality theory provide a universe of insight into the dynamic phenomenon of human personality.

Psychologists use tests (personality tests with no right or wrong answers) to determine the degree of control that an individual believes he or she may have over his or her own life. There are those individuals that psychologists label "internally controlled" and those categorized as "externally controlled." Internally controlled people believe they are in total command of their lives; they believe that what they do matters and they assume responsibility for their success or failure. Externally controlled individuals feel that they have no real personal control of their lives. It is always the fault of someone else or some other agency

Review

Personality: Four Schools of Thought:
Fill in the Blanks

This section discusses four reasoned approaches to the question, "Why are we the way we are?" According to the _____ model of human nature associated with 19th-century naturalists, personality is inherited and cannot be altered through human choice or behaviour. We are determined by heredity, not environment. We must play the cards nature has dealt us because we will pick up no others along the way.

A late 19th- and early 20th-century Viennese doctor named _____ revolutionized our perception of human personality by proposing an intricate model, referred to as the _____ model of personality, involving components which interact to determine personality.

The _____, our unconscious, is comprised of our pleasure drive (_____) and our drive towards aggression, hostility and destruction (_____). The _____ is our moral sense; the_____ is our self-awareness or consciousness, which negotiates between demands of the _____ and the expectations of the _____.

According to this school, the degree to which the _____ and _____ repress, alter, or fulfil biological drives determines personality.

when things go wrong. Parents, employers, boyfriends/girlfriends, etc., all make great scapegoats. Their destiny (happiness or unhappiness, success or failure) is perceived to lie in the hands of "others." They feel powerless insofar as they *believe* that what they do has little or no impact on anyone or anything.

Perhaps when viewed from this perspective, our paradox makes more sense. Those individuals who are "internally controlled" clearly fall into the humanist camp, while the "externally controlled" individuals belong in the behaviourist camp. Internally controlled people would probably vote and engage in other activities which would indicate their degree of *perceived* control over their own lives. Externally controlled people, predictably, wouldn't vote and might say: "What difference does my vote make anyway?"

Examine the paradox and you will probably find that our attitudes and beliefs are full of contradictions. In this case, perhaps, there is a continuum, ranging from "absolutely no control over my life" to "absolute control over my life." Maybe the behaviourist vs. humanist debate is better understood by first understanding our complex range of perceptions about how much of our lives we *believe* we actually control!

QUESTIONS

1. State what basic assumption is made about the nature of personality with the traditional biology school.

2. State the problems that exist with respect to the genetic engineering of so-called "good genes."

3. Relate the thinking of this school to: (a) taking personal responsibility for behaviour; and (b) parental input for gifted, delinquent or athletic children.

4. List and define in a short sentence each of the three distinct aspects of human personality according to Sigmund Freud.

5. List and define in a short sentence each of the two biological instincts contained with the *id*.

6. Define socialization/internalization using the terms *ego* and *superego*.

7. State what, according to Freud, are the psychological problems associated with: (a) too much *ego* repression; and (b) too much *ego* expression.

8. List the specific aspects of the "world of *id* " that give the Freudian school insights into the causes of personality.

9. Explain how the "talking" cures of Freudian psychoanalysis are supposed to work.

10. List the three assumptions that are made by the behavioural school.

11. State where emphasis is placed in this view of personality.

12. State what the Law of Effect is, using the term *reinforcement*. Illustrate your answer with the example of the child throwing a tantrum in order to receive candy.

13. State what assumption is made concerning behaviours that are delinquent, addictive or anti-social.

14. Define behaviour modification.

15. State the question behaviourists ask concerning inappropriate behaviour.

16. State the assumption that the first three schools share and contrast that with the thinking of the humanistic-existential school.

17. State the view this school holds with respect to the ability of the human personality to change.

EXERCISE

Remember, your task is to assess the relative impact or importance or merits of each school of thought.

Choose a behaviour and examine the analysis and assumptions made by each school with respect to the causes and treatments of the behaviour. For example, you can look at alcohol addiction and assume—

a. It is *biologically* based, caused by a genetic weakness or predisposition. Alcoholism is not the person's fault, and, therefore, treatment lies in understanding and correcting the biological imbalance. Any "talking" cures (psychoanalysis) would be totally useless and irrelevant to this view.

b. Alcohol addiction is *unconsciously* motivated, caused by misdirected *eros* or *thanatos* energy surfacing to *ego* in the form of an addiction to drinking. The person is consciously unaware of the cause of this "oral" dependency, and therapy would involve many hours of exposing the unconscious *(id)*, that is, of talking out one's feelings, anxieties and early life experiences.

c. Alcohol addiction, to the behaviourist, is a bad habit! It is a behaviour which has obviously been reinforced, in that the behaviour (response) of drinking has led to good things happening (reward). The consequences (reinforcement) of alcohol dependency must be altered so that abstinence leads to reward. Therefore, sessions of behaviour modification might be used to slowly change the reinforcers. (A drastic method of intervention, called "aversive conditioning," was illustrated in the movie, *A Clockwork Orange*.) In short, "bad" behaviours can be unlearned and relearned through appropriate conditioning (reinforcement) methods.

d. The humanist would assume you have chosen alcohol dependency as an escape; this is understandable in a world filled with stress and anxiety. Do you want to change? If you do, you have the power and control within you to make that choice. As one anti-drug campaign put it, "Say NO to drugs!" It's that simple— or is it?

"I'm getting him conditioned beautifully— every time I run through the maze, he throws me a bit of cheese."

•

The above theories and examples are presented in an oversimplified and non-technical way. In reality, of course, these theories and therapies do overlap and are more complex. However, we have presented them to you as separate and independent schools to promote analysis, insight and comparison.

Is one theory better than another? Should certain concepts from one theory be married to another theory? Do you yourself have some new clues about personality and human behaviour?

The adventure is to know more about yourself, for such insights often help you to understand how you relate to others, and how you may enrich your own life. Self knowledge, understanding some of the potential causes that make you a personality, also enables you to understand others.

We share with humankind that quality called "personality." It is an exciting, lifetime adventure to discover who we are—and why.

✓ A New Perspective on Biology

John Elias

Contemporary research into the biological aspects of human personality is changing our assumptions. There is an enormous debate amongst scientists on how to interpret and evaluate current genetic research. Some scientists take a deterministic and reductionist approach (reducing all explanation of human behaviour to genetic influence). Still others argue that we must recognize the limits of biological research in explaining personality.

Until quite recently, the biological school was often presented as a deterministic school which stated that personality was pre-programmed by our genetic code. The slogan, "Biology is Destiny," nicely captured the essence of this view. Sensational genetic breakthroughs have reinforced the deterministic image of this school. In particular, the efforts of the Human Genome Project to map the entire genetic code have added further weight to the view that the biological school alone will discover and reveal the secret of life.

paradigm—a framework or model.

Modern biology has developed a scientific paradigm which tries to integrate Darwin's theory of evolution with genetics in order to explain human behaviour. A growing number of dissenting scientists argue, however, that this paradigm needs to be revised in order to address the complexity of the brain and the richness of human experience. While they accept the validity of Darwin's theory of evolution and the findings of current genetic research, R.C. Lewontin, a geneticist at Harvard, and Gerald M. Edelman, a Nobel Laureate and neuroscientist, argue that we must understand the limits of science to describe human personality; they also reassert the uniqueness of human beings. Their position, grounded in a biological view, is both complex and realistic, and tries to account for the development of human consciousness, mind and freedom.

Lewontin and Edelman articulate the paradoxical view that we have been determined by nature to be free. They recognize both the influences of genes and the environment in shaping us. They cut

"Survival of the Fittest"

Charles Darwin

Charles Darwin (1809–1882), author of *The Origin of Species* and the major exponent of the theory of evolution, is regarded by many as the father of the biological school of personality.

Darwin claimed that God had not created all living things and species all at once and eternally fixed each species on the "chain of being," with humans at the pinnacle of creation. Darwin's voyages to the Galapagos islands and examination of the fossil record convinced him that species had evolved over millions of years through a mechanism which he called natural selection.

Darwin saw that there were a number of variations within each species; he deduced, therefore, that there was a struggle for existence within each species. Those members of a species which could best adapt to changing conditions in the environment would survive and reproduce. Darwin called this process of natural selection and adaptation the "survival of the fittest"—those beings who were best suited or "fitted" to the environment would survive and leave offspring.

The principles of evolution were, therefore, the mechanism of natural selection, adaptation, and struggle for existence or survival. The memorable line from the poet Tennyson, "Nature red in tooth and claw," symbolized the idea of evolution through natural selection. What Darwin had failed to understand, however, was the fundamental mechanism of heredity.

through the "nature versus nurture" debate by developing a new perspective that is based in biology yet aware of the complexity of human experience.

Edelman attempts to put the mind back into nature and argues that understanding the structure and function of the brain is central to gaining an understanding of the development of consciousness. He rejects the view that there is a predetermined genetic program which constructs our sense of self. Edelman calls his theory "Neural Darwinism" or "The Theory of Neuronal Group Selection" (TNGS). Neuronal Darwinism is a process by which an organism evolves a view of the world and acquires the skills necessary to deal with it. In other words, this form of Darwinism does not occur in a whole species over millions of years, but occurs within each individual organism, during its lifetime, through the competition of groups of cells within the brain. As the

Double Helix

DNA—Cracking the Genetic Code

The investigations and work of the monk Gregor Mendel (1822–1884) on crossing a variety of peas led to the basic understanding of the principles of heredity. It was not until 1909, however, that the term "gene" was used to describe the fundamental units of heredity which transmitted characteristics from one being to another.

By the 1920s it was known that it was the chromosomes which carried the genes and the information of heredity. However, it was not until 1953 that the major breakthrough occurred in chemistry. While working in Cambridge, James Watson and Francis Crick discovered the DNA molecule (deoxyribonucleic acid) which finally disclosed the fundamental mechanism of how heredity really worked.

The DNA molecule consists of a "double helix" which looks like two ladders twisted together. The DNA molecule in turn consists of smaller molecules called nucleotides which consist of four base elements or compounds: A (adenine), T (thymine), C (cytosine), and G (guanine). A gene is a section or substring of the DNA molecule; it consists of a combination of nucleotides which determine a certain trait or characteristic. The genes which carry the basic genetic information are located in the 23 pairs of chromosomes which determine an individual's physical characteristics and traits. Watson's and Crick's model of the DNA molecule finally explained how the DNA carried the genetic information and how it was reduplicated.

Many scientists working on the Human Genome Project are confident that given time, money and new developments in technology, they will be able to map the 100,000 genes which make up our genome, that is, all the genes located in the 23 pairs of chromosomes. By uncovering the secrets of heredity and understanding the genetic code, which they believe determines who we are, they hope to gather enough knowledge and information in order to detect "faulty" or "defective" genes which produce crippling diseases such as Huntington's disease, cystic fibrosis, Down's Syndrome, muscular dystrophy, and cancer. They hope that the genome map will give them enough genetic information to detect genetic abnormalities and to find cures and treatments for the over 50,000 diseases which are currently known to be caused by defective or faulty genes.

individual proceeds through the world, certain experiences stimulate particular groups of cells, thus selecting and developing some cell groups more than others. In this way, the individual evolves through a unique interplay of natural capacity (nature) and experience (nurture). It is this interplay that both grounds a theory of consciousness in our biology and accounts for the rich diversity of individuals. This theory rejects simple biological determinism in favour of a theory that coincides with our feeling of a complex, ever-changing, self-developing flow of awareness. Only a non-reductionist theory adequately explains the development of beings who become self-conscious and are able to question the nature and origin of their existence.

What is Mind?

Mind over Matter

"After all, mind is such an odd predicament for matter to get into. I often marvel how something like hydrogen, the simplest atom, forged in some early chaos of the universe, could lead to us and the gorgeous fever we call consciousness.

"If a mind is just a few pounds of blood, dream, and electric, how does it manage to contemplate itself, worry about its soul, do time-and-motion studies, admire the shy hooves of a goat, know that it will die, enjoy all the grand and lesser mayhems of the heart?

"What is mind, that one can be *out of one's*? How can a neuron feel compassion! What is a self? Why did automatic, hand-me-down mammals like our ancestors somehow evolve brains with the ability to consider, imagine, project, compare, abstract, think of the future?

"If our experience of mind is really just the simmering of an easily alterable chemical stew, then what does it mean to know something, to want something, *to be*? How do you begin with hydrogen and end up with prom dresses, jealousy, chamber music! What is music that it can satisfy such a mind, and even perhaps function as language!"

Edelman's previous research on how the immune and nervous systems work convinced him that we needed a new theory of the brain. Both the immune and nervous systems, he discovered, are systems of recognition. In order to defend the body against invading bacteria and viruses, the immune system has to distinguish between "self" and "non-self." Similarly, the nervous system selects and emphasizes different sensory experiences, which it then categorizes and perceives to be essential for survival. According to Edelman, a child does not come into the world as a blank slate but has an innate system of values (such as food, warmth, comfort), which enables him or her to distinguish and select what is necessary for survival. We do not have a predetermined genetic program, but what we do have is a fairly basic capacity to actively select and process information—to build a world of meaning and relationships.

In other words, we construct ourselves and our place in the world. As Oliver Sacks writes, "Experience itself is not passive, a matter of 'impressions' or 'sense-data,' but active, and constructed by the organism. Active experience 'selects,' or carves out, a new, more complexly connected pattern of neuronal groups, a neuronal reflection of the individual experience of the child." This process of selection begins with the primary neuronal units in constant communication with other nerve cells. This communication (which Edelman calls "reentrant signalling") allows us to organize information based on a variety of neuronal sources and form ideas of the world.

"There are ten billion neurons in the cortex of the brain which provide information to the brain and are connected to the external world through specialized neurons called sensory transducers. Each nerve cell receives connections from other nerve cells at sites called synapses. But here is an astonishing fact—there are about one million billion connections in the cortical sheath. If you were to count them, one connection (or synapse) per second, you would finish counting some thirty-two million years after you began."

Gerald M. Edelman

Mapping The Human Genome

One easy way to grasp the nature of the genome is to think of it as the surface of a planet.

A planetary surface is made of many different parts—mountains, plains, marshes, lakes, rivers, oceans, continents, and so on. From a great distance, one can see the Earth as a whole but cannot make out the details of its surface. From a closer viewpoint—say, a geosynchronous orbit some 22,300 miles out—one can still see the entire planet but can also make out more details.

Even closer in—say from a shuttle orbiting a few hundred miles out—an observer can see many surface details, but cannot see the entire sphere. Finally, from an airplane flying just a mile or so above the surface of the Earth, an observer can make out extremely fine details.

Geneticists today are still like astronauts looking at the Earth from a moderately far distance. They can see the planet in its entirety, and can make out some of the details of its surface. But they are still not close enough to see the fine details—rivers, the Grand Canyon, or fields of corn and wheat.

The Genome Project will produce maps of the "DNA planet." These maps will have different levels of detail, from the whole planet to the location of a duplex in Atlanta, Georgia.

Now consider the genome as an encyclopedia that contains all the instructions necessary to create a living person. The human genome contains about a hundred thousand "entries" found in one of 23 different "volumes." These entries are written with an alphabet of only four letters that are repeated some three billion times in about twenty combinations of three-letter "words." All of this information is packed into an area much smaller than the naked eye can see. This is an encyclopedia that can literally fit on the head of a pin, yet it guides the complex development of a human being.

From *Mapping the Code: The Human Genome Project and the Choices of Modern Science*, Joel Davis, John Wiley & Sons, Inc. 1990.

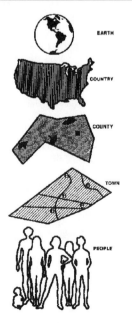

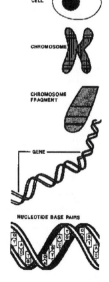

One way of understanding the scale of genetic mapping is to compare it to different maps of the Earth. Chromosomes are analogous to countries, chromosome fragments to states or counties, genes to cities or towns, and base pairs to individuals.

Reprinted from: U.S. Congress, Office of Technology Assessment, "Mapping Our Genes—The Genome Project: How Big, How Fast?" OTA-BA-373 (Washington, D.C.: U.S. Government Printing Office, April 1988.)

Behavioral Genetics

A Lack-of-Progress Report

CRIME: Family, twin and adoption studies have suggested a heritability of 0 to more than 50 percent for predisposition to crime. (Heritability represents the degree to which a trait stems from genetic factors.) In the 1960s researchers reported an association between an extra Y chromosome and violent crime in males. Follow-up studies found that association to be spurious.

MANIC DEPRESSION: Twin and family studies indicate heritability of 60 to 80 percent for susceptibility to manic depression. In 1987 two groups reported locating different genes linked to manic depression, one in Amish families and the other in Israeli families. Both reports have been retracted.

SCHIZOPHRENIA: Twin studies show heritability of 40 to 90 percent. In 1988 a group reported finding a gene linked to schizophrenia in British and Icelandic families. Other studies documented no linkage, and the initial claim has now been retracted.

ALCOHOLISM: Twin and adoption studies suggest heritability ranging from zero to 60 percent. In 1990 a group claimed to link a gene—one that produces a receptor for the neurotransmitter dopamine—with alcoholism. A recent review concluded it does not support a link.

INTELLIGENCE: Twin and adoption studies show a heritability of performance on intelligence tests of 70 to 80 percent. One group recently unveiled preliminary evidence for genetic markers for high intelligence (an I.Q. of 130 or higher). The study is unpublished.

HOMOSEXUALITY: In 1991 a researcher cited anatomic differences between the brains of heterosexual and homosexual males. Two recent twin studies have found a heritability of roughly 50 percent for predisposition to male or female homosexuality. These reports have been disputed. Another group claims to have preliminary evidence of genes linked to male homosexuality. The data have not been published.

Adapted from *Scientific American*, June, 1993.

"The process of reentrant signalling, with its scores—perhaps hundreds of reciprocal connections within and between maps, may be likened to a sort of neural United Nations, in which dozens of voices are talking together, while including in their conversation a variety of constantly inflowing reports from the outside world, and bringing them together into a larger picture as new information is correlated and new insights emerge." (Oliver Sacks).

The main point of Edelman's theory is that it presents a dynamic picture of the brain as consisting of a series of "maps" which are continuously rebuilding memories, feelings and thoughts. These maps are neural connections which relate points on the receptors of the body (skin, or retina of the eye) to corresponding points in the brain. Edelman writes: "Brains contain multiple maps interacting without any supervisor, yet bring unity and cohesiveness to perceptual scenes."

In explaining the nature of consciousness, Edelman distinguishes between primary consciousness and higher-order consciousness. He

Biological Determinism

Eugenics and Ideology

Eugenics is an ideology which claims to be scientific and has as its aim the study of heredity in order to "improve" the human race by purifying the human species through the elimination of undesirable genetic traits, which were believed to cause sexual immorality, criminal behaviour, and "feeble-mindedness." The most horrific and notorious example in human history is, of course, the attempt of the Nazis to create a "superior" or master race and to systematically exterminate Jews and other peoples who were deemed to be "inferior." The tragic history of eugenics can perhaps serve as a warning for us in the present of the potential dangers of genetic engineering.

Richard Lewontin is one of the most perceptive critics of the biological fictions which have been used to rationalize and legitimize competitive societies based on winners and losers. He argues that the "ideology of biological determinism" distorts Darwin's theory of evolution by turning it into a social ideology—Sociobiology and Social Darwinism—which characterizes human nature as the biological byproduct of innate and inherited differences. Social Darwinism, for example, paints a picture of human beings as biologically programmed by their genes to be selfish, greedy, and competitive; we are constantly at war with one another and trapped in a perpetual struggle for power, wealth, status and dominance over others. In the words of the great English political theorist Thomas Hobbes, we are in the state of nature where we are in "in continual fear, and danger of violent death; and the life of man, solitary, poor, nasty, brutish, and short."

The ideology of biological determinism and Social Darwinism can be used to justify the inequality of upper and lower classes by proclaiming that certain individuals are by nature superior, more intelligent and destined to rule over those who are inferior.

Richard Dawkins, the author of *The Selfish Gene*, goes as far as to say that we are selfish because "selfish genes" use us as vehicles to endlessly reproduce themselves. In his words: "We are survival machines,—robot vehicles blindly programmed to preserve selfish molecules known as genes." Lewontin argues that the ideology of Social Darwinism and selfish genes is absolute nonsense and propaganda which has no hard scientific evidence to back up its claims.

Lewontin states that I.Q. tests, for example, which claim to be objective and value-free in measuring innate intellectual abilities, are in fact full of social, cultural and educational biases which influence the results. He claims that there is no innate, fixed and unchangeable nature which can be divorced and known apart from nurture—environmental and societal influences. Lewontin states that many infectious diseases and viruses have been conquered, not by medical advances and new drugs, but by changes in the environment, society, nutrition and lifestyles, which have had a significant impact in decreasing mortality rates, making us healthier, and increasing our life span. For example, if a person doesn't smoke, then the chances of getting lung cancer are dramatically reduced; there is no smoking gene which predetermines a person to become a smoker and to die of lung cancer. Lewontin also insists that there are no genes predetermining us to become criminals, lazy, or alcoholics.

Lewontin and others claim that scientific thinking leads us to the conclusion that we are the product of the interaction between nature and nurture, genes and environment: one cannot exist independently of the other.

states that most animals have primary consciousness which allows them to be aware of their environment and to internalize mental images from sense experiences—their memories consist of a number of mental scenes which are constantly changing. Humans are the only beings, however, who as the result of evolutionary changes developed a higher consciousness which allows them to transcend the limits of the sensory present—the "here and now"—and to become conscious both of their past and their future. Humans are thinking and embodied subjects, who are not only conscious but also self-conscious, a state of awareness which integrates both our physical and our social selves.

transcend—to go beyond.

By developing a biological model of the brain, Edelman has been able to develop a theory of the mind which accounts for our sense of freedom, individuality, self-consciousness, and the unpredictability and ambiguity of life. His theory recognizes the important role that genes play in determining the physiological structures and functions of the brain. At the same time, however, Edelman avoids biological reductionism and determinism by claiming that human beings embody a "multilevel of consciousness," "linguistic and semantic capabilities," and a certain degree of freedom in determining who we are.

Nature may not have endowed us with wings to fly, as Edelman states, but it has given us the ability to think and to construct airplanes so that we can fly.

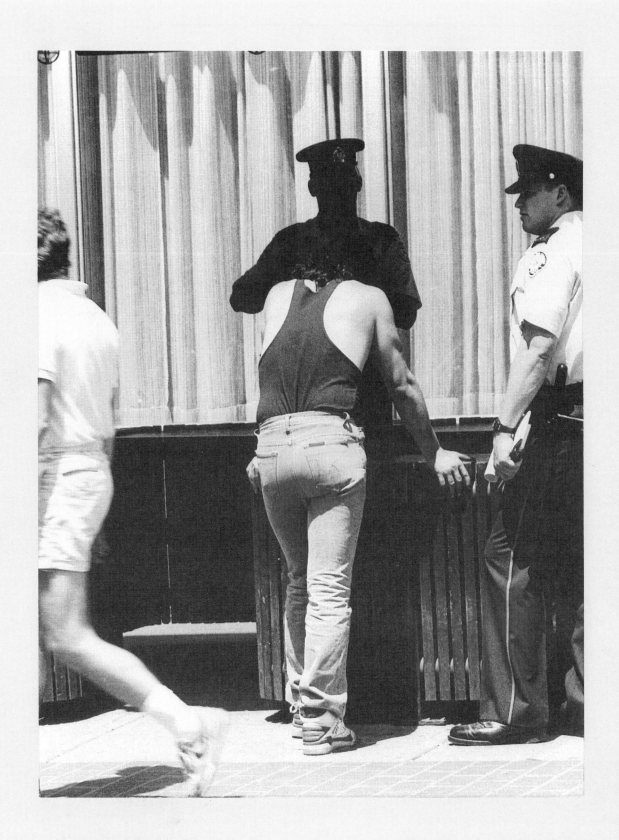

Freedom and Constraint

... if some day they truly discover a formula for all our desires and caprices—that is an explanation of what they depend upon, by what laws they arise, just how they develop, what they are aiming at in one case or another and so on, and so on, that is a real mathematical formula—then, after all, man would most likely at once stop to feel desire, indeed, he will be certain to. For who would want to choose by rule? ... for what is a man without desire, without free will and without choice ...

Dostoyevsky

I share genes with people in Japan; our physical resemblance is therefore striking. But the enormous psychological and behavioural gulf that separates me from those people is obvious the moment we open our mouths—environment has been the most important factor shaping our personalities.
The question of how much nature and nurture determine our personalities is rather trivial scientifically, but the social implications can be staggering, as victims of the Nazi concentration camps can attest.

David Suzuki

Am I Free or Determined?

Melanie Chaparian

Each of the five theories of personality discussed in Issue I takes a stand on the philosophical debate between determinism and libertarianism. On one side of the debate, determinism is the position that all human actions are determined, or caused, by natural and/or environmental forces beyond human control. According to this theory, people do not have any free will. Human beings are like sophisticated computers that can only perform the operations with which they are programmed. Although the traditional biological, psychoanalytic, and behaviourist schools advocate very different theories, they all agree that our personalities and, as a result, our actions are determined by forces outside our control. Thus, these three schools take the determinist side of the debate.

On the other side of the debate, libertarianism is the view that at least some human actions are free. Although many actions may be determined, there are some situations in which people can exercise their free will. Unlike computers, human beings are capable of making real choices between alternative courses of action. Only the humanist-existential school and Edelman's biological theory of personality take the position that people have free will.

An Argument for Determinism

Determinism may be defended on the basis of the following rather simple argument. Every event in the world occurs because of cause and effect. Like every other event, human actions must be determined by cause and effect as well. If all of our actions are caused, we cannot possess free will because the same action cannot be both caused and free at the same time. Therefore, all human actions are determined, and no human actions are free.

Let's look at this argument in more detail. Few people today question the universality of cause and effect in the natural world. Science teaches us that every natural phenomenon is the effect of a cause or set of causes. Indeed, science assumes a deterministic model of the world. It is the very nature of science to look for the causes of the phenomena it studies. The nature of causality is such that there is an *inevitable* connection between a cause and its effect: if the cause occurs, the effect *must* also occur. For example, if heating water to a temperature of 100°C *determines* the water to turn into steam, then every time water is heated to that temperature it *must* turn into steam. Heating water to 100°C is the *cause* and the water turning into steam is the *effect*. We never entertain the possibility that boiling water, or any other natural phenomena, occurs because of pure chance. Scientists always try to discover the causes of the phenomena they study. Indeed, when they are unable to identify the cause of a particular phenomenon, such as the memory loss suffered by people afflicted by Alzheimer's Disease, they do not conclude that no cause exists but rather that it simply has not *yet* been discovered.

But the deterministic view is not limited to the natural sciences such as physics, chemistry, biology, and medicine. Determinism is also assumed by the social sciences, such as psychology and sociology, which usually attempt to study and *discover the causes of human behaviour*. A determinist would agree that, although we may believe ourselves to be unique creatures, human beings are just as subject to the world of cause and effect as boiling water and Alzheimer's Disease.

The determinist argues that our distinctive nature only means that the causes which determine our actions are more complex, and therefore harder to discover, than those that cause other events. The *kinds* of causes determining human behaviour depend on the determinist's particular view of human nature. Some point to *nature*, such as hereditary or instinctual forces, as the primary cause of a person's actions. Those who adhere to the traditional biological school of personality, for instance, argue that genetics determines such traits as intelligence, talents, and temperament, which in turn cause an individual's actions. Other determinists argue that a person's behaviour is fundamentally determined by *nurture*, that is, by environmental factors. The behaviourists, for example, point to rewards and punishments as the causes of an individual's actions. Many, if not most, determinists, however, acknowledge that a *combination* of nature and nurture determines a person's actions. A Freudian psychologist, for example, believes that an individual's behaviour is caused by the way the *ego* moderates between drives of the *id*, which are determined by instinct or heredity, and the moral demands of the *superego*, which are determined by early childhood environment. Regardless as to the kinds of causes they point to, all determinists agree that all human actions are determined or caused.

do you mean
for all choices
or for some
choices.

No matter how long and hard we may deliberate between different courses of action, the "choice" we finally make has already been decided for us by hereditary and/or environmental causes over which we have no control. This applies to all of our actions, from the most trivial to the most significant.

According to the determinist, an analysis of the motivations of different people reveals the various causes that result in the difference in their behaviour. The determinist is quick to point out that you do not freely choose what interests you. Your interests are determined by your nature, your environment, or, most likely, by a combination of both. For example, you may have a naturally inquisitive mind. This is not an attribute that you freely chose to acquire. Or you may have been raised in a family that constantly debated whether or not people are forced into a life of crime because of social neglect and injustice. You have no more control over your upbringing than you do over your nature. You probably wish to pursue academic success. Why is this important to you? Perhaps your family has always encouraged academic success. Again, the determinist points out that you have no control over the values your family has bred into you. You may be aware that good grades are essential for the new graduate to secure a decent position in today's highly competitive job market. Once again, the determinist points out that you have no control over the increasingly high academic requirements demanded by employers. Nor do you have any control over the high unemployment rates that make today's job market so competitive. *Your* actual motivations for persevering through your homework probably include some of those discussed here as well as a number of others. But whatever they may be, the determinist argues, they reveal that you do not freely choose to study hard.

At this point, you may be convinced that *your* actions are caused by forces outside your control. But how does the determinist explain the actions of other students in your class who socialize at the expense of studying and consequently earn low marks? After all, most of them also come from families that stress academic success, and all of them want good jobs after they graduate. It *seems* that these negligent students are making a free, although foolish, choice.

Things are not always as they first appear. According to the determinist's theory, if your negligent classmates were subject to exactly the same causal forces that determine your behaviour, they would of necessity be studying as hard as you are. The very fact that they sacrifice study time to socialize indicates that their personal histories are very different from yours. Perhaps their families have not so much *encouraged* academic success as relentlessly *pressured* them to do well in school. If so, they may have been determined to rebel by going to all

the college parties instead of studying. Just as you have no control over the encouragement you receive, the rebellious students have no control over the pressure they suffer. Other students who neglect their homework may simply not have the maturity required for self-discipline. Having fun may be as important to them, or even more so, than earning good marks or preparing for their future. If so, the determinist points out that a person cannot simply decide to become mature. This is a developmental process that is determined by an individual's nature and upbringing. There is an entire host of other causes that may determine some students to neglect their studies. Whatever these causes may be in any actual case, the determinist argues that negligent students do not freely choose to ignore their homework. Although they may feel guilty that they are not studying, they simply cannot choose to do so. Neither

Some of these students will perform better in the classroom than others.

According to determinist thinking, educational achievement is the result of hereditary and/or social factors outside the control of the individual student—things such as natural talents, general economic conditions, family background, parents' income, and the like.

the diligent student nor the negligent student really makes a genuine choice between studying or not studying. The course of action each takes is determined by causes over which neither has any control.

Nor do we have the freedom to make genuine choices concerning even the most important aspects of our lives. Nature or nurture, or both, determine such things as which profession we pursue, who we fall in love with, and how many children we have. According to the theory of determinism, *all* human actions are the effect of causes over which we have no control; consequently, free will is merely an illusion.

Because we usually pride ourselves on our freedom, we may feel reluctant to accept the determinist's conclusion. But this in itself is not a good reason to reject determinism. It would be hard to deny that the deterministic model has helped to advance our knowledge of the natural world in general and the human world in particular. Discovering the cause of an event not only increases our understanding of that phenomenon but also allows us to *predict* and sometimes *control* its future occurrence. If, for example, we know that a virus causes an illness in the human body, we can predict that a person will become ill when infected by that virus, and, moreover, we can control that illness by finding ways to prevent the virus from infecting more people. Or, if we know that a moderate amount of parental pressure causes a student to succeed in school, we can predict that a student subjected to that amount of guidance will earn good grades, and we can control such successes by teaching parents how to provide the proper dose of encouragement. The deterministic model also helps us to make sense out of our personal lives. We are often remarkably successful, for instance, in predicting the actions of our close relatives and friends. If such predictions are not merely lucky guesses, the determinist argues, they must be based on our relatively extensive knowledge of the hereditary and environmental causes that determine the behaviour of those relatives and friends. The fact that we do not *like* the theory of determinism does not negate of the wealth of evidence for its accuracy.

James's Critique of Determinism

In his famous lecture entitled "The Dilemma of Determinism," William James, an American philosopher and psychologist who lived from 1842 to 1910, defends libertarianism, the theory that human beings have free will. Before he actually begins his argument for this theory, however, James shows that determinism — its appeal to science notwithstanding — cannot be scientifically demonstrated.

Science cannot really tell us, for example, if the negligent student's background is causing him to rebel. The fact that he does consistently neglect his assigned readings is not in itself conclusive proof that the student is determined to take this course of action. Moreover, *before the fact* — that is, before the student entered college — no one, not even the most learned determinist, could ascertain whether the student's background would lead him to socialize or to study. For instance, it would not have seemed inconceivable to suppose that the excessive family pressure would prompt the student to study harder than any other student. Nor would it have been unreasonable to surmise that this pressure would compel him to overcome his immaturity and set his priorities in a more beneficial way. *Before the fact*, this series of events seems as likely to occur as the events that actually came to pass; thus, James argues, *after the fact*, there is no way to prove that the student was determined to neglect his studies. The same argument applies to all human actions. James therefore concludes that the determinist cannot prove that all actions are the inevitable effects of prior causes. While this in itself does not disprove determinism, it certainly dispels the myth that determinism has the weight of science on its side, and, furthermore, suggests that libertarianism should at least be reconsidered.

William James

James's Argument for Free Will

Different libertarians disagree among themselves on how far human freedom extends. On one extreme, the existentialists claim that all human actions are free. On the other extreme, some libertarians only argue that actions performed in the face of moral demands are free. In this discussion, we will focus on the views of William James, who defends a relatively moderate version of libertarianism. According to James, we are free whenever we have a genuine choice between at least two possible and desirable courses of action. This does not mean, of course, that we are free to perform any conceivable action whatsoever. Nor does this even mean that we are free to do anything we may desire, for the action that we find most tempting may not be included within the choice before us. All that is required to render an action free is the existence of one other alternative action that it is possible for us to perform.

Essential to James's definition of free will is the existence of *possible actions*; that is, actions which a person is not inevitably determined to do but may perform nonetheless. If an action is the result of free will, then it is, before the fact, merely one of two or more genuinely *possible* alternative actions that the person can *freely choose* to perform; and, after the fact, it is correct to say that the individual *could have acted otherwise* by choosing another alternative. For instance, the negligent

"There is nothing more wholesome for us than to find problems that quite transcend our powers."
Charles Pierce

student may have freely chosen to spend his time socializing instead of at the library; and even though he made this choice, he could have chosen to study instead. It is the idea of possible actions that puts James in stark opposition to determinism, which states that every action is the *inevitable* effect of a cause.

We have already discussed James's argument that determinism cannot be scientifically demonstrated. He does not attempt, however, to disprove this theory nor to prove libertarianism true. This is because he believes determinism and libertarianism to be two alternative theories of reality, neither of which can be objectively proven true or false. Thus, he claims that the best we can do is to examine both theories to see which one offers us the most rational explanation of human behaviour. According to James, a "rational" theory should not only explain objective reality but must account for subjective human experience as well. James's defence of libertarianism consists in the argument that the free will position is more rational in this sense than determinism.

A significant fact of human life is the *feeling of freedom* that we often experience. James argues that any theory of human behaviour must adequately explain this feeling. Unlike determinism, libertarianism conforms to our ordinary experience: we often feel free to choose between alternative courses of action. Of course, the determinist argues that this feeling is merely an illusion because our course of action has already been decided for us by causes beyond our control. But the "illusion" persists in our inner, subjective experience nonetheless. For example, a good student probably *feels* that she or he could have chosen to go to more parties while a negligent student likely *feels* that he or she could have decided to study harder. In his or her practical affairs, even the most staunch determinist probably *feels free* to choose between alternative courses of action. No matter how solidly convinced we may be that determinism offers us a rational account of all natural phenomena and perhaps most human behaviour, we still find it difficult—if not impossible—to *believe* subjectively that we are never free. Thus, determinism requires us to reject as illusory a universal human experience. Libertarianism, on the other hand, acknowledges the feeling of freedom as a natural part of the experience of exerting our free will. According to James, this is a good reason to adopt the free will thesis. While he concedes that determinism is a rational theory of reality from an objective standpoint, James argues that libertarianism is an even more rational position because it can account for our inner, subjective experience of freedom.

Another important fact of human experience that James believes a rational theory must explain are *feelings of regret*. Our dissatisfaction

To Study or To Party?

Free Will Re-considered

Suppose you have an examination tomorrow and a friend asks you to forgo studying and spend the evening at a party. Your friend does not urge or threaten or coerce you. You consider the alternatives, and after a moment's thought, decide to give up studying for that night, and go to the party. We would ordinarily say that you are responsible for your decision. We think of such cases as actions in which you are free to decide one way or the other.

Contrast this to a situation in which a headache leads you to lie down and fall asleep on your bed instead of continuing to study. In this case it would not make sense to say that you are free to decide one way or the other about studying. The dispute between advocates of free will and advocates of determinism is basically a dispute whether incidents like the two so cited, which feel so different, are really radically and essentially different when viewed objectively.

Whereas the advocate of free will would perceive these two sorts of acts as essentially different, the determinist would not. The determinist might argue that although you may believe that your decision to stay home to study for the exam was an expression of free choice, nevertheless closer scrutiny would reveal that your behavior was not really free after all. What you thought was a free choice was really a choice dictated by your desires, which in turn spring from your character, which in its turn is fashioned by the forces of heredity and environment, which are clearly beyond your control.

The central affirmation of determinism is that every event has a cause. By an analysis of the causes of any one of your actions, the determinist would cause your so-called freedom to vanish in a chain of causes that stretches back into the remote recesses of your heredity and environment. Nature and nurture, genes and society — those are the factors that made you what you are and cause you to act the way you do. The notion that you are free is really a misapprehension, an illusion.

Adapted from *An Introduction to Modern Philosophy* by Donald M. Borchert.

with the world, especially with human behaviour, leads us to regret; that is, to "wish that something might be otherwise." After receiving a poor mark in the course, for instance, the negligent student may *regret* that he chose to spend all his time socializing. And because we regret the actions of others as well as our own, you may also *regret* that he had not studied. The most significant regrets concern the moral sphere. We do not accept as inevitable the senseless murders, rapes, and cases of child abuse we read about in the newspaper; instead, we judge such acts to be bad or immoral to the highest degree and regret that they are part of our world.

A regret implies that something is bad, and "calling a thing bad means … that the thing ought not to be, that something else ought to be in its stead." When we label someone's action immoral, we imply that it

---

Review

Am I Free or Determined?

This article by Melanie Chaparian explores one of the most basic philosophical dilemmas: does an individual possess free choice or is the path a person walks determined by circumstances beyond his or her control?

The author cites the work of the American philosopher/psychologist William James (1842–1910), who espoused the doctrine of "libertarianism." An advocate of free will, James argued that the theory that all human actions are the effects of prior causes cannot be scientifically proven.

James also observed that human beings have the capacity for feeling regret, and to regret an action implies an awareness of our ability to create consequences. Since we know we could have acted otherwise, we must assume the existence of free will.

---

should not have been done and that the person should have acted otherwise. For instance, when we proclaim that a murderer is guilty of the highest moral offence, we mean that he should not have committed homicide and should have instead settled the grievance with his victim in a peaceful, humane manner. Regrets obviously assume the existence of free will. For this reason, libertarianism offers us a better explanation of our regrets than does determinism.

The source of our deepest regrets is the recognition that the world is fraught with immorality. According to determinism, even the most heinous crimes are as much the result of cause and effect as the routine activities we do every day. Knowing the causes of immoral actions does not eliminate our regret that they occur, but it does make our regret merely futile hope. Libertarianism, on the other hand, recognizes immoral actions as the result of free will and, as such, acknowledges that other actions could have been performed instead. Since this applies to future as well as past actions, there exists the possibility that the world—although certainly imperfect—may be made a better and more moral place through free human action. Thus, from the libertarian viewpoint, regrets may virtually be taken at face value—as expressions of our belief that immoral actions *can* be avoided and *should not* take place. This, according to James, renders libertarianism a more rational theory of human existence.

James admits from the outset that his defence consists of the argument that libertarianism is more rational than determinism because it offers a better account of our feelings of freedom and regret. This is not a claim that can be proven objectively, but one that can only be "verified" by consulting our inner, subjective sense. Although James argues that determinism is also incapable of objective demonstration, he acknowledges that determinism appeals to a different kind of rationality, perhaps what we might call a scientific rationality. Even though James finds libertarianism to be more rational than determinism, it remains for each of us to study both theories to see which of the two *we* find to be the most rational.

"I WANT TO BE AN ENGINEER JUST LIKE MY MOM"

Ontario
Women's
Directorate

Mavis Wilson
Minister Responsible
for Women's Issues

480 University Ave.
2nd Floor
Toronto, Ontario
M5G 1V2
(416) 597-4500

107C Johnson Ave.
Thunder Bay, Ontario
P7B 2V9

(807) 345-6084

UNIT 2

CHANGE IN THE SOCIAL WORLD

■ **ISSUE 1:**
Dynamics of Social Change

■ **ISSUE 2:**
Public and Private Roles

Equal pay demonstration in Ottawa, Ontario, 1991.

Dynamics of Social Change

We make history ourselves, but, in the first place, under very definite antecedents and conditions. Among these the economic ones are ultimately decisive. But the political ones, etc., and indeed even the traditions which haunt human minds also play a part, although not the decisive one ...

Frederick Engels

Though women do not complain of the power of husbands, each complains of her own husband, or the husbands of her friends. It is the same in all other cases of servitude; at least in the commencement of the emancipatory movement. The serfs did not at first complain of the power of the lords, but only of their tyranny.

J. S. Mill

We are here to claim our right as women, not only to be free, but to fight for freedom. That is our right as well as our duty. It is our privilege, as well as our pride and our joy, to take some part in this militant movement which, as we believe, means the regeneration of all humanity.

Christabel Pankhurst

Introduction

John Steckley and Michael Badyk

What do we mean by the term "social change"? We mean that within a group of people at least one aspect of life has been altered significantly. For example, when we say that in Canada no households had televisions in 1951, while 90% did in 1963, we are talking about one form of social change taking place.

When speaking about social change, we often use the term "society." It can be used to refer to groups of people at a number of different levels: (a) a group within a country (e.g., French-Canadian society); (b) the country itself (e.g., Canadian society); or, (c) a unit beyond the level of a country but still recognizable as one group (e.g., North American society or Western society). So, society is just a particular group of people. Society itself is not uniquely human; many animals exist in social units. It aids them in their survival, and it was likely a necessary part of early human survival. We have retained this characteristic to this day.

Usually when we mention society we also use another term—**culture**. Culture is a totality of a way of life. It includes food, art, history and just about anything else that you can think of. Culture is passed from generation to generation. The process by which children acquire their culture through learning is called *enculturation*.

Culture is not passed down from generation to generation entirely intact. There are always changes caused by innovations and innovators within the culture or society. Change can also occur when one culture has contact with another. They trade ideas and materials. These two points (innovation and trade) are known as *acculturation*.

Social change is similar to change in the life of an individual. Alter one aspect of a person's life, and other elements are affected. We can see this when a person leaves high school and enters college. It is not just the education level that changes, but the person's entire life experience. There are *material* changes as well. The environment that the person encounters is different. The college student may have to travel further, by a different means of transportation, to an area he or

CULTURE
Culture is a totality of a way of life. It includes food, art, history and just about anything else that you can think of. Culture is passed from generation to generation.

she might not know. Locations of classrooms, offices, cafeterias and washrooms must be learned.

There are also changes in the student's *social* world. The population of the college is drawn from a broad area, and includes ethnically diverse groups. The student is drawn into new friendships with other people in the same program.

The student's world of ideas, or *intellectual* sphere, changes as well, and not just in what is taught in class. For example, the student learns to think of time in different ways. He or she may have more "free" time outside of the classroom, but must learn to budget that time to deal with a greater workload. The student also encounters new ideas, both inside the classroom and among friends, and develops a different perspective in this world.

Eventually these changes end up creating a set of social or cultural **values**. Values are those things that our society perceives as good, or wise, or right. In many ways these values are the items that allow us to recognize a particular society or culture.

There is also conflict within the society as competing groups having different aims struggle to have their interests represented. Those who own and control resources are interested in maintaining and benefiting from their ownership. Other individuals or groups see new, or what they feel are better, ways of doing things and challenge the existing methods. This challenge sometimes takes place in the context of technological change such as the development of stone tools, the invention of the combustion engine and the widespread use of the computer. In the case of computers we have seen a remarkable growth of their use and a proliferation of competing companies, systems and software systems.

Even though social change is inevitable, it is not always welcomed by everyone. People tend to be comfortable with the society they are familiar with. Sometimes this resistance to change can lead to serious problems of adjustment. These adjustment problems happen frequently when different cultures come into contact with one another for the first time.

There is a tendency to view things from the perspective of one's own culture. In other words, we tend to place our culture ahead of others that we come into contact with. This is known as **ethnocentricity**. Unfortunately ethnocentricity frequently involves stereotyping, discrimination, racism and prejudice. Probably the best example of this is the legacy of European/Native dealings over the past four or five hundred years. All too often we were taught that the Native Canadian cultures were primitive, made up of savages with nothing to offer the Europeans.

VALUES

Values are those things that our society perceives as good, or wise, or right. In many ways these values are the items that allow us to recognize a particular society or culture.

ETHNOCENTRICITY

Ethnocentricity is the tendency to view things from the perspective of one's own culture, placing one's own culture ahead of others that we come into contact with. Unfortunately, ethnocentricity frequently involves stereotyping, discrimination, racism and prejudice.

Part of a demonstration during the Oka crisis outside the parliament buildings, Queen's Park, Toronto.

The Europeans also felt that they altered all aspects of the Natives' lives for the better. Technology, language, religion, and agriculture from Europe were all considered to be improvements. In truth, the aboriginal people were very sophisticated in all of these areas. Most of the people living in Southern Ontario were growing crops—corn, beans, and squash—then unavailable to Europeans. They also had a more nutritious diet than that of most people living in Europe during the 16th and 17th centuries, and, as a consequence, were generally taller than most Europeans. Their axes, knives and arrowheads were manufactured from flint often obtained through complex Native-only trade networks. They spoke languages filled with terms and concepts for which European languages were silent. The fields, forests and waterways were alive with spirits, whereas Europeans just saw the physical world. But still the Europeans felt that they were superior.

But acculturation works both ways. What did the Native peoples give the Europeans? Many things; for example, their crops would eventually make up most of the food crops grown in the world, as they are today. One particularly important cultural trade item was the potato. It seems to be an insignificant item but it has changed the whole world. Over much of Europe the crop most frequently grown in the past few centuries was wheat. Wheat doesn't grow well in all places, either because of cold or wet summers, or a combination of both. Whenever the wheat crop failed starvation was widespread. The potato would thrive in the cold wet conditions because it had originated in the cold, wet mountains of Central and South America.

Potatoes are also much more nutritious than grains and they offer a big dose of Vitamin C, which was generally lacking in most Europeans' diets. Starvation was reduced, people were healthier and they lived longer.

In Russia, and what is now Poland, the potato was viewed as the "food of the devil" because of its almost magical health properties. The Empress, Catherine The Great, realized the importance of this crop and by royal decree forced the people to plant it. Now it is part-and-parcel of Russian culture, being used for food but also to make vodka, another Russian tradition.

Elsewhere it was adopted more readily. In Ireland, it caused a profound change. In 1754, Ireland had a population of 3.2 million; by 1845 the population soared to 8.2 million, plus another 1.75 million had emigrated out of Ireland. This population growth can be attributed directly to better nutrition from the potato. Irish dependence on the potato was so complete that when a potato blight (a fungal infestation) ruined the potato crop in the 1850s, thousands and maybe millions starved. They had no other crop to fall back on. Their lives were now tied to this foreign food.

We associate Ireland and potatoes to this day. Indeed, the package of potatoes we buy from Prince Edward Island shows a cartoon character consisting of a potato with an Irish hat in one hand and a shamrock (an Irish plant that is considered a good luck charm) in the other. This use of symbol is somewhat ironic since the potato originates here in the Western Hemisphere, not in Ireland.

In summary, trade in culture goes both ways. We end up with something new. In the U.S.A. you are almost forced to assimilate into what is known as the "American melting pot." You are an American first, and your ancestral background comes second. This decrease in cultural diversity is known as *assimilation*. Here in Canada we are more multicultural. You are encouraged to maintain your heritage.

Should we encourage people to assimilate into Canadian society? If so what exactly is Canadian society and culture when we have such a diverse grouping of citizens? These are difficult questions to answer. One way to get some clues about the influences on our society is to look at somewhat less complex or geographically isolated societies.

Change and the Family Meal

John Steckley

We tend to look at change in two ways. If the change is technological, we usually think it is good, taking us closer to "Star Trek: The 21st Century Generation." If the change is in the social world, we seem to feel it is bad, taking us away from an earlier, better time. Yet both types of change are quite similar and are often closely linked. Neither technological technique nor social form are carved in stone, not etched in our DNA (genetic programming). It is just as natural for humans to have different types of families as it is for us to have varied means of sending messages—through words spoken, written by hand, typed, printed, faxed or flashed over video screens.

Both types of change enable us to gain something new and compel us to lose something old. We are well aware that technological innovation brings with it new skills, but we often overlook the fact that it can sound the death knell of old skills as well. One reason we hold feats of ancient large-scale construction in awe (and sometimes foolishly assume the ancients could not have done them without the help of aliens) is because we have lost their technological expertise. Take, for example, that 4,000-year-old marvel, the enormous stone rings of Stonehenge in England. Without our modern moving equipment we could not move the smaller 8,000-pound stones of the inner circle of Stonehenge the torturous 300-mile journey they took from the Presely Mountains in Wales (where the stone was quarried) because we have lost the knowledge of how to do it.

Change in the social world can bring gains that we applaud as well as the losses we more typically mourn. Child labour laws in 19th-century Britain (such as the Act of 1833 that reduced the maximum work week of a child under 11 to 69 hours, and of a young adult under 18 to 84 hours) substantially reduced the presence of children in textile mills and other factories. Only the more short-sighted factory owners and shareholders wore black at the funeral of that social form.

The connections between technological and social change are strong. Change in one area affects the other (with the former often driving the latter). The industrial revolution of the late 18th and 19th centuries brought new and much more powerful sources of energy (initially coal-fired steam) and the monster machines driven by this energy to the world of manufacturing. This had a powerful effect on the family, as thousands left the countryside and went to work in the factories, mines and other newly-developing businesses in the cities. As countries industrialized, people waited longer to get married—they could not depend on getting a piece of the family farm, so they had to save enough money to establish a household. In Canada, during the great industrialization period of 1851 to 1891, the average age of first marriage went up from 23.8 to 26.1 for females and 26.8 to 29.2 for males. It is not higher than that today. The number of children in a family began to drop because children were no longer as much in demand; there were cheap, home-grown farm labourers, and more women entered the work force prior to marriage. (It has been estimated that in 1891 in Canada, one out of every eight paid workers was a woman, suggesting that perhaps at least one-quarter to one-third of all Canadian women worked before getting married.)

Let's look at the family meal to illustrate the linking of technological and social change. The changes in the family meal also show how change in the family is a natural adaptation to changing conditions rather than a lamented deterioration in life.

First, we need some kind of definition of what the family meal is. For our purposes here, the family meal is an event in which all of the family members get together at one time and place to eat the largest meal of the day. As a daily event it is very much the product or innovation of a society in which farming is the main food-producing activity. Such daily feasts were relatively unusual in the earlier established lifestyle of hunting and gathering societies where eating occurred more casually whenever food was available, a person was hungry or someone was visiting. Large-scale family meals in such societies typically involved more than one family, perhaps the whole community, and it was usually a ceremony celebrating the success of the hunt. (Think of the scenes in the movie *Dances with Wolves* after the Lakota Sioux and Kevin Costner had returned from hunting the *tatanka* [buffalo]).

Industrialization altered this act of family life as much as any other. The time shifted for one thing. Instead of being a massive midday meal it became a night-time affair. Lunch was born. Many of us have learned about the differences between city and country meals after going to the country to visit grandparents. The midday meal is often called "dinner" and it is huge; the night-time meal is called "supper" and it is usually merely big.

The role of the father also changed. The father on the farm was not usually far away from the other members of the family. He often saw, worked and talked with his wife and children during the day. When dad went to work alone in the industrialized city he became isolated from the rest of the family. The family meal was one time in which he could become reacquainted with his wife and children. But it was also the long-awaited and dreaded time for "Wait until your father gets home"—new tension entered the family meal.

Tension also came from other sources as the family meal moved into the twentieth century. "Scientific" child-raising of the first few decades dictated that children should not be pampered by getting their own way, but needed firm discipline. "Let them cry; don't give in to them or you will fail as a parent," the books said. The family meal became an experimental test area for that theory and "making them eat the right things" also became important.

The majority of Canadians didn't live in cities until the second decade of the twentieth century. This move changed children's eating habits in a number of ways. The economies of food alter when food is purchased in the city rather than grown on one's own farm in the country. Meals will have less volume and less variety at any one sitting. This made life tougher for children with fussier appetites. Opportunities for alternatives more suited to a child's particular tastes—junk food— also became available. Corner stores were close by. Part-time work and allowances as payment for work done at home meant that children had money to spend on "treats." "Spoiling your appetite" became a new sin.

The test for the new meal-time experiment began with the words, "You're going to sit there until you're finished your brussels sprouts. There are starving children who would love to eat them." Children who did not finish their food were sometimes forced to remain at the table in a battle of wills with their parents.

Anthropologists say that behaviour becomes ritualized when its performance takes on a significance that is more symbolic than a reflection of something practical. For example, in Western society wearing ties is a ritualized activity, symbolizing that a man is formally dressed, no matter what else he is wearing. During the twentieth century, the family meal became ritualized and parents became custodians of the rituals, the ones responsible for the rituals being performed correctly. An important part of this job was to see that the family meal was a certain length of time, like in "more cultured times when we (the parents) were young."

Radio became the first great iconoclast (ritual or symbol breaker). The children had their favourite radio shows that they did not want to miss. Parents had them too, but they didn't want the "meal heathens" to know that. In many homes across Canada, the "great radio compromise" must have taken place. The sacred words of this important contract were "We will turn the radio on for your program while we are eating if you promise to be quiet and to eat at least some of your brussels sprouts." It was the beginning of the end for the traditional family meal.

Many families in North America have developed lifestyles that depend upon fast-food restaurants.

And then came television. The wandering eyes of the viewer would follow the restless ears of the listener. Family members began a migration towards the TV, a move that cut a path across the time territory of the family meal. Eventually, television even came with its own meal and it own table—the frozen TV dinner and the TV tray!

All this is somewhat ironic. Television tries hard to push the so-called traditional family. Commercials preserve the housewife whose world revolves around the three c's—cooking, cleaning and curing. You see more such women on the screen than in your neighbourhood.

Studies show that the more television children watch, the more traditional views they have towards female roles. And yet the networks try hard to keep the airwaves "clean" during "family viewing hours." You'll not see significant nudity nor hear words from the street (or the schoolyard) during prime time.

Still, television promotes the move, or should one call it the trek, from the family table at dinner time by offering some of its most enticing programs for the entire range of family members. Here's the schedule for six o'clock, Wednesday, May 1, 1991: for the little ones, "Polka Dot Door;" the next age group has YTV's "Rock'n Talk;" one group older has Much Music's "Spotlight;" then for all ages, "Star Trek: The Next Generation" and the "Cosby Show;" and finally, for the more elderly, fantasy traveller (for they are the true "cruisers"), "Love Boat." Did the networks miss anyone?

Our cooking technology has joined the family meal revolution. Consider the following scene from an episode of "Star Trek: The Next Generation." Commander Riker has just prepared a "real" omelette rather than making one the usual way with a food replicator. Data, the android, questions why Riker would go to such trouble rather than have a computer instantly produce the same omelette from whatever raw material the replicator uses. Doctor Polaski replies that cooking your own meal was an important part of an ancient twentieth-century ritual, linking long preparation with the eating of a meal together as a significant social occasion. The implication was that with individuals being able to produce instant meals to their own tastes whenever they wanted, the family meal became obsolete.

In a sense she was right, even for today. We have a kind of instant food replicator now: the microwave oven. No longer is a family forced to have dinner together because the cooking apparatus is taken for long periods of time—even half an hour can be long if you are hungry—just to prepare one basic dinner. We now have more choice. With rapid-fire microwave ovens, separate meals can be prepared quickly whenever a person wants, whatever that person wants (as a variety of "microwaveable" dishes become available). Children soon learn its operation, often faster than adults do. New technology such as this benefits best the new-of-mind, with no traditions to get in the way.

Should we mourn the decline of the family meal? Think of it this way. One of the indignities of being in a hospital, one of the most depersonalizing aspects of hospital life, is that you are forced to eat at hospital dinner time and to take whatever is being served (because "it is good for you"). Do we miss that when we return home? Isn't that a lot like the traditional family meal?

Perhaps the present author is prejudiced. I grew up dreading the family meal. I remember the shame of my bad marks being announced at dinner for the whole family to hear, sisters not too sympathetic (parents neither) to the excuses I gave. I recall my father constantly watching and judging my sloppy eating habits and wondering out loud why I couldn't eat like a "normal human being." I firmly believe that my family meal experiences are why I eat so quickly now and why it took me a long time to learn how to eat at a "leisurely" and "civilized" pace in a restaurant, rather than bolting down my food and bolting out the door to "freedom."

What does that leave us with? Let's look first to the hunters and gatherers discussed earlier. In traditional hunting and gathering cultures people shared food when circumstances permitted. It was something special, a willing decision of the participants. Perhaps that is where we are going today, with family meals being infrequent, but desired on special occasions.

And maybe technology is offering us solutions, if we choose to see them. With video rentals being a rising phenomenon, more and more families are watching films together. Along with that comes a technologically produced "family snack," popcorn made in a microwave. The shared experience of movie and popcorn is usually an enjoyable one. Perhaps our childrens' grandchildren will look back to that as the family meal that makes them feel sentimental; by then there might be food replicators, and new social forms.

The author admits that so far he has been overstating his case. The important thing is this: it should not be forgotten that in virtually all change there are both positive and negative aspects. In stressing one, you should not ignore the other.

At the beginning of this article we looked at great historic technological enterprises such as Stonehenge in terms of skills lost through change. That does not mean that we should see that change in purely negative terms. We are fortunate that we have the new heavy moving machinery and don't have to resort to the "tricks" of the past (which probably involved strenuous labour on the part of a lot of people).

Likewise, the decline of the family meal as we have come to know it is also two-sided, both good and bad. Perhaps the negative aspect lies foremost in the area of values, a kind of intellectual change. The family meal taught, among other things, that the family had a significance beyond that of the individual, that a family need could be more important than an individual need sometimes and that some compromise is necessary in life. Those are important lessons. You don't have to go to the extreme of a Thomas Hobbes to believe that too much individualism can be destructive to society. Acting like good cooperative family members would certainly look good on us all—from powerful politicians and corporate leaders, to high-salaried athletes, and the rest of us.

Family Values—The Bargain Breaks

The Economist

Marriage is a bargain between men and women. That bargain is increasingly broken by divorce. The sufferers are men, women and children.

Once the rock on which society was founded, marriage is being increasingly chiselled away. All over the industrial world, more couples are choosing to live together and even to start a family without marrying. More of those who do marry subsequently divorce. This article examines these trends. It argues that women increasingly see marriage as a bad bargain; but that divorce may not be a better one.

First, the trends. Men and women are marrying later. In the 12 countries of the EC the mean age of marriage for women is now just over 25, two years older than in the late 1970s. In the United States by the end of the 1980s, the age of marriage for American women stood at a 20th-century high. To some extent, the decline in marriage has been offset by a rise in cohabitation. The prevalence of cohabitation varies enormously. In northern Europe people tend to live together for long periods. In America such partnerships are shorter. In Italy people hardly ever cohabit.

Births out of wedlock are not always births to women living alone. In Sweden more than half of all births are to unwed mothers, but perhaps three-quarters of these are to women living in "consensual unions"—i.e., stable partnerships. Such households are also common in Britain, where 30% of all births are out of wedlock, but much rarer in America, where one in four births of all babies (and 60–65% of black babies) is to a single mother.

People enter marriage later; they leave it earlier. By far the highest divorce rate in the industrial world is that of the United States. On current rates, about half of all American marriages will be dissolved. In Europe, if present rates continue, two out of every five marriages in Britain, Denmark and Sweden will end in divorce, but only one in ten in some southern European countries. "Even in Japan," says John

EC—European Community.

Family Matters

Family Values and Social Change

Change is everywhere around us. Whether we like it or not it is a part of life.

Communities all around the world are made up of families who take care of their individual members. People are born, grow up, fall in love and care for one another. Part of every stage of life involves people making decisions about organizing, collecting, producing and choosing how to get access to or manage the resources available.

The first article in this section "Family Values" describes some of the changing expectations that are taking place within the family itself. The division of labour where men work in the public realm while women take care of the private sphere is no longer a reality for most families. The majority of women are now participating in the "paid" work force leading to a double work load for many. At the same time, the so called "typical" nuclear family is no longer as typical as it once was. Blended families and single-parent families are common.

Ermisch, professor of economics at Glasgow University and author of a recent book on lone parenthood[1], "on present trends one marriage in five will eventually end in divorce."

In many countries the divorce rate picked up in the 1960s and accelerated in the 1970s. In the United States the rate doubled between 1966 and 1976. Now it shows signs of levelling off in several countries, including the United States and Sweden (it has fallen in both), Britain and Holland.

More births out of wedlock and more divorce mean more children spending at least part of their youth in one-parent families. In the United States a quarter of all families with children are headed by one parent; in Britain, one in five; in Sweden and Denmark, one family in seven. Divorce is the main reason. In the United States, half of all children are likely to witness the break-up of their parents' marriage; in Britain, a quarter; in Norway, a third.

Breaking Up

Does a common cause lie behind these changes in the importance of marriage, and particularly in the increase in divorce? Some see a

---

[1] "Lone Parenthood: an Economic Analysis." National Institute of Economic and Social Research.

pervasive cultural change, an erosion of morality that has accompanied the decline of religious belief and the rise of materialism. Others point to changes in the laws which have made divorces easier to obtain. Still others see a link with the rise in women's employment.

A change in attitudes to divorce has certainly taken place. In 1945 and again in 1966, national samples of Americans were asked if they thought the divorce laws in their states were too strict or not strict enough. In both years, the most popular response was "not strict enough." But at some point after 1968, a sharp change in attitudes took place. In 1968 and 1974, a sample of Americans was asked whether divorce should be made easier or more difficult. Between the two sample years, the number replying "easier" rose by 15%, while the number who said "more difficult" declined by 21%. Since then, the proportion who thought divorce should be more difficult has been increasing once again; by 1989 it accounted for a majority of Americans.

But what people believe and what they do may be quite different. Andrew Cherlin, author of a riveting book[1] on American marriage, draws attention to a group of young mothers who were interviewed several times between 1962 and 1977. At first, half the women agreed with the sentiment: "When there are children in the family, parents should stay together even if they don't get along." But the women who agreed were almost as likely as those who disagreed to divorce in the following 15 years.

Changes in attitudes may have accompanied or followed the rise in divorce, rather than caused it. The same may well be true of changes in the law, although each time a divorce law is made more permissive, the divorce rate tends to rise a little. But for underlying causes it may be wiser to look at the job market rather than the courts.

Since the end of the second world war, the proportion of women in paid employment has risen dramatically in every industrial country. Increasingly, women now go out to work even while their children are toddlers. Almost two-thirds of all women in the OECD have paid work, and in Sweden the proportion (four out of five) is almost as high as for men.

OECD (Organization for Economic Cooperation and Development)— 24 of the industrialized countries.

The expanding employment of women is a theme that runs through many of the changes occurring in the family. Gary Becker, professor of economics at Chicago University and winner of the 1992 Nobel prize for economics, has encouraged people to think of the economic forces that influence people to get married and have children. He believes they are as powerful as the forces that govern decisions to buy a new

---

[1] *Marriage, Divorce, Remarriage.* Harvard University Press

In the past the traditional patriarchal family held a secure and unquestioned place at the centre of society.

car or change jobs. The better the opportunities for women to earn, the greater the costs of giving up work to have children, and so the later women are likely to start their families and the fewer children they are likely to have. "Children are cheaper during recessions," Mr Becker observed when he gave his presidential address to the American Economics Association.

Mr Becker was by no means the first to point out that women's employment might affect marriage. Back in 1919 one Arthur W. Calhoun argued that "the fact of women's access to industry must be a prime factor in opening to her the possibility of separation from husband." A number of studies, mainly of American women in the 1970s, have shown that married women with jobs are more likely to divorce or separate than those who stay home.

Mr Ermisch, whose book analyses the economic forces behind the break-up of marriages in Britain, establishes that the more time British women spend in paid work, the more likely their marriage is to end in divorce. Of course, it is unlikely that the mere act of getting a job makes women unhappy in their marriages—although, as Mr Ermisch puts it, "Their employment may provide better opportunities for meeting another partner who compares favourably with their present one." But women with an income may worry less about the poverty that generally comes with divorce; and those in unhappy marriages may see employment as an insurance policy.

Fathers Don't Do the Ironing

Once women earn, one of the oldest advantages of marriage is undermined: economic support. Another, sex, is safely available without marriage, thanks to effective contraception. As a result, couples—or rather, wives—are likely to care more about the other potential benefits of marriage, such as emotional support or help in the home.

The extra emphasis on marriage as an emotional partnership may make it more vulnerable. That men and women expect different things from marriage has been the stuff of good novels for many years, but the differences are now minutely picked over by sociologists. Penny Mansfield, a member of One plus One, a British research group, has been studying a group of 65 London couples who married in 1979. Interviewed in the sixth year of their marriage, each partner was asked to describe a range of social and family relationships, and then to say to whom they felt closest. Several husbands (but no wives) were baffled by the question. "I don't know what you mean, 'feel closest to'," said one. "People of most importance in my life? Who I'd be most worried by if something happened to them?"

The gap between expectation and reality grows wider once children arrive. The sort of partnership advocated by romantic magazines is hugely time-consuming. Finding space for all those candle-lit dinners and meaningful conversations is difficult enough when both partners have jobs; it is harder still when they have children as well. True, husbands—at least in the United States and Britain—boast to sociolo-

The proportion of women in paid employment has risen dramatically in every industrial country.

Increasingly, women now go out to work even while their children are toddlers.

gists like Miss Mansfield that they play a bigger part in running the house than their fathers did. Sadly, as Kathleen Kiernan, of the Family Policy Studies Centre in London, points out in the latest issue of British Social Attitudes, reality is usually different.

She has looked at couples where both partners are employed, and compared men who disagree with the statement, "A husband's job is to earn money; a wife's job is to look after the home and family," with men who agree. The "egalitarian" men are more likely than the fogeys to share household tasks. But whereas half share the shopping and the evening's washing up, only a third share the cleaning or preparation of the evening meal, and only 12 percent share the washing and ironing. The proportion of couples who think such tasks should be shared has increased since 1984, but the practice has hardly changed.

Washing up the evening dishes seems to be, she reports, "an idiosyncrasy of the British male, or a success story for the British female." Seven out of ten British men do at least some of the washing up, compared with an EC average of four out of ten. Maybe this foible of British husbands explains the extraordinary reluctance of their wives to acquire automatic dishwashers. In 1990 only 12% of British households owned dish-washers; 20% had a home computer and 50% a microwave.

Men seem to be more willing to help with looking after children than with household chores. Miss Mansfield, drawing on British and American research, argues that "men who become involved with their children often do so because their partner is working. They tend to have better relationships with both their children and their wives. Indeed, women seem to find it very sexy when men care for their children. It creates a new bond in the marriage." But if the husbands do not help much in the home, and the job market beckons, some women may wonder what they gain from being married. The costs of divorce may then seem smaller than the costs of staying in an unsatisfactory marriage. The trouble with that siren song is the evidence that divorce is bad for people: for men, for women and, above all, for children. Married people tend to be healthier people. At every age, as a recent study of Britain by One plus One records, men and women are more likely to die prematurely if they are single, divorced or widowed than if they are married. These differences partly reflect the lower incomes of those who are not married. But whatever adjustments are made, it is clear that people suffer physically from not being married—and, incidentally, men suffer more than women.

Wanting Out

As ever, some of the links may run both ways. For example, among both sexes, the divorced are the group most likely to be admitted to mental hospitals. This may simply prove that the unstable make difficult partners. Similarly, in Britain divorced men are the heaviest drinkers. But alcoholics may be less likely to marry and more likely to be thrown out by their partners than those who drink moderately.

Divorce also affects living standards. Men may actually see their disposable incomes rise, especially if they pay little or no child support. Official American figures for 1989 found that 41% of all divorced and separated women living with children under 21 received nothing from their former husbands; the rest received on average just over $3,000 a year.

The predictable upshot is that women and children are poorer. A study of American families who have been interviewed each year since 1968 finds that separated and divorced women suffer an average fall of about 30% in their incomes the year after their marriage breaks up. Worst hurt are middle-class wives who have stayed at home. But 31% of all wives whose incomes were above average when they were married found that their living standards fell by more than half in the first year after their marriages collapsed.

To cope with poverty, divorced mothers go out to work. Their working patterns are different from those of their married sisters. In most countries (but not in Britain), they are more likely to have paid work. Even so, they make up a large and growing proportion of the poor in most industrial countries. It may be a struggle to bring up a family on a single male wage with the free child care that a stay-at-home wife can provide; it is harder still to raise children on a single female wage, especially if they are young enough to need to be looked after.

Moreover, the poverty does not end when the children grow up. For a woman, divorce often means losing pension rights, as well as income; in the next century, some of society's poorest people will be elderly women whose marriages broke up in middle age, especially if they had stayed at home to care for the children. The problem could be particularly severe in Britain, where pension rights are rarely divided at divorce.

Heather Joshi, a British economist, has estimated that the lifetime earnings of a married mother of two may be little over a quarter of those of a similarly qualified married man. Marriage, she points out, is often a bargain: the husband can earn more because the wife gives up employment opportunities to care for the home. The labour market is employing the couple, not the husband alone. Pensions legislation, she argues, should recognize that reality. Divorce makes men unhealthy and women poor. But it also seems to be worse for children than was once thought. Oddly, the long-term effects of divorce on children is an area where little research has been done, and most of the evidence comes from the United States and Britain. It would be helpful to know whether the effects are the same in, for example, Sweden, where lone parents are less poor and single-parenthood seems to be more socially acceptable.

Children Suffer

A dramatic account of the effects of divorce on children has come from work by an American, Judith Wallerstein, who studied 131 children from 60 recently separated families at a counselling centre in Marin County, California. She paints a dismal picture. Ten years after their parents' divorce, the boys were "unhappy and lonely;" they and the girls found it hard to form relationships with the opposite sex. Unfortunately, her study was confined to problem families; and as no control group of children in intact families was monitored, it is impossible to know how many of these young Hamlets would have been miserable anyway.

More convincing than such impressionistic research is the work conducted in America and Britain on surveys of random groups of children as they grow up. In the United States, Sara McLanahan has shown that children who grow up in single-parent families are more likely to drop out of school, marry during their teens, have a child

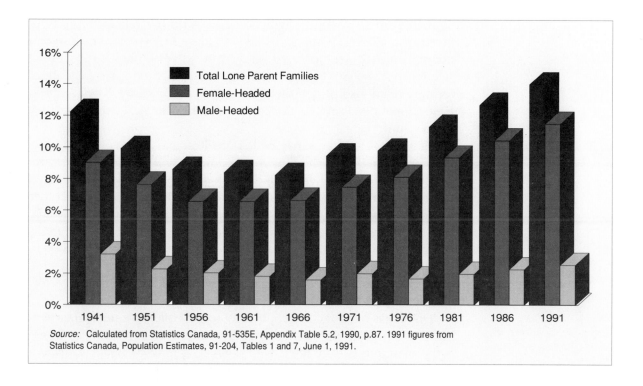

Source: Calculated from Statistics Canada, 91-535E, Appendix Table 5.2, 1990, p.87. 1991 figures from Statistics Canada, Population Estimates, 91-204, Tables 1 and 7, June 1, 1991.

before marrying and experience a breakdown of their own marriages. Some of these consequences—perhaps half, she estimates—are related to the poverty of single parent families. But the rest do indeed seem to be the other consequences of divorce.

Lone parent families in Canada, by type, 1941-1991.

Similar results have been found from surveys of British children born in a single week in 1946 and 1958. One study, by Ms Kiernan, found that girls brought up by lone parents were twice as likely to leave home by the age of 18 as the daughters of intact homes—and three times as likely to be cohabiting by the age of 18 and almost three times as likely to have a birth out of wedlock. Boys seemed to be slightly less affected than girls, but were more likely than their sisters to leave school by the age of 16 if they came from a one-parent family. Martin Richards, a Cambridge psychologist, has looked at the children born in 1958 and concludes that the chance of a child going to university is halved by a parental divorce. All these effects, incidentally, are either weaker or nonexistent when a father has died.

Mr Richards also notices another effect. When their mother remarries, the children of a divorce may no longer be poor. But the other effects of divorce are either unchanged or even strengthened. In particular, girls who live in step families are much more likely to leave school at 16, to leave home because of friction and to be married by the age of·

20 than even girls whose divorced mothers do not remarry. And boys in step families are particularly likely to leave home early because of a quarrel, and to set up home early. "In surveys," he reports sadly, "teenagers from divorced homes say sensible, cautious things about forming relationships; yet they do exactly the opposite. They seem to have a great need for affection, and when they find a relationship, they jump into it."

Many of these effects may be the result not of the divorce, which is easy to record, but of the thunderous atmosphere of a rocky marriage. An important study of children on both sides of the Atlantic appeared in *Science* in June 1991, by Mr Cherlin, Ms Kiernan and five other authors. It argued that "a substantial portion of what is usually considered the effect of divorce on children is visible before the parents separate." For boys in particular, most of the effects usually ascribed to divorce seem to appear before the parents actually break up.

Ask Mr Cherlin what he thinks today about the effects of divorce, and he responds thus:

"Divorce is bad for children, but not for all children equally. It is very bad for a small group of children, and moderately bad for many more. If the marriage is truly filled with conflict, it may be better to have a divorce. But here in the United States, many marriages that could limp along end because people are bored. I'm not sure that children are harmed in such marriages."

Language and Social Change

Jill Le Clair

Social change often affects even the language we use. As a result of major social changes taking place in society—in particular the increasing involvement of women in the labour force and the changing ethnic composition of Canada—many people are now more critical about the written material they encounter. They are beginning to re-evaluate it for *bias* and *stereotyping*.

Biases in writing can take many forms. Possible biases you might find are described below.

Bias against women. Sexism (androcentricity) refers to seeing the world as male centred or through mens' eyes. Often authors write as if there is one perspective and that is male. Clearly, half the world is made up of women, so it is important to understand a woman's point of view. Examples of male sexism are: writing from a male viewpoint or framework; suggesting that males are the people who do things, whereas women are the people things are done to; omitting to discuss women, so they become invisible; and trivializing problems experienced by women. In preparing her book *Nonsexist Research Methods: A Practical Guide* (Boston: Unwin Hyman, 1988), Margrit Eichler was not able to find examples of reverse sexism in contemporary journals.

Bias against ethnic or racial groups. In ethnic or racial biases, assumptions are made about specific groups of people based on stereotypes. The focus may be on the ethnic group of the individual or it could be based on skin colour. *Stereotyping* is when a person assumes that one individual will behave in the way a specific group has been expected to behave. An example of stereotyping is when a male student is on holiday in Europe and the hosts expect the Canadian student to be an excellent hockey player, when it is entirely possible that the student's preferred sport is basketball. Similarly, assuming that a person who has a black skin and comes from Kenya and lived in a small rural "undeveloped" village is jumping to conclusions. Many Kenyans, Nigerians, South Africans, etc., live in highly urbanized, modern cities.

Language and Change

Spot The Bias

Read the following statements and see if you can find anything in these quotes that leads you to think there may be something biased or overlooked.

SEXISM

1. *Sociologist Van den Berghe ... interprets intergroup warfare as a rational means of gaining livestock, women and slaves, gaining or keeping territory, or gaining, controlling and exploiting new territory." (Shaw quoted in Eichler, 1988: 22)*

This is a male point of view; intergroup assumes that the group is male, although the group does include women. Women are described as objects gained through warfare.

2. INTERVIEW QUESTION:

Agree or disagree with this statement:

It is generally better to have a man at the head of a department composed of both men and women employees. (Eichler, 1988: 43)

Here the choice in answering the question is restricted. How can the person answering the question disagree or support the opposite view that women might make better heads of departments?

3. *The journalistic fraternity is very concerned about protecting its sources.*

The language assumes that journalists are male—the "journalistic fraternity." The group is not referred to as a sorority or sisterhood.

4. *If a freshman student wants to register early he may apply at the registrar's office.*

The term freshman excludes freshwomen. The assumption is that the new student is male.

5. *The nursing department is manned by twenty people.*

Such a department obviously includes women. A more appropriate term would be staffed.

6. *God is viewed by Christians as all powerful. He can understand all that takes place in the world.*

The assumption here is that God is male.

7. *Jacob Mincer ... finds, for example, that quit rates in the union sector are about one-half as large as in the nonunion sector for young men and about one-third as large for men over 30.* (Frank quoted in Eichler, 1988: 28)

Women are totally overlooked in this example. Sexism by omission is a very common form of discrimination.

ETHNIC/RACIAL/CULTURAL

1. *Christopher Columbus discovered America in 1492.*

There were already communities in North America. A more accurate description would be: "Columbus was the first European to arrive in the Americas". Also his name is Anglicized—that is not how he spelled his own name.

2. *Canada was created in 1867.*

By 1867, the First Nations had lived for many centuries in the territory we now know as Canada. The British government created the origins of the political unit we now call Canada in 1867 (excluding Newfoundland of course).

3. *The primitive Indian game of lacrosse was far from being the slaughter too often conceived in the history of sport classes. Rather it was a game of great skill, which demanded a high degree of stamina and endurance, and which was played with passion. It*

was a noble game, although a vigourous one. (Jette quoted in J. Oxendine, *American Indian Sports Heritage.* Champaign, Illinois: Human Kinetics Books. 1988: 47)

It is unnecessary to describe the Indian game as primitive. Would the author describe English soccer games of the 19th century as primitive as well?

DISABLED

1. *In the past crippled persons were not permitted to participate in regular sport activities.*

Today the term "crippled" is not used. The word "disabled" is preferable.

SEXUAL ORIENTATION

1. *Some homosexuals tend to seek out a single relationship, hoping to gratify all emotional needs within a one-to-one exclusive relationship. Such twosomes are usually based on unrealistic expectations, often accompanied by inordinate demands; in most instances, these pairs are caught up in a turbulent, abrasive attachment. These liaisons are characterized by initial excitement which may include exultation and confidence in the discovery of a great love which soon alternates with anxiety, rage and depression as magical expectations are inevitably frustrated. (Bieber quoted in Isay, 1990: 146).*

The assumption is that somehow homosexuals have "weird" or unusual sexual relationships. The research does not support this view. Change the term homosexual to heterosexual and hopes for a great love are not any different.

Bias against the disabled. Often in the past those with disabilities were isolated from society or even physically hidden away. Even twenty years ago, people would talk about the "crippled," the "dumb" and the "retarded." Today it is expected, and it is the law under the Human Rights Code, that everyone is treated with respect. The most healthy and active person can become disabled in the few moments it takes for a car to go out of control on a road.

Bias against homosexuals. *Homophobia* is when people have a fear of people whose sexual orientation is to a person of the same sex. In many countries, homosexuals are labelled mentally deviant, put in jail or even put to death.

Do Men Speak Another Language?

Penney Kome

Over my desk hangs a photo torn from a men's fashion magazine, showing a tousle-haired fellow in tweedy country clothes. "Elegant and Easy," reads the caption. I wonder if any women's magazine would suggest fashions to make a woman look "easy." "Easy" is just one of the hundreds of words that takes on a sexual connotation when applied to women. English (as well as French and most other languages), is full of words that have different meanings for women than for men.

The difference is so great that I have come to think it represents two different languages: Manspeak and Womanspeak. Within every language there are words and phrases that mean different things when said by a woman or a man. When a man says, "I'm easy," he means he's agreeable; when a woman says, "I'm easy," most men hear it as an invitation. To succeed in men's world, most women have to learn Manspeak, though they may not realize that that's what they're doing. Men, conversely, rarely learn Womanspeak, because they seldom feel a need for it.

Language affects us in several ways: in how we use language rules, how we define words, and how we are defined by them. Until about 10 years ago, women were almost defined out of existence in everyday language, occupying a fringe space as distant relatives of "Mankind."

With feminism there came awareness that personal oblivion reflected political domination. Women realized that all women had to strain to make themselves heard by men, that what each woman had experienced privately as her own inarticulateness was actually a valid perception of a functional barrier to communication with men. Scholars suggest again and again that the only logical conclusion is that women and men use different languages.

Sociologically, the evidence collected over the past 10 years indicates clearly that the genders employ different tones of voice, styles of speech and body language when they attempt to communicate. As well,

A different language for a different world?

according to researchers such as Australian feminist Dale Spender, women and men are heard differently (especially by men) even when the words are identical.

For instance, a wife might say to her husband, "We really must spend less money next month, don't you think so, dear?" Many people would agree with the linguists who analyze such "women's" phrasing as weak, tentative, and the tag question at the end as indecisive. Let's turn the situation around, and have a husband say to his wife, "We really must spend less money next month, don't you think so, dear?" Now the phrasing appears to be a strong, decisive instruction, and the tag question can easily be interpreted as a veiled threat.

The way men speak conveys power, but it has other serious limitations on the speaker's self-expression. Consider this typical scene, where both parties end up dissatisfied:

She: Do you like my new dress?

He: Sure, it's nice.

She: Nice? Is that all you can say?

He: Okay, it's very nice. What do you want?

She: Well, if you don't like it, I won't wear it.

This couple's problem is that she's asking him to talk like a woman, and he can't. "Nice" is among the higher compliments available to most men; this fellow may praise his colleagues by saying they're "hard-hitting" or "top notch," but those words can hardly be used to describe a dress. Women's talk, on the other hand, is full of descriptive phrases and adjectives like "stunning," "fabulous," "divine," "smashing," which may sound effusive to the male ear, but which comfort and cheer men as well as women, nonetheless.

Of course, the existence of Womanspeak and Manspeak reflects our conventional expectations about women and men. Generally, we expect women to try to coax and persuade men and children to listen to them. Therefore we hear women's talk as indecisive and eager to please. Men's talk, on the other hand, sounds confident and authoritative, even when there's no substance to the words. Men usually can get women's attention right away; they need only to clear their throats. Women must make much more effort to be heard.

This is partly because men's language and women's language have different rules for conversation, as well as different meanings for individual words. According to the language rules men learn, conversation is a competition, like everything else in their lives. Women are taught to be helpful; to them, conversation is a collaboration.

"In conversations between women and men, women act as Band Aids, patching up gaps of the conversation," says Maryann Ayim, an associate professor of philosophy in the Faculty of Education at the University of Western Ontario. "Men are like wet sponges, in that they have a dampening effect. Far from being supportive, men frequently blatantly ignore female input, and change the topic at whim."

Pioneering studies on how women and men share conversations were reported by Candace West and D.H. Zimmerman in 1975. Researchers studied hours of "natural setting" conversations tape-recorded in the homes of volunteers. They found that men monopolized the conversations, talking more and longer than women did; that men interrupted women 96 percent of the times that women spoke; that women introduced 62 percent of conversation topics but were ignored by men 64 percent of the time; that women pursued 96 percent of topics men introduced. In short, men used Manspeak in order to "win" by controlling the situation. Womanspeak was ignored. These results have been replicated in many studies since then.

Perhaps the most surprising finding in all the empirical research is that women talk much less than men, popular myths to the contrary. This helps explain why, despite men's complaints that women never let them get a word in edgewise, despite all the jokes about how women can't keep secrets, women's lives through the ages are shrouded in the secrecy of the invisible, the ignored, or the forgotten. Dale Spender speculates that devaluing women's talk also served to keep safe men's secrets. Until recently, an enforced silence hid the "unspeakable" horrors of some women's home life: wife battering, child abuse, incest, and spousal rape.

Do men speak another language?

Children learn women's language long before they understand men's talk; but, oddly enough, boy children (deliberately?) forget Womanspeak as they grow up—some are sent to expensive schools to have it drummed out of them—so that as adult men, they can only hear when addressed by other men. Some Manspeakers pride themselves on never taking Womanspeakers seriously.

Sometimes women's speech patterns are so proper that they sound precious. Men have joked for generations about women who exclaim "Oh, fudge," or, "Dear me, good gracious," when the situation calls for a stronger exclamation. People responded without hesitation when linguist Robin Lakoff asked them to identify the sex of the speaker in each of the following two cases: "Oh dear me, I made a mistake," and "Shit, I made a mistake."

"Ladies'" reputations used to depend on their being protected from words like "shit." Women's language prevailed inside proper homes; cursing was banned, along with such profane topics as politics and commerce. Like an immigrant living in a neighbourhood full of people from the old country, or a Franco-Ontarian living in a French town, a woman can still manage almost every aspect of her daily life speaking only to other women, without having to raise her voice to be heard by men. As long as she knows her place, and sticks to her own kind, she can get by.

French-speaking men, as well as women, in private discussion have drawn the political analogy between feminism and language rights. In both cases, the status quo is maintained by the majority's seemingly wilful inability to understand what the minority says. Members of the language minority group must become bilingual in order to survive, and even then they may face discrimination. Members of the language majority have no urgent need to learn the minority language, and usually don't even realize what they're missing. Feminists are often told that they undermine their own arguments by being too shrill or too emotional or too womanish. In the same way, minority group members who try to communicate in their own language with the majority may be told peremptorily to "speak white."

Francophone women I've contacted agree that they use French differently from men. "Absolutely. We have two different languages in French. For one thing, women have a much richer vocabulary," says Madeleine Gilchrist, a nurse. "We see it all the time in the emergency ward: Women have 20 words to describe what's wrong with them, but men just point to where they hurt." Gilchrist cites another parallel with bilingualism: "Men don't learn women's language for the same reason that Anglophones don't learn French. They're afraid of making a mistake and looking foolish."

For women learning Manspeak's nuances, of course, the risks are doubled. Men's language assigns certain roles to women, and certain cues for taking turns in conversation. One major difference I've noticed is that a smile means different things to either gender. When a man is talking and somebody starts to respond, usually he will smile to assert that he wants to keep the floor, and then he'll keep talking. Women's smiles, on the other hand, signal submission. A talking woman who smiles at a man's interruption is likely to be cut off in mid-sentence, because he will interpret her smile as a signal to go ahead.

Women's and men's talk are different in every culture and class. "The growing body of studies on the language use of women in a variety of settings and cultural groups provides convincing evidence that differences will exist in the speech of men and women in every social group," according to sociolinguist Patricia Nicholos. She concludes that among all the factors (class, region, education) that shape the way we speak, power is the key factor that determines how women and men talk together. The powerless had better be either silent or polite. Men's language tends to accord courtesy by rank. Men are usually very courteous to their superiors, reasonably polite to their peers, and capable of incredible rudeness to those they think they control. "I've been nice to other people all day," one husband said to his wife, "and when I come home, I don't feel like being nice anymore."

As the language of the powerless, Womanspeak accords courtesy regardless of rank, to children and men alike. In order to be able to live with men's combative style of coexistence, women have developed ways of avoiding or resolving conflicts without open clashes.

The hesitancy and defensiveness that characterizes women's talk serve to protect women from men's competitiveness. To the alert ear, more than the message is transmitted when a woman phrases her request to a man thusly: "I was wondering if you would mind if I asked you to drive me to the store for diapers and groceries, if it's not too much trouble." She's saying, please please please don't be angry at me. Women speak hesitantly because they often bear the brunt of men's anger, when men don't want to hear what they're saying.

More and more women (especially in the business world) are learning to understand and speak men's talk. An individual woman can learn enough to get by in men's world. She can smile when the junior store clerk calls her "dear," and call him "dear" right back. (I've been doing it for years, and clerks usually switch immediately to "ma'am.") She can march into the employment office and say, "Give me a well-paid job," instead of, "I don't imagine you have anything for me today, do you?" She can learn to lower her voice for the telephone, or raise the volume by projecting her voice to fill a hall. Individually and collectively, over the past 10 years, women have learned enough Manspeak in several languages to pierce the silence that historically has concealed women's existence.

However, it is not enough that women learn how to speak like men. It is just as important that men learn how to understand and speak Womanspeak. If we wish to preserve the institution of marriage, men must learn to speak the language of caring; otherwise, for too many women, the threat of economic hardship is the main incentive keeping them in punitive relationships. If we want children to grow up knowing they are loved by both parents, men must learn that they can talk with youngsters without worrying about who's "winning."

A synthesis with women's language, which would eliminate some of the friction built into men's language, could save us all a lot of time—time we could spend on important matters, like admiring men pictured in fashion magazines. I stare at the photo over my desk, longing to meet this fellow in the country tweeds. The caption is partly correct: He certainly is elegant. I wonder what "easy" means in Manspeak.

Posters like the one above, published by the Ontario
Women's Directorate, may reflect an ideal state of affairs,
but they are also an effective means of changing
assumptions about race and gender.

Notes of a Black Canadian

Adrienne Shadd

It always amazes me when people express surprise that there might be a "race problem" in Canada, or when they attribute the "problem" to a minority of prejudiced individuals. Racism is, and always has been, one of the bedrock institutions of Canadian society, embedded in the very fabric of our thinking, our personality.

I am a fifth-generation Black Canadian who was born and raised in a small Black farming village called North Buxton, near Chatham, Ontario. North Buxton is a community comprised of the descendants of the famous Elgin Settlement of escaped slaves who travelled the Underground Railroad to freedom in Canada in the 1850's. As a young girl growing up in the fifties and sixties, I became aware of the overt hostility of Whites in the area when we would visit nearby towns. Children would sometimes sneer at us and spit, or call us names. When we would go into the local ice cream parlour, the man behind the counter would serve us last, after all the Whites had been served, even if they came into the shop after us. Northern Ontario may as well have been below the Mason Dixon line in those days. Dresden, home of the historic Uncle Tom's Cabin, made national headlines in 1954 when Blacks tested the local restaurants after the passage of the Fair Accommodation Practices Act and found that two openly refused to serve them. This came as no surprise, given that for years certain eateries, hotels and recreational clubs were restricted to us, and at one time Blacks could only sit in designated sections of movie theatres (usually the balcony), if admitted at all. Yet this particular incident sent shock waves through the nation, embarrassed about such evidence of racial "intolerance" going on in its own backyard.

Somehow, this kind of racism never bothered me. I always felt superior to people who were so blind that they could not see our basic humanity. Such overt prejudice, to my mind, revealed a fundamental weakness or fear. Although, instinctively, I knew that I was not inferior, there was not one positive role model outside our tiny community, and the image of Blacks in the media was universally derogatory. Africans were portrayed as backward heathens in the Tarzan movies we saw, and Black Americans were depicted through the characters of Step'n Fetchit, Amos 'n Andy, Buckwheat of "Our Gang" fame, or the many maids who graced the television and movie screens in small bit parts. (Black Canadians were virtually non-existent in the Canadian media.) I used to wonder if it could really be true that Black People the world over were so poor, downtrodden, inarticulate and intellectually inferior, as the depictions seemed to suggest.

At the age of ten, we moved to Toronto. In the largely White neighbourhood where we lived, I was initially greeted by silent, nervous stares on the part of some children, who appeared afraid of me, or at least afraid to confront me openly. Later, as I began to develop an awareness of the Civil Rights and Black Power movements through my readings, certain friends would respond with a frozen silence if I brought up the name of Malcolm X, or, for that matter the latest soul record on the charts. Looking back, I can see that things ran fairly smoothly as long as the question of race could be ignored, and as long as I did not transgress the bounds of artificial "colour blindness" under which I was constrained. This, apparently, was the Torontonian approach to race relations.

I share these reminiscences to illustrate the different forms which racism has taken over time, and in varying locales in Canada, whether in the form of overt hostility and social ostracism as in southwestern Ontario, or in the subtle, polite hypocrisy of race relations in Toronto in the sixties.

But how, you may ask, do these personal experiences represent examples of institutionalized racism! Do they not depend on the attitudes of people, which vary from individual to individual? Are not our Canadian laws and policies very clear about the fundamental rights of all people to equal treatment and opportunities?

The problem with this line of thinking is that it fails to recognize how powerfully attitudes and behaviour are shaped by the social climate and practices around us. If the only image you have of Black women is derived from the one on your pancake box, then there is something wrong with the media portrayal of racial minorities. If there are no visible minorities in the boardrooms of the corporate world, and few in positions of influence and authority in the work force, this sends a message far more potent than the human rights legislation set up to create a more equitable distribution of rewards and opportunities. When generation after generation of school children continue to be taught only about the accomplishments of White Europeans in Canada—mostly men—the myth that this is "traditionally a White country" as I heard a reporter say the other day, will persist unchallenged.

The selective recording of some historical events and the deliberate omission of others has not been accidental and they have had far-reaching consequences. Blacks and other people "of Colour" are viewed as recent newcomers, or worse, "foreigners" who have no claim to a Canadian heritage except through the "generosity" of Canadian immigration officials, who "allow" a certain quota of us to enter each year.

But this myth that Canada is a White country is insidious because, on the one hand, it is so ingrained in the national consciousness, and on the other hand, so lacking in foundation. There is a tendency to forget that Native peoples were here first; Blacks, first brought as slaves in the 1600 and 1700's, were among the earliest to settle on Canadian soil; the presence of the Chinese is traced to the nineteenth century. In fact, people from a wide variety of races and nationalities helped to build this country. Unfortunately, this reality is not reflected in our school curricula.

The long Black presence and contribution to Canada's development continues to go unacknowledged. People are surprised to learn, for example, that ten percent of the Loyalists who migrated to British North America after the American Revolution were Black. Their descendants, particularly in the Maritimes, have been living in quasi-segregated communities for over 200 years. Blacks were one of the largest groups to enter the country during the nineteenth century when 40–60,000 fugitive slaves and free people "of Colour" sought refuge in Canada West (Ontario) between 1810-1860.

Standard textbooks never mention that in 1734, part of the city of Montreal was burned down by Marie-Joseph Angelique, a Black female slave, when she learned of her impending sale by her slave mistress. Most Canadians are not even aware that slavery existed in this country. Women's history courses fail to acknowledge that the first newspaperwoman in Canada was a Black, Mary Ann Shadd, who edited a paper for fugitives between 1853–1859 in Toronto and later Chatham, Ontario. Heartwarming stories such as that of Joe Fortes, a Barbadian born sailor who came to British Columbia in 1885 and subsequently, as the lifeguard of English Bay, taught three generations of young people to swim—such stories are all but forgotten. Fortes is considered a true Canadian hero to those who are still around to remember him, but it seems that many younger British Columbians believe Fortes was a White man. And did any of you know that the term "the real McCoy" was coined after the inventions of a Black man, Elijah McCoy, born in Harrow, Ontario in 1840? From his mechanical work on railway engines, McCoy invented a lubrication cup or graphite lubricator used on locomotives. This invention made it unnecessary to stop the machine for oiling, hence arriving 7 minutes earlier per 100 miles of travel. In the years that followed, 45 patents were awarded to him, all but 8 pertaining to lubrication devices for heavy machinery.

Today's students, Black and White, look to the United States for information regarding the Civil Rights movement, unaware that a gripping saga exists right here in Ontario. In the forties and fifties, organizations such as the Windsor Council on Group Relations, the National Unity Association of Chatham-Dresden-North Buxton, the Brotherhood of Sleeping Car Porters, and the Negro Citizen's Association of Toronto fought segregation in housing, accommodations and employment, as well as racist immigration laws. Much of the anti-discrimination and human rights legislation that we now take for granted are a direct result of the struggles which these groups waged.

Certainly, these few bits of information alter our perception of what has traditionally been taught in Canadian history textbooks. At the very least, they lead us to question the prevailing assumption that Canada was settled and built strictly by White Europeans.

The educational system could be at the forefront in dispelling many of the myths and stereotypes which fuel racist thinking today. Instead, it aggravates the problem by channelling disproportionate numbers of Black children into low-level academic courses and ultimately, dead-end positions in life.

The point I am making is that racism is not simply a phenomenon which afflicts the minds of individuals and causes these individuals to perform discriminatory acts. Racism is something which afflicts an entire society; it is ingrained and reinforced in all the major and minor institutions of the society. Even in the most seemingly "objective" of undertakings, such as the writing of our national history, racism has operated to exclude minority groups from the historical landscape, thus rendering their accomplishments invisible, and therefore insignificant.

Second, racism is not something which simply affects its victims in various adverse ways. It also benefits all those against whom it is not directed, by affording certain privileges. Just remember that for every visible minority who is denied a position because of his/her colour there is a majority group member who is awarded that same position because of his/her colour. Many well-intentioned White Canadians fail to recognize that their lifestyle and position in society is based on a system of class and race privilege. Of course, men enjoy additional privileges based on their gender. Rather than focusing energy on helping the victims of racism, some of these people should examine the problem from the standpoint of their own situations of privilege.

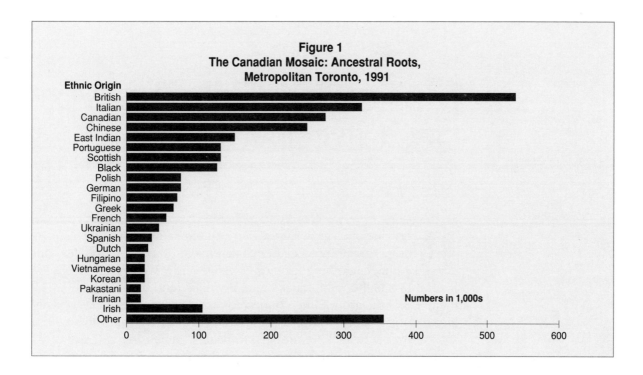

Figure 1
The Canadian Mosaic: Ancestral Roots,
Metropolitan Toronto, 1991

On a more personal level, even the most subtle and polite forms of racism can be detrimental, especially as they affect children. In my own case, when we moved to Toronto I was made to feel different, alien, even though no one specifically referred to my racial origin. It is a feeling which has never fully left me and perhaps explains why to this day I do not feel comfortable in the company of a group of White people. And when some Whites think they are paying Black people a compliment by saying, "We don't think of you as Black," as my sister's friends have told her, this is not just a misplaced nicety; it is an insult. We are not seeking "honorary" White status.

Before we as a society can liberate ourselves from the grip of racism, we have to acknowledge that it exists, and that it is not something which has been blown out of proportion; neither is it the figment of some people's imaginations. If we can do this much, we will at least have moved out from under the heavy shroud of self-delusion and deceit. That in itself would be a refreshing step forward.

Multiculturalism: The Mix of Cultural Values

Jill Le Clair

Every one of us grows up within a certain cultural context. *Culture* comprises all those elements that make up our way of life—our language, clothing, economic values, how we live and what we live in. In small communities cultural values tend to be shared by all members of the group. Interconnectedness pervades all aspects of daily life. In larger, more complex societies, however, we often live within sub-cultures where there are shared values. Increasingly, many of us grow up or spend much of our lives within such different "societies" or sub-cultures, and sometimes the shared values of these sub-cultures may conflict or not be totally in line with those of the wider society.

Recent census information shows that today the majority of students in the Toronto school system were born outside of Canada. This fact, of course, confirms our own impressions of living in increasingly multicultural cities. Parents bring many of their cultural values with them when they move to Canada. Sometimes there is family conflict between parents who insist that their children come home early, shouldn't have dates, or insist on attendance at community or religious events. Meanwhile their children are arguing for the right to do what they want and may prefer to listen to "inappropriate" music and eat pizza or at MacDonalds rather than do things the "traditional" way?

Increasingly we are seeing a mixing of cultural values. *Acculturation* is the term used to describe the coming together of different cultural groups. In music, for example, we have seen a blending of styles and sounds from American rock and roll, Jamaican reggae and East Asian bhangra (with performers such as the English Apache Indian).

Canada is committed to multiculturalism and there is much heated debate on this issue. On the one side, people argue that one of Canada's strengths is the recognition that Canadians can have a dual identity—that of being Canadian and that of their country of origin. On the other side, people argue that every Canadian should be a Canadian without a hyphen (Irish-Canadian, Chinese-Canadian, etc.).

HUMAN RIGHTS

The Ontario Human Rights Code is an example of legislation designed to protect individual rights. It clearly states that every Canadian should be free from any form of discrimination.

"Every person has a right to equal treatment with respect to services, goods and facilities, without discrimination because of race, ancestry, place of origin, colour, ethnic origin, citizenship, creed, sex, sexual orientation, age, marital status, family status or handicap."

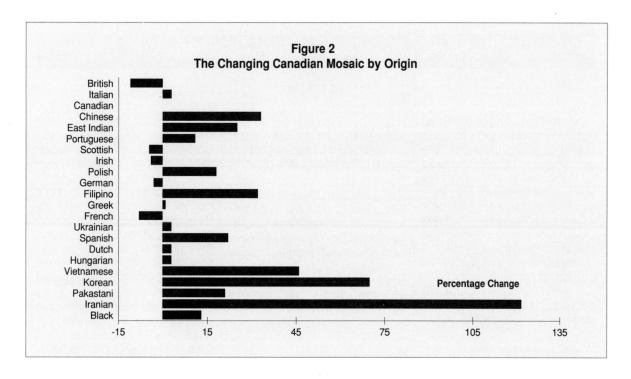

Figure 2
The Changing Canadian Mosaic by Origin

At what point does someone become a "genuine" Canadian—after three generations, four, five or at the point you are a Canadian citizen? Should Canadians focus on those elements that bring us together rather than stress our differences? Others maintain that the whole debate about multiculturalism masks the real issue—one of discrimination based on racism.

How do people define themselves and use their cultural identity to say who they are?. In Canada's recent national census researchers were surprised at the answers to the question about ethnic background. Canadians were asked to define who they were by ethnic background, so if your parents or grandparents were born in Italy you were expected to write down the word Italian as your ethnic origin. To the surprise of the statisticians, there was a huge increase in the number of individuals who wrote down "Canadian." Many people want to define themselves as Canadian rather than as so called hyphenated Canadians.

The following selections depict the thoughts and experiences of several Canadians grappling with multicultural experiences and identities in Canada today. These voices are typical of hundreds of thousands of Canadians, young and old. It is individuals like Jenny, John, Zina and Angella who will shape Canada in the next century and beyond.

"I feel that I am not considered the typical member of my culture. Then again, does anyone fit the "norm?" Even though I am a WASP, I behave in a manner which many people refer to as weird ... I also must consider the fact that whomever I compare myself to, probably does not entirely represent her cultural group either. Therefore, in interviewing someone from a different culture, I cannot compare my group to her group—it must remain person to person ..."

From an Interview with a college student.

Multiculturalism—The Cultural Mix

JENNY

My family came to Canada from Hong Kong as landed immigrants two years ago. We are Chinese, born and raised in Hong Kong. Our parents were born in China, but they went to Hong Kong in 1949 when the Communists took over mainland China. We decided to leave before the Communists take political control of Hong Kong in 1997. We have chosen Canada because it is a free country and it tolerates multiculturalism.

We are adapting to the Canadian culture; however, in no way do we want to give up our own identity as a distinct ethnic group. We are proud of our ethnic heritage and we want our children to learn and uphold it. On the other hand, we are aware that it is important to learn the values of Canadians in order to integrate into the mainstream of the society. We feel ourselves at the crossroads, trying to find out a good balance between the two value systems—the one we were brought up with, and the one we are confronting at the moment.

The majority of the Canadians are Anglo-White, and we are a Chinese Yellow minority. We know that no amount of cultural adaptation can completely eradicate our racial distinction. We find that being a minority means we are in a disadvantaged position in political, economic and social standing. Nevertheless, we want to be good citizens here and we want to prove that we are worthy members of society.

I am writing this essay as an individual and as a parent. My racial and ethnic origins have bearings on my values and attitudes and manifestations in my behaviour in terms of what I do, what I plan for my children, and what I expect from them.

The Value of Retaining Our Own Ethnic Identity

It is a common view among the Chinese parents here that they do not want their children to be like "bananas"—yellow-skinned yet white inside. I am a supporter of this viewpoint. I believe that it is important to retain our own ethnic identity through maintenance of the Chinese language, familiarization with Chinese history, celebration of the Chinese festivals, and linkage with the Chinese community.

1. *Maintenance of the Chinese Language.* Language is an important means of differentiation for it distinguishes us from other ethnic groups. At home, we talk to our children in Chinese, and expect them to answer in the same language. We ensure that they can read and write Chinese by sending them to heritage school every Saturday.

2. *Familiarization with Chinese History.* China is an ancient country with thousands of years of cultural heritage. We want our children to be familiar with the roots of our culture. We expose them to story books and videos about the great deeds of the great men/women in Chinese history, and explain to them what we can learn from these celebrated people.

3. *Celebration of the Chinese Festivals.* The Chinese festivals, for example, the Chinese New year, the Mid-Autumn Festival, and the Winter Solstice have special meaning because they bring all members of the family together and promote kinship and common bonds. We value these celebrations and encourage our children to participate.

4. *Linking with the Chinese Community.* By visiting Chinatown, attending events organized by the Chinese community, reading Chinese newspapers and magazines, and communicating with relatives and friends back in Hong Kong, we keep ourselves informed of the happenings in the Chinese community, and we expose our children to these aspects of the Chinese culture to supplement what we teach at home.

JENNY—*continued*...

The Value of Learning from Confucius' Teaching

Here in Canada, we find that at the grassroots level, there is a general lack of seriousness towards work. At school, there is a liberal attitude towards students' academic achievement, and at home, there is little respect for parents and grandparents compared to that in Chinese families. We would feel threatened if our children should pick up these attitudes, and to counteract them, we find it useful to emphasize the teaching of the great Chinese teacher and philosopher, Confucius. Specifically, these values are spelled out as follows: (1) the virtue of filial piety—the love and respect for a parent; (2) the virtue of industry—the need to excel through hard work; (3) the virtue of being an all-round educated person, the need to be trained in the mind and the body, for education is the foundation of a future career.

The Value of Learning the Canadian Culture

Being in Canada, I believe that it is equally important to learn the Canadian culture in order to live a meaningful life. At the moment, I believe in the importance of mastering the English language, learning Canadian sports, celebrating the Canadian festivals and enjoying family life.

1. *The Importance of Learning the Language.* I will continue to polish my English so that I can communicate well with people in the workplace; we want our children to learn both English and French so that they can do well in school.

2. *The Importance of Learning the Canadian Sports.* Sports have become part of the Canadian way of life, and a topic for conversation. We are learning how these sport games are played, and we want our children to be able to play hockey, baseball, soccer and learn skating, skiing and swimming.

3. *Celebration of the Canadian Festivals.* We celebrate the Canadian festivals such as Easter, Thanksgiving, Halloween, and Christmas like other Canadians. I think this is important, as we want our children to be able to share and talk about the joy of these festivals with their friends at school.

4. *The Importance of Family Life.* I observe that most Canadians put a lot of emphasis on family life. Sunday is regarded as an important day for family gathering and religious worship, and the issue of Sunday shopping is attacked vigorously. Having been here for two years, I am used to the idea of going to church on Sunday morning, and spending the rest of the day with my family.

I observe that in one way or another, I am changing my behaviours and lifestyle. Though striving to uphold some of the values I have brought from my mother country, I am gradually assimilating the values of the Canadian culture. I am sure that in a few years I will subconsciously pick up more of the predominant values of the Canadian society.

Multiculturalism—The Cultural Mix

ZINA

An immigrant Canadian, I am a part of the much talked about Canadian ethnic mosaic. I epitomize the diversity of this mosaic: a Kutchi by race, born and raised in East Africa (a second generation African), a practising Shiite Ismaili Muslim and with a working knowledge of three languages (East Indian, Swahili and English). A Tanzanian national by birth, I left my country in 1971 as a result of political considerations for a four-year stay in the United Kingdom prior to immigrating to Canada in 1978.

It was during the sixties that Tanzania (known as Tanganyika then) and the other countries in the region attained independence from Britain. The colonial affiliation meant that up until 1970 the school system, the judiciary and other institutions were modelled along those in Britain. For example, the medium of instruction in schools and the predominant language of commerce and government was English. I was therefore brought up with an understanding and appreciation of British culture—the predominant culture I subsequently found in the U.K. and in Canada.

A strong part of what I am is the Ismaili community I belong to. The Ismaili faith, one of the 72 sects of Islam, takes the Islamic concept of religion as a way of life (i.e., unlike the strict Augustinian distinction between material and spiritual, Islam considers both equally important) even further. The community encourages and has developed major programs in education, social and economic development. Higher education, excellence in commerce and the professions is put at par with prayers as is enterprise with a conscience and self-help. My faith has instilled strongly in me the existence of God, and a balance between the pursuit of material things with prayers for the soul.

Culturally, I consider myself a Canadian Ismaili. This would not be different if I were asked this question on a visit to Tanzania or at JK (JK—commonly used abbreviation for jamatkhana, the Ismaili prayer/community house). As minorities in all countries they reside in, Ismailis' first loyalty is to the countries they reside in—there is no Ismaili code of conduct, They adopt language and dress code for the respective countries. As an "unhyphenated" Canadian I see myself as a citizen, sharing with other Canadians, the same future, all equal and without special privileges.

As someone who left her country because of political reasons, I am able to appreciate the stable political environment, democratic values and institutions, and the various freedoms (of expression, religion, etc.) far more than Canadians who were born and raised here. This is reflected in my active participation in, and support of civic affairs; e.g., the fact that I always vote in all elections, my membership in a political party, my open mindedness in accepting various differing opinions, my interest in reading newspapers and in particular editorials and opinions, and my support and respect for law and authority.

Similarly, I am able to appreciate the "high" standard of living in Canada, having lived in a third-world country where electricity and running water were considered (and are still considered) luxuries. I place a high premium on education. It was a luxury "back home" both in terms of user fees and availability. Tanzania, with a population of 25 million, has one university.

Although I was born and raised in relative luxury, the poverty and lack of opportunities to most Tanzanians is a permanent reminder that to most of the people in the third world getting three meals a day remains a major preoccupation.

These "backgrounds" have also instilled in me a high regard for the work ethic and self-help. Social security programs (medicare, pensions, etc.) do not exist in Tanzania or India (the country of my great

ZINA—*continued*...

grandparents' birth) and therefore this dependence on government is an alien concept for me. Although as a liberal-minded social democrat, I support the UIC and welfare systems, I would find it difficult to collect from these programs; work ethic, pursuit of excellence and self-help are reinforced in all my background influences (nationality, ethnic and religious). As a parent, I expect to pass along to my children these values and related ones of thrift and of carrying as little debt as possible.

Another major influence is my being a member of a visible minority which is fre-quently negatively stereotyped. The ignorance of my fellow Canadians as to the very many different peoples generalized as East Indians (a Tanzanian Ismaili like myself has as much in common with a Tamil from South India as a WASP would have with a Ukrainian—they are both White) is disappointing. I am frequently drawn into the role of an educator, explaining about different Eastern cultures and religious backgrounds.

Unfortunately, the only thing many Canadians know about the world's second largest religion (Islam has one billion followers) is the political violence and terrorism in the Middle East, which is like equating Christianity with violence because of the struggle in Ireland between Catholics and Protestants. People lose sight of the fact that Moslems, like everyone else, can be poor or rich, tolerant or intolerant, honest or dishonest, illiterate or scholarly. In personal terms, this has cultivated a tolerance for other cultures, a desire to learn more about them and a sympathy for the negative stereotyping they might be subjected to.

Multiculturalism—The Cultural Mix

ANGELLA

I was born in Guyana, South America as were my parents. And as far as I know four generations before them were also born Guyanese. Therefore, my nationality is Guyanese, while my ethnicity is East Indian. My ancestors came from India. My original language is English.

Life in Guyana was very simple. I realized this when my family moved to Canada. I was ten years old when we came here, and the differences were clear to me right away. Where I was used to having mom at home, now she was working. Women back home did not work as much as they do here. I noticed both my parents to be very uptight all the time, which is something I never saw back home. Life over here was all work. They were always worried about house payments and all kinds of bills. They never owed anyone money in Guyana.

Being a ten year old and coming to this country was horrible. First of all I came halfway through the school year in the midst of winter. Not only was it hard to adjust to school, but also the weather, my new friends and speaking English the Canadian way.

It took me a long time to get used to all of this. At home I was Guyanese in that I still spoke the same way and ate the same foods. But at school I tried very much to be Canadian. Somewhere along the way I decided I did not want to be Guyanese anymore and that I was going to try the hardest I could to be Canadian, like my new found friends, and disregard my Guyanese heritage. For a long time I wished I was White. Life just seemed simpler—you didn't have to lie or make excuses or even apologize if your skin colour was white. I really envied White people.

I did meet up with prejudice. I can remember taking the long way to school just to avoid running into people who would call me racial names. However, there were people that would say to me, "Well, you are White in the way you think and act." I used to take it as a compliment, but as I grew older I started to understand that there's not a more terrible thing a person could say to me. I think it's adding insult to injury when someone says that.

My Mom and Dad brought us up by Guyanese standards—very, very strict. The emphasis was on getting a good education and eventually getting a good career—absolutely no socializing. That was when I started rebelling. I wanted to go out just as all my friends did but I wasn't allowed. I was torn between the two cultures. By day I was at school being very much Canadian in the way I acted.

I used to get very depressed and hurt over this because my parents couldn't understand what I was going through. It was only when I was 19 that my parents started to let me go out. I felt a lot of resentment and hate for a long time towards my parents for this, but my four older sisters seemed to be better able to accept this.

My parents are both very hard-working people who always wanted the best for us. As my father has said to us so many times, "You can do anything or be anything you want in this country." That's why he brought us here—for a better life and I really do believe that. I live my life today by those words.

We were never religious. By tradition we are Hindu, as most Indian people take on that religion, but my parents never practised it. Therefore any religious beliefs I have are just from what I've learned over the years, and I do have a very strong belief in God.

Although Canada is multicultural, at times I am still very self-conscious of my colour. Mom and Dad have always taught us to be objective and to think about other people's feelings, to take people for who they are, not what they look like. So I can feel for all other minorities in this country. Not just in skin colour but any-

ANGELLA—*continued*...

one who is discriminated against for whatever reason. I can honestly say I know how they feel. And from being a minority, I've learned to appreciate all people regardless of race, creed, ethnicity, etc. because I have been on the receiving end of it. Therefore, my skin colour coupled with my parents' influence has made me a better person.

I've adapted to Canadian culture very well but I still have Guyanese in me. I think I'm a bit of both. I dress Canadian, I eat Guyanese foods, my friends are Canadian and Guyanese.

The places I go to are very much Canadian—the bars I go to or the events I participate in socially. I've only gone out with White guys and this is a preference and maybe a prejudice. I can't explain it other than saying I've never been attracted to any other guys except Whites.

I now feel a great admiration for my parents for coming to a new country and starting all over again, and for being extremely successful in doing so. I now realize it was just as hard for them to adjust as it was for me. If anything, I feel ashamed for all the problems I caused them. I know I'm a better person for all they've taught me. There's a lot of love and respect for them on my part. I don't deny myself my Guyanese heritage anymore; as a matter of fact, I am very proud of it.

In conclusion, I would like to say that I feel very privileged and lucky to be able to have two cultures. Although it was a struggle in the beginning, now it's a blessing. I have been given the opportunity to take what I like best from both.

Multiculturalism—The Cultural Mix

JOHN

Upon meeting a person from a different culture, a daily occurrence in today's multicultural melting pot environment, both individuals are superficially aware of the other's uniqueness. Skin colour, accent, and dress all form an initial impression of the "outer self" of that person, but very rarely do we get to delve into their thoughts, beliefs and value systems. This, of course, is where the true heart of the person beats. Education, traditions, family rearing and societal influences are all elements which help to shape and mould the human into the special being that he or she is and it is through the examination of these elements that we can gain valuable insights into our "ethnic" neighbours.

Quite recently I had the opportunity to meet and interview Bill, who is racially and ethnically a Native Indian. Before our meeting, I, of course, had predetermined certain facts and thoughts concerning him and I am sure he probably had done the same about me. We both, however, were in for an educational experience. Although we did have our inevitable differences, it was the similarities we shared that I found fascinating. Both of us, having been raised in Canada, would have had some similar experiences, however, even culturally we had some distinct parallels. It is the similar-

ities and differences that I shall examine in this paper and I will maybe shed some insights into how these racial and ethnic differences and similarities allow us to appreciate each other's individuality.

Bill spent his early formative years on an Indian reserve in Northern Ontario and, although he moved to Toronto before his tenth birthday, he considers the North to be his true home and the major influence on some of his thoughts and feelings. Conditions at the site were not very hygienic, and living quarters, he remembers, were generally more like upgraded cabins than houses. He recalls it with a sense of fondness, however, because of the remembered warmth of family memories. He stated his belief that family is very important to the Indians and that "family" included very close friends who were related by values and beliefs. He indicated that the exile a lot of Indians felt was due to the isolation of the reservations from the rest of the populace and this encouraged the close-knit supportiveness that was, in fact, necessary for him to function emotionally. He found separation from family very detrimental to the individual and was in awe when I related my family upbringing.

Although I had been brought up with the belief that the family unit is an extremely precious notion from which

support, love and encouragement flow, experience was somewhat different. I was raised with love and sensitivity but never felt the bond of which Bill spoke. To him, his family was his mainline, but to me it was quite often a group of people that I sometimes loved more out of duty than desire. Upon the examination of two other ethnically English families with whom I have had repeated contact, it seems that although the family is respected, it is also somewhat distant and not terribly demonstrative. Perhaps that can be attributed to the British upper-class aloofness and the well-established boundaries of class and respect. Nevertheless, it seems to be prevalent in the three English families I know intimately. Conversely, Bill related that his family, and the Indian families he knew, were very close and expressed as much physical love as they did verbal love. Even though we both had a strong belief in the family, I came to recognize that while his was a physical reality, mine was more of a concept, and I envied him his ties.

Religion is usually a major influence on a person's development and values, as is lack of religion. Both Bill and I had been raised with the belief in an Almighty Creator and that this Creator should be revered and worshipped. In my religion, Christianity, the Creator is

JOHN—*continued*...

known as God while in Bill's the Almighty is referred to in Sioux tongue as Wakan. Wakan differs very little from God; both created the Heavens and the Earth and all creatures great and small, and both are fervently worshipped by followers of the faith. It is the other aspects of the two religions that illustrate their differences.

Bill devoutly believes that all objects found on Earth have an essence, be it a tiny stone or a mighty waterfall. He believes that all the creations are whole, and that any discord which ensues after an object is removed or destroyed should be righted by the return or replacement of a similar article. In his opinion, man should always be as one with the environment and sensitive to the natural aura of the Almighty's creations.

He doesn't feel that a place of worship, like the Christian church or the Jewish synagogue, is a necessity, because faith is an ongoing process and an individual should show this faith in daily settings and actions and not just obeisance on a given or acknowledged day.

My new friend went on further to say that it was his conviction most Indians adhered to the ancient beliefs, and through rituals like the "vision quest," a solitary, cathartic journey into one's inner space helped to ensure new genera-tions would be cognizant of the old ways and would ensure their continued existence.

I similarly believe that a place of ritual worship is not a prerequisite for perpetuating one's beliefs, but I am at odds with the dogma of my leaders. The high Anglican church states that church attendance is an essential part of faith, and it considers non-attendance and lack of involvement in the religious community unacceptable. While I carry forth my convictions, this is one aspect of the church with which I do not agree and therefore am considered somewhat unworthy in the eyes of the ministry.

The two of us discussed this notion, and Bill chuckled that the solution was obvious. Since I agree with most of the Indian beliefs on which he had elaborated, he jokingly argued that I should convert to "Wakanism." Although I can well imagine a devout Anglican blanching at the thought, after careful examination, I discovered that even after taking into account the varied differences, the two religions are more alike than I would ever have thought.

Even though Bill, in reality, is the "true" Canadian, my White, Anglo-Saxon, Protestant culture has made me, in the eyes of the majority of Canadians, the recipient of the "true Canadian" title. Because I am a White, English-speaking male from an upper middle-class family, I have never had to be concerned with how my ethnicity would affect job prospects, housing enquiries, in short, how others would view me. Because of my social and cultural identity, I am almost guaranteed success in any field I choose. This option is not always available to all members of today's "modern" society and Bill very ably illustrated this point to me.

Bill is considered a half-breed—he has an Indian mother and a White father, and consequently he has the physical attributes of both. His skin is a little paler than that of his mother, a true Sioux Indian, but nevertheless from a visual standpoint he is certainly far removed from Caucasian colouring. His straight hair is jet black and certain facial features, although somewhat softened by his father's genetic influence, are evocative of the Indian stereotype.

I have referred to his physical features because he feels they have a significant impact on the treatment he sometimes receives. He told me that occasionally people would take a second look in attempting to determine his racial background. By himself, he said he encountered very little prejudice, but if seen with a group of Indian friends, the

JOHN—*continued*...

reactions were not always so subtle. Ladies clutching their purses a little tighter if the group came near, obvious sneers directed toward the group, and blatant slurs voiced just loud enough to carry, are all experiences Bill and his friends have endured. "I don't know what they think we are going to do," he relates to me, "but there often seems to be this tension in the air between US and THEM."

As he recounted certain incidents, I realized that although I had never behaved outright in such a manner I was guilty of harbouring certain similar misconceptions, and I almost felt like apologizing. I let him know this and he laughed; he said he expected people to have certain preconceived notions of Indians due to books, stories and films, and he had learned how to adapt to it.

He suspected any minority would agree with his view that adaptation and enlightenment would help to curb such petty ignorance and that, hopefully, in a time not too distant, the aforementioned situations would lessen and then cease to be altogether.

Upon conclusion of the interview, I began to reflect on some of the instances we had discussed. We are two human beings from extremely different backgrounds, yet there was always a common thread of agreement to be found in most of the topics on which we touched. Although I could never expect to fully comprehend his cultural identity, nor he mine, the opinions of one so far removed from my own upbringing were extremely enlightening. I was better able to see my own prejudices. Although I still tend to see things ethnocentrically from time to time, understanding my own and then another's culture, I believe, is the first step to breaking down some of the racial and ethnic barriers erected so long ago.

A respect must be engendered for the differences of our many cultural heritages, for it is only in this manner that we can learn from and grow with each other. An acknowledgement of our similarities should be recognized because norms, values and beliefs, although varied, are all based upon love, friendship and understanding. Only after

a careful examination of a different culture can we begin to see that although we appear dissimilar outwardly, there seems to be a sameness which is only evident if we make a conscious effort to discover each other's individuality within.

Change, Law and the Workplace

Kathy Casey

Compared to twenty years ago, today many more women, visible minorities and disabled employees can be found in offices, schools, industries and medical centres. These workers are qualified for their positions and work productively at their jobs. However, some feel disadvantaged, that they are not receiving equal treatment in the workplace. Others are discriminated against and harassed, even though it is public policy that every person is free and equal in dignity and rights and can expect to live and work in an environment that is exempt from discrimination and harassment.

In order to understand why people are treated differently and, in some cases, unfairly, let's examine what discrimination and harassment are and review how the legislation in Ontario attempts to prevent unfair treatment and remedy the effects.

Now, *discrimination* is a tricky word. Sometimes, definitions of the term are devised to accelerate the interests of those people who claim they are being discriminated against. However, at its simplest level, discrimination merely means making a choice, and making choices is an essential part of everyday life for individuals and organizations. These choices are governed by many factors including attitudes, traditions and rules. When these factors have the effect of limiting the opportunities of certain groups of people because of their sex and colour, for example, then the problem of discrimination arises.

When our different treatment of people is based on stereotypical perceptions rather than real characteristics, then we are illegally discriminating. For instance, some women are not hired or promoted to senior management positions because of the attitude that women have family obligations and therefore won't make good senior managers. As well, some blacks are not hired or promoted because of the attitude that blacks are lazy and won't make good employees. Ultimately, illegal discrimination is based on prejudiced attitudes about people that result in unfair treatment of people.

Discrimination may also be defined as an action or behaviour that attaches exaggerated importance to physical differences between people. When we assume that people have certain characteristics because of their skin colour, disability or sex and then treat them unfavourably, we have created a situation of illegal discrimination.

Harassment may be defined as repeated vexatious or distressing conduct or behaviour that is known or ought to be known as unacceptable and unwanted. Harassment takes many forms: for example, sexual, racial, gender, age and ethno-cultural. However, what is important to note is that all forms of harassment are uninvited and unwelcome. Furthermore, harassment is a form of discrimination. It occurs because people have internalized the stereotypes and prejudices that exist in our society.

Harassment is based in the abuse of power—real or perceived. It is generally carried out by members of a dominant group against members of a minority group. Incidents of harassment tend to be repeated and to grow in intensity. Victims often say nothing because of fear or embarrassment. The person doing the harassing then feels a distorted sense of power and continues his or her demeaning treatment of others. It is important to note that, because people often accept the stereotypes and prejudices of the dominant culture, a person can harass another person or group of people of the same gender, race or ethno-cultural background as himself or herself.

Despite public policy, there are many indications that racial and sexual harassment are on the increase today. Signs and buttons presenting "Keep Canada White" have been displayed in public. Also, anti-female slogans have been heard on some post-secondary campuses in opposition to women studying in non-traditional programs.

Acts of discrimination and harassment are illegal in Ontario. All persons in the province are protected under the *Ontario Human Rights Code*. First enacted in 1962 as a consolidation of various anti-discrimination provisions, the *Code* provides, among other matters, that every person has a right to freedom from discrimination and harassment in a number of areas and various different grounds. The areas are services, goods, facilities, accommodation, contracts, employment and membership in associations and trade unions. The grounds are race, ancestry, colour, ethnic origin, citizenship, creed, sex, handicap, age (18–65), marital and family status, receipt of public assistance, record of offences and sexual orientation. For example, you cannot be denied accommodation because of your colour, denied education because of your handicap, or denied employment because of your religion (creed). As well, according to the legislation, you cannot be the object of harassment which could consist of slurs, jokes, stares, isolated treatment and/or suggestive touching or remarks.

If you think that you have been discriminated against or harassed by someone in your workplace, then there are a number procedures to follow. If you work in a unionized environment, you can speak to your union representative. Alternatively, or as well, you can file a complaint internally through the Human Resource Department in your company or externally with the Ontario Human Rights Commission.

Another type of legislation in Ontario has come about because of the historical undervaluation of the work that women workers do. It is the *Pay Equity Act*. Historically, men and women have tended to do different work, and the work that is performed by women has not been paid as well. This undervaluation has resulted in a wage gap: the difference between the average earnings of men and women. Currently, the wage gap in Ontario means that women earn 30.4 percent less than men.

A lot of the mistaken ideas about the role of women in the workplace and the worth of their work are based on the assumption that women are secondary workers. Some believe that women's contribution to the economy is less important than that made by men and that women don't really need employment income. Moreover, a lot of the jobs available to women are secondary jobs—part-time, temporary, dead-end and poorly paid.

This idea of secondary workers and secondary jobs—secondary, meaning less important—has caused some people to undervalue the work that women do. This is one of the main factors contributing to the wage gap. Though the wage gap stems from a number of reasons (such as difference in education, differences in experience, prejudice, job ghettos and hours worked), a third of the wage gap exists because of the myth that the work women do is of less value.

To bridge the wage gap, *Pay Equity* was enacted as of January 1, 1988. The Act requires an employer to pay men and women the same wage for work that is different but of equal value. Pay equity is not to be confused with "equal pay for equal work" which means that if a woman is doing the same job as a man she will be paid the same wage.

Pay equity compares different jobs to see if the jobs are of equal value to the employer. Although the jobs may be different, their contents may be similar and therefore comparable.

To compare jobs, the criteria used are skill, effort, responsibility and working conditions. The *Pay Equity Act* requires employers to compare female job classes to male job classes using the four criteria. When it is found that the female and male job classes are of the same value, yet the female jobs are paid less, compensation in the female job class must

HARASSMENT

Harassment may be defined as repeated vexatious or distressing conduct or behaviour that is known or ought to be known as unacceptable and unwanted.

Harassment is based in the abuse of power: real or perceived. It is generally carried out by members of a dominant group against members of a minority group.

be improved. Both men and women within the underpaid female-dominated jobs will receive adjustment.

If you currently work in a female-dominated job class (one in which 60 percent or more of the members are women), and if you are interested in seeing how your position has been compared, your employer is required upon request to show you the evaluation method used. If you are concerned that you are not being paid fairly, you can ask the Pay Equity Commission for assistance.

The *Ontario Human Rights Code* is an example of legislation that has been enacted to prevent unfair treatment of all workers in the province. The *Pay Equity Act* is an example of legislation to remedy past discriminatory treatment of all workers in female-dominated job classes. Nevertheless, some pro-active employers have not waited for legislation. Instead, these employers, as well as adhering to provincial legal requirements, have voluntarily created employment equity programs within their company. Employment equity is a planning process adopted by an employer to examine how women, the disabled, visible minorities and native persons are recruited, hired, trained, promoted and represented within an organization. It seeks to identify and eliminate illegal discrimination in a company's processes and policies and tries to remedy the effects of past illegal discrimination. These remedies may include programs aimed at changing representation within and across occupational groups so that target group members are appropriately represented throughout the workplace. Canadian and Ontario laws specifically require that programs designed to change the effects of past discriminatory behaviour are not in themselves discriminatory.

Employment equity is a voluntary program undertaken by an organization to ensure that non-discriminatory employment practices are carried out within the workplace. By having such a program, an employer is broadcasting that discrimination based on sex, race and disability is no longer acceptable. Recognizing that certain groups within our society have a tradition of being unfairly discriminated against, employment equity programs counter the long-term effects of such discrimination to give these groups real equity of opportunity in the workplace.

Change is difficult for every generation. We hear that we are losing what has been important, that other areas will also change, that we must adjust and learn new ways when we are already comfortable with what we know. However, change is the norm of the human condition. We must confront the paradox. While we are always seeking new knowledge and new ways of being, we resist change. However stubborn our resistance may be, one thing is evident. The workplace

Uncovering Bias

Application Forms

It is not appropriate to include on application forms any questions that relate directly or indirectly to the following prohibited grounds of discrimination: race, ancestry, place of origin, colour, ethnic origin, citizenship, creed, sex, sexual orientation, record of offenses, marital status, family status or handicap. (The terms "disability" and "person with a disability" are used throughout this document instead of "handicap" or "handicapped person." Although the term "handicap" is used in the *Code*, many people with disabilities prefer the term "disability".)

	Permissible Questions	Prohibited Questions
Race; Colour	None.	Inquiries which elicit information about physical characteristics such as colour of eyes, hair, height, weight, or requests for photographs.
Creed	None.	Inquiries as to religious affiliation, churches attended, religious holidays, customs observed, willingness to work on a specific day which may conflict with requirements of a particular faith (e.g., Saturday or Sunday). Requests for character references that would indicate religious affiliation.
Citizenship; Place of Origin; Ethnic Origin	Are you legally entitled to work in Canada?	Inquiries about Canadian citizenship, landed immigrant status, permanent residency, naturalization, requests for Social Insurance Number. (A S.I.N. may contain information about an applicant's place of origin or citizenship status. A S.I.N. may be requested following a conditional offer of employment.) Inquiries as to memberships in organizations which are identified by a prohibited ground (e.g., Anglo-Canadian Association.) Inquiries as to the name and location of schools attended.
Sex	None.	Categories on application forms or inquiries such as maiden or birth name; Mr., Mrs., Miss, Ms.; relationship with person to be notified in case of emergency or insurance beneficiary.
Sexual Orientation	None.	Categories on application forms or inquiries such as married, divorced, common-law relationship, single, separated; Information about spouse (e.g., is spouse willing to transfer); relationship with person to be notified in case of emergency or insurance beneficiary.
Marital Status	None.	Categories on application forms such as married, divorced, common-law relationship, single, separated; maiden or birth name; Mr., Mrs., Miss, Ms.; information about spouse (e.g., is spouse willing to transfer); second income; relationship with person to be notified in case of emergency or insurance beneficiary.
Record of Offences	Have you ever been convicted of a criminal offence for which a pardon has not been granted?	Inquiries as to whether an applicant has ever been convicted of any offence; has ever spent time in jail; has ever been convicted under a provincial statute (e.g., *Highway Traffic Act*) or been convicted of an offence for which a pardon has been granted.

Selected from: *Human Rights: Employment Application Forms and Interviews*, Ontario Human Rights Commission.

THE VALUE OF HOUSEHOLD LABOUR

Much work, time and energy is invested in the maintenance of the household (cleaning, laundry, cooking, repairs, shopping) and in the care and nurturing of household members.

Research shows that the majority of work in the home is done by women, even in households where both the woman and the man are working outside the home.

Obviously, this is an arena for much negotiation, debate and change in coming years.

Female to Male Earnings Ratios for Full-year, Full-time Workers, 1980-1991

Age Group 15-24 years
Age Group 25-34 years
All age groups

Source: Statistics Canada, Cat. No. 13-217.

has changed from what it was just a short time ago, and not only the government but also individual employers have responded to that change in a variety of ways. New legislation and new programs have been created in response to the multicultural, multinational, dual gender workplace that we now have. Examining our own behaviour in an attempt to understand and change, rather than to defend, allows us a new perspective on a changing environment, a perspective that will allow us to accept how others differ, to respect those differences, and to value ourselves and others as unique individuals who have a worthwhile contribution. As a result, we all grow in our understanding of ourselves and each other, an understanding that will increase our ability to live and work together in harmony.

Sex, Statistics and Wages

Globe & Mail Editorial, January 21, 1993

Give the Canadian media some credit: they didn't make as much of a hash of this story as they usually do. The subject is the much ballyhooed "wage gap" between men and women, documented annually by Statistics Canada, and eagerly lapped up by the nation's newspapers and television news shows. Faint praise is in order this year, however, because three ingredients that are essential to understanding the wage difference—education, hours worked and marriage—receive at least passing mention in some of last week's coverage.

It was reported that women's wages rose to 69.6 per cent of men's in 1991, from 67.6 per cent the year before. But what does that mean? For starters, it does not mean, despite the obfuscatory efforts of those who ought to know better, that women are being paid nearly one-third less to do the same jobs. A recent ad campaign by the Ontario Women's Directorate, for example, asked Toronto bus and subway passengers, "How much would they pay a man to do your job?" The slogan, and the text that followed, suggested to female readers that, by the simple virtue of being male, a man at their firm is being paid one-third more to do precisely the same job. He isn't. Sex discrimination in wages—paying a man with the same qualifications more than a woman to fill exactly the same position—is against the law, and has been ever since Bob Rae was in short pants.

Statscan's numbers are, of course, an average of millions of Canadians, with different ages, levels of and types of education, skills, years of work experience and jobs. An average focusing solely on gender tends to obscure the degree to which all sorts of other factors come into play. (Keep in mind also that the following statistics refer to full-time workers only.)

One would expect that, since society's attitudes towards women's work and education have changed relatively recently, the difference in average wages would be least among the young. And that is precisely what one finds: The hypothetical full-time working woman over age 55 earned 63.6 per cent of the income of her male counterpart in the same age bracket, while her granddaughter, aged 15 to 24, earned an average of 86.4 percent as much as a man in the same age group.

Crunch the numbers a bit further, and other interesting facts pop up. Education, for one thing, matters. Women with a university degree earned more, not less, than men with lower levels of education. When one considers that a majority of those enrolled in Canadian universities are female (55.3 per cent of full- and part-time university students are women) it's hard to imagine a future in which the wage difference will not continue to narrow.

But there is already almost no wage gap between single men and single women. In 1991, single women's average earnings were 91.1 per cent of those of their male counterparts. For some women, there was even less of a difference. Data compiled by Statistics Canada at The Globe and Mail's request show that the income of single women age 35 to 44 was 94.5 per cent of that earned by men of the same age. And looking only at the most educated members of that age group, single females with a university degree—women actually made six per cent more money than single, 35 to 44 year-old, university-educated men. (In fairness, the margin of error in Statscan's survey is large, so these last two percentages could be off by these several points.)

All of these numbers refer, of course, to full-time workers. But not all full-time workers work the same number of hours. On average, men work more than women: 40.4 hours vs. 35.2 hours a week. In other words, the average man works 12.9 per cent longer, explaining a large part of the wage gap.

But the biggest factor is marriage. The earnings of single women, single men and married women working full-time are roughly comparable. But the earnings of the average married man rise above those of everyone else. That is the only real "wage gap." Whether or not it is a problem is a subject worthy of discussion. Its existence suggests that, as one would expect, married men and women choose certain career and life paths, different from those chosen by singles. But why is it that many married women work only part-time, or adopt less time-consuming (and less well-paying) full-time careers? Are they forced to by their husbands? By circumstance? By entrenched social attitudes? Do many, for a whole variety of unquantifiable reasons, freely choose this path, thinking it best for their families?

In the debate that ought to take place around this issue, answering these questions would be a good place to start.

A Response to the Globe & Mail Editorial

Are Women's Salaries Behind Men's?

The *Globe and Mail* made extended editorial comment on the fact that, as reported by Statistics Canada, the earnings gap between women and men closed slightly in 1991. Readers should not be misled into believing that the position of women in the labour market is improving significantly, even relative to that of men ("Sex, Statistics And Wages"—editorial, Jan. 21). It is true, as Statistics Canada reported, that the earnings of full-time, full-year women workers in 1991 were 69.6 per cent of the earnings of men working full-time, full-year, up from 67.6 per cent in 1990.

This mainly reflects the fact that the loss of full-time, full-year jobs in 1991 disproportionately took place in manufacturing and construction, sectors where relatively well-paid jobs are held disproportionately by men.

Most importantly, it should have been noted that just 51 per cent of working women are employed on a full-time, full-year basis, compared to 68 per cent of working men. For the 49 per cent of women working on less than a full-time, full-year basis, Statistics Canada reported that average earnings fell by 6 per cent from 1990 to 1991 (more than the 5.1 per cent fall for the 32 per cent of men who did not work full-time, full-year). The important fact that wages fell significantly for the 49 per cent of women who did not work on a full-time, full-year basis was prominently reported by Statistics Canada in the summary of the publication from which the "closing of the earnings gap" story was extracted. It was generally ignored by the media. Why? It is true that many women "choose" not to work on a full-time, full-year basis, though this choice is shaped by the fact that, in the absence of a national child-care system, women bear a disproportionate burden of family responsibilities. Exclusion from full-time, full-year jobs is not, however, just a matter of choice. Between one-fifth and one-third of part-time women workers regularly report to Statistics Canada that they work part-time only because they cannot find a full-time job.

It is important to understand that the overall deterioration in the labour market in the recession has affected women in specific ways. Women have not suffered quite as much as men from massive industrial layoffs, but hundreds of thousands of women have been marginalized through unemployment and underemployment, and earnings have clearly fallen for almost half of the women in the labour market. It takes a rather perverse perspective to interpret all this as a step toward equality. We are, of course, very far from equality. The Statistics Canada study shows that just 3.7 per cent of women earned more than $50,000 in 1991, compared to 15.7 per cent of men. At the other end of the spectrum, 37 per cent of women earned less than $10,000, compared to 23.9 per cent of men.

Nancy Riche, *Executive Vice President, Canadian Labour Congress, Ottawa. Reproduced from the Globe & Mail.*

Public and Private Roles

It is understood that in a developed society *needs* are not only quantitative: the need for consumer goods; but also qualitative: the need for a free and many-sided development of human facilities, the need for information, for communication, the need to be free not only from exploitation but from oppression and alienation in work and leisure.

A. Gorz

The Re-Organization of Work

Hugh Armstrong

It would be difficult to overstate the importance of paid work. It is, of course, the central factor shaping our income levels. Moreover, it exerts a vital influence on where we live; who our friends are; our health, safety and longevity; our opportunities for lifelong learning; and how we see ourselves and others see us. The "long arm of the job" extends not only to our material well-being, but also to our social contacts and to our sense of self. We are, and are seen to be, productive members of society largely through our paid work.

To be sure, the significance attached to paid work has its shortcomings. Measuring value by means of money means devaluing the contributions of those who do unpaid housework and volunteer work. Because most housework and volunteer work are still done by women, it means that women themselves tend to be both devalued in society and placed at a disadvantage when they work for pay.

To point out the negative effects on women (and others who do the housework and the volunteer work) of our society's "value system," does not alter the fact that paid work is central to our lives. In examining this enduring reality, the first observation to make is that change seems, paradoxically, to be the sole constant in the workplace. New technologies, new forms of organization, new expectations and requirements are introduced at a pace that appears to be dizzily accelerating. We are enjoined to work longer, harder and smarter preparing for and performing our paid jobs. We are counselled to anticipate frequent shifts between careers, between jobs and between tasks. More and more of us are getting "re-structured" out of secure, full-time employment and into part-time and limited-term jobs, when we can find paid work at all.

True, for many Canadians, economic insecurity has long been a familiar reality. Professional actors have not been the only workers with too much time "between engagements." And the dramatic movement of millions of women into paid employment has in many ways meant

In this clothing factory clothes are assembled using mass production techniques.

more of the same, as they continue to be slotted into segregated jobs at or near the bottom of the labour force heap. Moreover, for some women and for some more men, the good times continue to roll, as their wealth and privileges steadily accumulate.

This article concerns how best to understand these workplace changes and continuities. It starts by suggesting when the changes began and then sketches the most fundamental of them. In a subsequent section, it points to some of the most important workplace continuities and then discusses the key implications of both the changes and the continuities, notably for the education and training of students and workers.

Fordism and Benettonism

Following the Great Depression of the 1930s and the Second World War, a long economic boom took hold. With uneven impact across the globe, it was centred in North America and centred on the mass production of goods. The most important of these goods was the automobile, which in turn consumed vast quantities of steel, rubber, glass, textiles and other supplies in its manufacture, and vast quantities of petroleum in its operation. As measured by standards of durability, safety or fuel consumption, the quality of what was produced may have been indifferent, but demand was high and prices were low. As both a precondition and an effect of the rise of the automobile, enormous investments were made in the construction of suburbs, shopping malls and roads.

Although relatively brief and minor recessions were periodically felt throughout the period following the Second World War, the predominant pattern until about 1970 was one of sustained economic growth. Then, quite suddenly in retrospect, the long postwar boom ended, and profound changes began to be felt throughout the Western industrialized world in general (with equally profound implications for the rest of the world) and at workplaces in particular.

During a few short years in the late 1960s and early 1970s, the United States ceased to be seen as the world's dominant economic power. This was signalled by its decision to no longer sustain the gold standard, by which the value of the U.S. dollar was fixed at $35 per ounce of gold, making the U.S. dollar the stable international currency, much to the advantage of those holding such dollars. At the same time, the U.S. was also in the process of losing the Vietnam War. With the rise of the Organization of Petroleum Exporting Countries (OPEC), the users of petroleum products were introduced to the "oil crisis," and its chilling effects on fuel consumption. Meanwhile, Western governments stopped introducing new welfare state measures and started to face, if not successfully deal with, a "fiscal crisis" of the state. They have yet to figure out whether, to what extent, and how to deal with massive budget deficits and accumulated public debt. "Stagflation," a term referring to the novel combination of economic stagnation and inflation, was introduced to the vocabulary. And large, private-sector unions stopped growing, and started to shrink in terms of size and influence.

These profound changes were felt and reinforced in the workplace. In recognition of the assembly line mass production system pioneered by Henry Ford, the old way of organizing production is often termed "Fordism." Its origins go back long before the postwar boom. Early in this century, Ford had adapted the "disassembly line" of the Chicago meat packers to the complex matter of assembling automobiles. Workers remained stationary at fixed points along a moving line, repetitively performing standardized tasks using standardized tools and standardized parts to make small, incremental contributions to the assembly of a standardized product. Ford reputedly announced that you could buy his Model-T automobile, first introduced in 1913, in any colour you wanted, as long as it was black.

The assembly line was complemented by other production innovations associated with Fordism. Firms exploited "economies of scale," lowering their costs through such practices as the bulk purchasing of

Workstations that isolate and buffer the individual from distractions are designed to maximize the efficiency of the modern office.

supplies, the development and use of specialized or dedicated equipment in long production runs, and mass advertising. They held large buffer stocks of supplies to keep the line moving without interruption, and large inventories of finished products ready for distribution when surges of demand warranted. They also sought increased market control through "vertical integration," or the attempt to own and control every stage of the production process from the extraction of raw materials to the sale of consumer products. Thus, for example, a retail food chain might have had its own sugar refinery (or even its own sugar cane plantations), its own soft drink bottling plants, and its own warehouses and trucking fleets. At the other end of the cycle, it might have developed the shopping malls in which its supermarkets were the prime tenants and in which it placed its own discount department stores and snack bars. Or a newspaper chain might have owned everything from pulp and paper mills and railways to newsstands. These huge firms were resource-driven, scrambling world-wide for raw materials, and used enormous amounts of cheap energy.

In the factory, and increasingly in the office or store, more and more jobs were broken down in a detailed division of labour whereby workers were required merely to carry out simple instructions in loading, adjusting and unloading machines in repetitive fashion without much thought or judgment being encouraged, or even allowed. An everyday example is the fast food restaurant, where the pre-packaged hamburgers are grilled until the buzzer goes off, and the cashier may even speak from a prepared script. "Will you have fries with that?" The firms established distinct research and development units to work on new products and processes, which were then imposed from above on local managers as well as production workers. Quality control, such as it was, took place after production, as sub-standard products were picked out and rejected.

Within this system of "scientific management," the practices of management rather than the abilities of workers were made responsible for the labour process. Trade secrets became enterprise secrets. The conception of this work rested with management, which used efficiency experts to study each stage of the labour process, and then issued precise instructions to those actually doing the production work. Management itself was rigidly hierarchical, consisting of fine gradations of rank and authority from top to bottom. And its focus was on the present, on the smooth running of the current operation, on the production of more of the same at less cost, and on the direct control of the worker.

Although many firms remain today resolutely Fordist in their outlook and practices, the dynamic sectors of the economy are increasingly characterized by new approaches to production. Firms here seek "niches" where the demand for customized goods and services can be found or created. Given the pace of change, they stress the capacity to shift nimbly from one product to another, exploiting economies of scope rather than economies of scale. To do so, they engage in sub-contracting (a process of "vertical disintegration"), and make use of programmable equipment that can be readily switched to meeting new customer specifications or even to turning out entirely new products without much "down time." They try to replace buffer stocks and inventories with "just-in-time" methods, by which parts and supplies arrive at the plant just as they are needed, and the particular good or service is produced in response to the customer's order rather than in anticipation of it. A premium is placed on accurate and timely information.

Workers often experience these changes as a move away from the endless repetition of the same narrow tasks to an emphasis on "multi-skilling" or, less ambitiously, "multi-tasking." They may find themselves organized into teams or cells where "intelligent co-opera-tion" is stressed as they control, monitor and maintain machines, and are expected to analyze and apply data generated, processed and stored by information technologies. They may be told to view their co-workers in other teams as suppliers or customers, and may face the prospect of having their phase of the production process contracted to an outside firm or shifted to another division of their own firm if insufficient "value added" is deemed by management to be coming from their team.

Quality control is likely made integral to every step of the production process, and made the responsibility of every worker.

Management, under this new system, is usually "flattened" by the elimination of one or more layers from the former hierarchy. Those managers who remain are expected to serve as mentors and models in firms that are "learning organizations," to develop "partnerships" with suppliers and customers, and to bid on contracts within the firm as well as between firms. The elimination of "waste" from the production process is if anything a more pressing management concern, as "lean production" and "flexible specialization" become new watchwords. And management becomes more focused on strategic directions, or on the formulation and making of choices about future directions for the firm.

This new approach often goes under the unimaginative label of "post-Fordism." Perhaps "Benettonism" would be more apt. At a trivial level, "Any colour you want, as long as it's black" is replaced with the "United Colours of Benetton." More profoundly, Benetton has a very well-developed information system to spot which styles and colours of leisure wear are selling well in which of its retail outlets across the globe. It is then organized, partly through sub-contracting arrangements with a diversity of suppliers, to get the right clothes into the right stores very quickly. In addition, it positions itself in an expanded marketplace by blurring the distinction between advertising and objective news coverage, with controversial mass advertising campaigns that are "launched" at colleges of art and that bring together the private consumption of sweaters with social concerns over Third World poverty, environmental degradation, racism, and the AIDS epidemic.

Implications

Fordism was more than a system for mass producing standardized goods. It also meant a range of complementary institutional arrangements. Most significantly, mass production required mass consumption, which was not unconnected to the relatively high wages paid at least many of the men working in the mass production industries and represented in most cases by large industrial unions. To compensate for business cycle fluctuations, it also meant the postwar adoption, to varying degrees by the central governments of most Western industrialized countries, of economic policies designed to keep the demand for goods and services steadily high. Budgetary deficits were drawn up and justified on the grounds of providing economic "stimulus." And Fordism also meant a variety of welfare state measures.

Chart 1: Fordism and Benettonism: A Comparison

	Fordism	Benettonism
1.	Economies of *scale*	Economies of *scope*
2.	*Mass* production	*Niche* production
3.	*Standardized* goods	*Customized* goods *and services*
4.	*Dedicated* equipment	*Programmable* equipment
5.	*Large buffer* stocks and inventories	*Just-in-time* production
6.	Quality control *after* production	Quality control *as part of* production
7.	*Resource*-driven and *energy*-intensive	*Demand*-driven and *knowledge* intensive
8.	Detailed *division of labour*	*Multi-skilling*
9.	*Loading, adjusting and unloading* machines	*Controlling, monitoring and maintaining* machines
10.	*Operational* management	*Strategic* management
11.	*Hierarchical* organization, vertical integration	*Flattened* organization, sub-contracting
12.	Scientific *management* (Taylorism)	Intelligent *co-operation*

Now, along with the workplace changes, the Fordist institutional arrangements seem to be falling apart. As job insecurity intensifies, unemployment insurance and other welfare state provisions are cut back, the collective bargaining process is assaulted, and private sector unions in particular are weakened. Faced by mounting debt and the increased mobility of firms to set up shop across the globe, governments retreat from previous commitments to full employment. As "de-regulation" and "privatization" take hold, market considerations increasingly pervade the workings of the public sector itself. School systems bid for training contracts, and through "magnet" schools market their specialized programs to high school students and their parents. Hospitals not only develop "product lines" (heart and circulation, ageing, etc.), but also compete to provide laundry services to restaurants and hotels.

Amid all the economic and institutional uncertainties associated with current changes, there appears to be widespread agreement on one thing: the importance of education and training. Although drop-out rates are still cause for concern, the issue is not solely viewed as a matter of preparing youth for subsequent employment. The emphasis is increasingly on lifelong learning, so that we can readily and repeatedly adapt to rapidly changing workplace circumstances. Instead of narrowly training youth once and for all to fill specific, static jobs, schools and colleges are both broadening their curriculum and welcoming back adults for continuing education. More attention is being devoted to the development of generic skills (communication skills, numerical skills, critical thinking skills, interpersonal skills, and perhaps computer skills) that will be useful whatever the shifting occupational structure and whatever the lifelong learning requirements.

There is a danger of placing too much faith in education and training as the solution to workplace problems. It can easily become a way of "blaming the victim," of suggesting that current and potential workers are inadequately prepared, when the real problem is a shortage of decent jobs. The solution to contingent (or temporary and casualized) employment may be for individuals to develop job-seeking skills from resume writing to statistics, but it may also be for employers and for society to make employment relations more secure. Not much training is required to shift from performing one menial task in a mass production system to performing a range of slightly different menial tasks in a niche production system, especially if in the process production becomes leaner with ever more "waste" motion eliminated.

The workplace features continuities as well as changes. Firms have always competed with one another, even if the global competition has in recent years intensified. The organization of work has continually been revolutionized, even if with new information technologies the pace of change has accelerated. Employers have always sought new ways to motivate workers to remain diligent at what often remain boring and yet stressful jobs. On balance, however, the recent workplace changes do seem to be sufficiently interrelated, and sufficiently different from those that immediately preceded them, to warrant a new label.

The changes between the regimes labelled here Fordism and Benettonism are summarized in the adjacent chart. Of necessity, a chart like this sets out the changes quite starkly, perhaps too starkly bearing in mind the continuities that are also to be found. However, by comparison with the changes underway in the broader environment within which paid work is performed, the patterns of workplace change are decidedly clear and coherent.

On the Meaning of Work

Mitchell Lerner

There's a story told about a young man who brings the ruler of a peaceful kingdom a secret method of making bread without labour. At first everyone, ruler included, is delighted because it seems that hunger will be gone and the need to work will vanish. Then, painfully, reality sets in. What will people do with time on their hands? The king orders the young man killed. "The devil," as the saying goes, "makes work for idle hands." As the king belatedly understands, work is a necessity, an inescapable part of the human condition.

No civilization can survive without work. But what is the nature of this activity that by necessity is part of your life and mine? This essay presents several interpretations of work from ancient to modern times.[1]

One of the earliest interpretations goes back to the Judaeo-Christian roots of western civilization to the first story in Genesis. Eve having eaten from the fruit persuades Adam to do the same and together they are banished from paradise to "a life of toil and sweat of the brow." This kind of work means drudgery, repetition, punishment and suffering.

> Accursed be the soil because of you.
> With suffering shall you get your food from it.
> Everyday of your life
> It shall yield you thorns and thistles and you shall eat wild plants.
> With sweat on your face shall you eat your bread
> Until you return to the soil
> As you were taken from it.
> For dust you are
> And to dust you shall return.

---

[1] In these considerations I have been generally influenced by Hannah Arendt's discussion of work. I am also indebted to some theological interpretations and to some concepts of Peter Berger.

In this fundamental Judaeo-Christian understanding of work, humankind did not deserve the gift of paradise, the gift of a complete world. We got instead an incomplete world—filled with necessity and condition. To survive, we must work. It is not a very pleasant role we have to play since according to this view work is a punishment.

At face value this interpretation of work as punishment is intolerable. Every religion has a work ethic because few can imagine work without some reward. We view work as a mixed blessing—something people love to hate, but can't see doing without. Therefore, we redefine work in both religious and secular philosophies so that work offers something positive. So, this early view gets modified.

Rational moral thought does just that. It holds that our expulsion from paradise and the subsequent necessity of work has a reason: to develop moral character. We attach certain values to work. Work keeps us out of trouble. It reduces the wastefulness of idleness. Work challenges us to use our talents and abilities, and helps develop personality. It is said to reduce self-centredness and arrogance, moderating the excessive lifestyle in favour of the modest one.

Work separates the authentic from the image. Think of two bike riders on the street: same racing gear, same bikes, same clothes. You cannot tell one from the other. Only in the race is the true racer distinguished from the hopeful novice. Without exception, the real thing, not the appearance, shows through work.

So, in rational moral thought, the Fall from paradise becomes advantageous since work fosters positive qualities in us: generosity, because by working we give; faith and good will because we hope without knowing that the fruit of our labours will be good. In fact, work mirrors our human condition. We strive in the face of the unknowable, we seek means to great ends, we are forever impatient with the pace of our progress. Ultimately, work is a supreme test for all of us. Through work we succeed or fail; become great or small; are judged to be worthy or petty, good or bad, high or low.

The trouble is, though, that this profound and ennobling view of work doesn't fit easily into our modern experience, so we must look further. This brings us to our next interpretation.

Labour or Work?

Hannah Arendt, the influential modern philosopher, wrote much about the meaning of work in her book *The Human Condition*. She suggested that our understanding of work goes back as far as the ancient Greeks. Greek culture distinguished between craftsmen, those who made things, and labourers, those who worked with their bodies.

In ancient Greek society, slaves and women laboured, performing menial tasks. Labouring was in Aristotle's description "the meanest, because the body is most deteriorated."

Arendt points out that this distinction between work and labour exists in many languages. In French it is *travailler* and *ouvrer*, and in German it is *arbeiten* and *werken*. The German word *arbeit* originally referred to farm labourers. In English, the word *labour* connotes a sense of drudgery and suffering as found in the biblical story of Man's Fall, while the word *work* connotes effort that is directed toward the accomplishment of making something. So we get phrases like "the works of Shakespeare, Beethoven, and the Beatles" and by contrast the "labours of Hercules" that involved back-breaking physical tasks.

This distinction between "work" and "labour" helps us to think about what we will be doing the rest of our lives. Will we be labouring, which suggests a kind of slavery? Or working, which suggests a more meaningful connection to the activity and the possibility of producing something? For the most part, we share with the ancient Greeks the feeling that physical labour is a menial occupation holding little status in society because labour leaves little trace behind.

So, working is making something that stays. For us and our friends in ancient Greece, where modern civilization was born, work holds status because it means leaving a trace of your existence, a "body of work." On the other hand, labourers, who make neither a complete thing nor leave any notable contribution to humankind, are relegated to the periphery of society. In the last century, labourers sought to correct this flaw in the scheme of things by organizing into collective political units. As a result of the labour movement, the status of labourers was raised, both intellectually and socially. This was something the ancient Greeks never accomplished.

For the ancient Greeks the highest form of work allowed for as much leisure time as possible for the pursuit of philosophy and virtue. In our day, the labourer is equally entitled to leisure, protection, dignity and an OHIP number, while the philosophers, and some craftsmen, are often relegated to the unemployment lines.

Wisdom is best pursued when food, shelter and other basic human needs are met, even though, according to some, we gain much wisdom from scrambling to meet our basic needs of survival. In ancient Greece, where the pursuit of wisdom became an ideal, only twenty percent of the eligible population could participate in politics, philosophy and pure thought, while eighty percent had to work.

Our next interpretation of work demonstrates that wisdom derives not from the luxury of philosophy but from the experience of the common labourer.

Karl Marx on Work

Karl Marx, the 19th-century socialist philosopher, had much to say about this question. Marx believed that industrialization turned labour into a product to be bought and sold in the marketplace. He called it labour power. And every individual had about the same share. As the factories of the industrial revolution churned out more and more product, more and more labour was required. People abandoned the land because increased agricultural efficiency freed them to move to cities where a better life was possible. People moved from being generalists, capable of many things, to being specialists, capable of one or a few things only.

When people sell their labour, they are exchanging an essential part of themselves for money. And this process of trading labour for a wage leads to measuring self by the wage, not by ability. Even people who define themselves as workers rather than labourers are not immune. On the industrial assembly line, in the steel or textile mills, in many human spheres, work became increasingly subdivided into limited operations performed by separate workers. While this maximized productivity, it minimized craftsmanship. Workers became increasingly adept at repetitive tasks as the various aspects of the work became disconnected.

When work is divided into component parts—we call this the *division of labour*—the individual worker finds it increasingly difficult to improve through work. He or she therefore seeks self improvement elsewhere. Aware of a growing split between public and private roles, the worker may attempt to integrate the two, with some success. However, the division of labour ultimately requires a division of self. And the modern struggle becomes one of composing one's identity.

For example, a doctor's social identity is distinct from his or her private self which is found at home. The patients know nothing of that doctor's private life. The sphere of work is geographically and socially separate from the private sphere where the "real person" is known.

So, fragmenting the production of a thing into isolated tasks has consequences beyond the workplace. The worker in a sweater factory who only sews labels day in and day out, may feel detached from the product, from the manufacturing process, and from himself as an individual capable of more than repetitive tasks. This detachment is called *alienation*. And it is not restricted to the assembly line but is a social fact found in middle-class occupations as well. We have assembly-line education, medicine and law where teachers, doctors and lawyers are so specialized that they are attached to small parts of the overall process.

WAGE LABOUR

Karl Marx, the 19th-century socialist philosopher, believed that industrialization turned labour into a product to be bought and sold on the marketplace. When people sell their labour, they are exchanging an essential part of themselves for money.

Alienated work leaves no trace of our presence as individuals. The industrial division of labour redefined workers as labourers because they no longer make a whole thing but a part of it. This notion of "alienated work," of being fragmented into parts in the process of production, and in ourselves, has been the negative side of work since the industrial revolution.

Marx wrote his ideas in the 1800s when working conditions were absolutely intolerable, when owners of mines would hire children because they were small enough to dig coal in the smallest seams and workers died early in life from breathing metal dust in cutlery factories. His ideas have never gone away. The long sweaty hours in unhealthy conditions that characterized the working environment of the past can still be found in the developing countries.

"Modern" Work

Work remains a constant but the kinds of work change with the times. Today, we need to be seduced to work by an illusory guarantee of security, fulfilment and advancement. The promise of "making it" is deceptive because it doesn't remove the necessity for having to work, but only sweetens it. Winning the lottery doesn't mean you no longer have to work. "Making it" refers to having it all now; and even though it is a culturally esteemed value, it is not the same goal as "making something." It is ironic but people who focus on making something often end up having really made it.

Today many occupations seem to offer more freedom from having to labour to meet our basic daily needs. Machines take the place of manual labour. Motors replace the strain of lifting and pulling. Workers operate and monitor machines that do everything from cutting metal to stitching leather. In an explosion of technological change, photography, telephones, radio, television, nuclear power, rubber and plastics, medicine, and computers redefine lifestyles at a pace never before experienced, leaving little time to reflect and plan.

Alienation is still a reality in the modern world. And along with it comes the challenge of finding meaning in work.

The Meaning of Work

Finally, whether work implies suffering and drudgery, or leaving a trace of your existence, or if work means alienation, the work you choose is probably the most important decision you will make. There is something irrevocable about that choice. Your lifestyle gradually envelopes and defines you and you become whatever occupation you have chosen: technician, accountant, housewife, teacher, nurse, farmer, truck driver, writer. The work we do folds us into various known and unknown quantities: measurable players in the game of life. It is inevitable; even if we remain idle, we are defined.

To many of us, ultimately, work means maturity. It helps us to identify and accept ourselves: to teach us our limits and possibilities on the testing ground. It is not enough to be a "good person," or a "promising individual." Work, in the final analysis, defines a person, clearly and mercilessly, for all the world to see. As the humanists say, we have some control over the circumstances of our lives—we have some choice of occupation, of deed. In the end, our lives are measured by what we accomplish and leave to memory. We all strive, secretly and openly, to make a difference, to make our existence worthwhile for others to benefit from. So the challenge laid down to Adam and Eve, to the ancient Greeks, and to us is the same—to make something of value when nothing of value is possible without engaging the human condition, without modifying the world; that work is the ultimate pain and pleasure of life, both necessary and desirable.

Being and Becoming

Earl G. Reidy

Who am I? What am I? These fundamental questions are commonly asked by people throughout the world many times during their lives. They are complex questions related to who and what we are as individuals and as part of groups. There are no simple answers. Each of us is unique, the result of a combination of many experiences and conditions, some learned, others influenced by our biology. In the natural and social sciences, the issue has often been over-simplified as a question of "nature" or "nurture." Frequently, today, those terms which relate to how we become who and what we are have been replaced by "essentialism" (the result of our nature or biology) and "social constructionism" (the result of social forces strongly influencing the construction of our identities), although the argument remains fundamentally the same.

Relatively early in our lives we begin to recognize, from urges within ourselves (our biology) and from external social forces (our family, peer group, the media, etc.), that our sexuality is a powerful force that helps to define our self concept, one which, as young people, we often find difficult to understand and manage. What we are usually unaware of is the degree to which social institutions play a crucial role in conditioning our biological urges and fashioning them into socially acceptable sexual behaviours which are always framed in a heterosexual context. In other words, we are taught through social influences by the family, the school, religion, the media, political, economic and other institutions to become erotically and affectionally attracted to persons of the opposite sex. There is a great deal of debate within the social scientific community about the extent to which our sexuality is the result of deliberate social engineering.

Until recently, there has been an almost unexamined assumption that human beings are naturally attracted (a result of our biology) sexually to persons of the opposite sex. Cross-cultural and cross-species studies have seriously challenged those assumptions. For example, Gilbert Herdt, an anthropologist studying a group he identifies as the Sambia in New Guinea, has documented social practices where all Sambian men are actively involved throughout their lives in what we would classify as same-sex (homosexual) behaviours which are socially acceptable and even necessary for the maintenance and survival of their society. A number of other studies illustrate similar situations in other societies and among our closest non-human, primate relatives.

Others have suggested that our sexual and affectional selves are the result of biology; that our sexuality is programmed either fully or largely by genetic factors. For example, a recent and highly controversial study by Simon Levay, an American pathologist, suggests that there may be some differences in brain size between gay and non-gay men. It is important to note, though, that Levay himself does not make any claims that this can be generalized to the total population. This, though, if proven, would indicate that we are "born with" certain potentials over which, as individuals, we have no control.

Sexual orientation, regardless of our gender, is a critical and complex part of who and what we are. To whom we are sexually and emotionally attracted is not a static one-time decision which we consciously make, although it may appear so. Most of us accept, without question, our society's assumption of heterosexuality. Some of us don't. A number of women and men throughout the world and throughout time have recognized that their sexual, affectional and erotic desires lean toward persons of the same sex either for a lifetime or for varying periods of their life. The sexual identities available to us in Western culture include heterosexual (opposite sex), gay (male same-sex), lesbian (female same-sex) and bisexual (attraction to both sexes). It is important to note, though, that while a sexual/affectional identity is crucial in a person's life, it should not be the only criteria by which we evaluate ourselves or other people. We are all multidimensional.

It is unclear whether the process of self-definition is the same for all people even within a single culture. For example, a number of factors such as gender, social class, racial and ethnic group, and age, influence how we recognize, develop, accept or deny sexual and affectional feelings and desires.

Another difficulty in assessing our sexual and affectional identities is tied in with learning our gender roles. The social presentation of a male identity in Western culture, for example, often includes behaviours which deny males the opportunity to express emotional and affectional ties toward each other. Our culture tends not to do that to women as much; they are often encouraged to express their emotions. It has been suggested that this restriction is placed on males as a result of "patriarchal" (male dominated and controlled) social institutions which set up strict expectations of masculine behaviour as a means of defending and reinforcing male privilege and power. Such a defensive

The *Ontario Human Rights Code* prohibits all types of discrimination against people on the basis of sexual orientation.

KNOW YOUR RIGHTS

SEXUAL ORIENTATION AND THE HUMAN RIGHTS *CODE*

 he Ontario Human Rights *Code* prohibits discrimination on the basis of sexual orientation in services, goods and facilities; accommodation; employment; contracts; and vocational associations. This means that a person cannot be treated unequally in these areas because he or she is gay, lesbian, heterosexual or bisexual, for example.

The *Code* prohibits all types of unequal treatment, from the denial of a job, service or accommodation to comments, displays and jokes which may make an individual uncomfortable, because of his/her sexual orientation.

· If you were denied a service or treated unequally by a store, restaurant, theatre, club, government agency, school, hospital, dentist's or doctor's office or other provider of services, goods and facilities because of your sexual orientation ...

· If you were denied employment or treated unequally in your place of work because of your sexual orientation ...

· If you were denied accommodation or treated unequally by your landlord because of your sexual orientation ...

contact your local office of the Ontario Human Rights Commission. You may be able to file a complaint.

position produces very strong and negative attitudes towards males who may display any behaviours which are considered to be feminine, and thus weak. This, many feminist theorists tell us, supports the status-quo, male power arrangement and keeps women subservient and males "in line." George Smith, a sociologist at the Ontario Institute for Studies in Education, says that one of the most important ways that North American society maintains a strict interpretation of masculinity is through what he calls the "ideology of fag." Perhaps you can recall using the term "fag" or hearing others use it. It is a powerful heterosexist[1] and homophobic[2] weapon used to force males to conform to the dominant interpretation of acceptable masculinity. When a male begins to recognize that he is sexually and affectionally attracted to other males, he quickly realizes that he must hide this from others because he becomes vulnerable to physical and verbal abuse. This form of self-protection is often referred to as being "in the closet." Women also report that they experience homophobic verbal and physical abuse which calls their femininity and sexual identities into question. The

---

[1] Heterosexism is usually defined as the assumption that everybody is heterosexual, and if they aren't, they should be.

[2] Homophobia is defined as an irrational hatred or fear of gay men and lesbians. Homophobia, as both a condition and a practice is, like sexism and racism, often well entrenched in social institutions and can be used to justify verbal and physical violence against lesbians and gay men.

female equivalents of "fag" include "lezzie" or "dyke," derogatory and hurtful terms which are also used to reinforce male power since, according to patriarchal notions, women are supposed to seek and find their identity only in relation to males.

When does a person begin to recognize that they may not "fit" the expected heterosexual norm? That is a very difficult question to answer, since each person's development is so unique. However, it is important that we distinguish between same-sex feelings and a gay or lesbian identity. The Kinsey studies on male and female sexual behaviour, although flawed, are the most comprehensive and important pieces of research we have regarding the sexual behaviour of North American men and women. Kinsey and his researchers found that a number of men and women may have erotic or affectional feelings for people of the same sex for short or long periods of their lives, but never develop or assume a gay or lesbian identity[1]. Laud Humphreys, an American sociologist, discovered that many men who firmly identify as "straight" often participated in impersonal, same-sex behaviours. These findings reinforce the idea that how humans construct their sexual identities is very complex.

Current research indicates that recognition of a gay, lesbian or bisexual identity depends on a number of factors. My own studies of gay, male community college students regarding the development of their sexual identities confirms reports that males tend to realize earlier than females that their primary attraction is to persons of the same sex. Males report that they often knew about their difference during their elementary school years, but generally did not know what it meant nor even what to call it. Many of them said that since such feelings preceded any social knowledge of a gay identity, they believe they were "born that way." Females, on the other hand, report recognizing their lesbianism much later, sometimes after they had married and produced children.

Early recognition of a gay or lesbian state often produces, especially for young people, a great deal of confusion and pain as they begin to experience the negative, social response to gay and lesbian people which results in a stigmatized status. These youths feel isolated because they don't know others like themselves and there are few visible role models to help them construct their sense of self as a lesbian or gay

---

[1] Results of a 1993 American study of American males, reported in *Time Magazine*, disputes the Kinsey findings. That survey, by the Batelle Human Affairs Research Centres in Seattle, Washington, noted that only 2.3% of the sample reported having sex with men in the past 10 years. The study has been widely criticized as being methodologically unsound. No figures were reported for females.

person. Most feel that they cannot turn to their families, friends, schools or other social groups for help. A 19-year old male college student reported that when he told his mother he was gay, she told him, "I wish I had never given you birth."

Studies of Canadian and American gay and lesbian youths indicate that many of them consider, attempt or commit suicide as a result of extremely negative social pressures. A fortunate few, mostly those who grow up in big cities, may have access to gay and lesbian support groups, but many young people have to struggle, mostly alone, without the benefit of accurate information, to construct, deconstruct (as they get access to more information) and then reconstruct their identities, sometimes many times over. Among the many questions the youthful gay male or lesbian must grapple with, in addition to other concerns of growing up, are, am I gay or lesbian; what is a gay or lesbian, what is it like to be gay or lesbian; how does my gender identity as a male or female "fit into" being gay or lesbian, am I a bad person; what will this mean to my life, my relationships and my future; can I live with this identity? For gay males, the fear of HIV disease must also be confronted. This growth process can be made even more difficult as a result of religious, racial and ethnic group membership. Some gays and lesbians have been abused or rejected by their families, in extreme cases being declared actually dead, as a result of religious beliefs or because of attitudes which their families or other members of their racial/ethnic communities have brought with them from other cultures or social groups.

It is crucial to understand that a sexual identity is not just about sexuality; it becomes part of the person's core, inner-being and helps to structure how they see themselves and their relationships with the rest of the social world. Identities also differ for men and women. Once people work through the painful and difficult process of accepting their sexual identity, they need to integrate it with other aspects of their personality. This is the coming-out stage which results from social interaction. Most major cities in the world have gay and lesbian communities which offer a variety of support services including groups for young gays and lesbians. It is within these communities that people begin to learn that they are not alone, that there are role models available to help in constructing their identity. Coming out is not a one-time event; it can be never-ending. There are parents, other family members, friends, business associates to tell or not tell. Gays and lesbians have to learn how to structure and live their partner relation-ships outside the social construction of marriage and how to explain their partner when they are asked to participate in social events and family gatherings. It can get very complicated.

For young men and women who identify as bisexuals, their lives become even more problematic. Drawn sexually and emotionally to people of both sexes, they are often misunderstood and shunned by the lesbian, gay and heterosexual communities.

Conditions for lesbians and gays in North America, and in some European countries, have improved significantly in recent years. This has largely been the result of political activities by lesbian and gay groups. In Canada, there is now federal and provincial legislation prohibiting discrimination; many union contracts contain anti-discrimination clauses; and almost every employment category—including the military and many religions—is now open to lesbians and gays. Popular culture, including literature, film and television, is now beginning to portray lesbians and gay men more positively, thus informing the public, helping to reduce negative and harmful stereotypes and producing more realistic role models for isolated youth. However, there still is resistance to providing accurate information to young people, especially in schools.

Unfortunately, it has also been necessary for police departments in some Canadian and American cities to develop "hate crime" units because of continuing violence, often referred to as "gay bashing," against lesbians and gay men who become scapegoats for others' insecurities. Systemic homophobia, often combined with sexism and racism, continues to be a problem for North American societies.

Conclusion

In the development of "who we are," some men and women must come face-to-face with the recognition that they don't fit taken-for-granted expectations of a major part of their personality—their sexual identity. The process of "becoming" a sexual person, whether straight, bisexual, gay or lesbian is complex and may involve both biology and social learning acting in complicated and, as yet, largely unknown ways. For those who do recognize they do not fit the assumed heterosexual pattern, the development of their self-concept, their very identity as a person, frequently becomes, because of hostile social responses, extremely difficult and painful. More accurate and available information, support from family, friends and social institutions—especially schools—and greater social intolerance of homophobic verbal and physical abuse would make their lives far less problematic. Society must seriously question whether it can afford the incredibly high personal and social costs of prejudice and discrimination whether directed against racial, ethnic or sexual minorities.

The Gender Dance: Learning the New Steps

Wendy O'Brien-Ewara

Walk into any bookstore and look in the psychology section and you will find row upon row of self-help books. There are books which will help you find the right mate, keep your mate happy and survive your mate's death. With titles such as *Dances with Intimacy, Women Who Love Too Much,* and *Necessary Losses,* these books claim to improve your self-image, your sex life, and your communication skills. They promise to resolve your supermom complex, your Marilyn dilemma or Peter Pan syndrome. Why do such books line shelf after shelf in bookstores and libraries? Why do such titles continually top bestseller lists?

In what follows, I argue that the popularity of self-help books reflects the changing nature of gender relations. As traditional sex roles have eroded in response to the dissolution of belief in inherent sex differences, it is no longer clear what roles men and women ought to play. Nor is it clear how they ought to interact with one another. Self-help books address these issues, providing answers to questions about the nature of masculinity and femininity and offering guidance on how to structure and conduct interpersonal relationships. However, I caution readers to carefully evaluate the advice such books furnish. Understanding what it means to be male and female in the 1990s requires critical reflection on the assumptions we make about gender roles, on the nature of sexuality, on the value we place on our physiology and on quick and easy remedies for resolving our gender troubles.

Every day we are bombarded with images of what it means to be male and female in contemporary society. They are relayed to us on television programs as diverse as *Designing Women* and *Home Improvement,* in advertisements for everything from cleaning products to cars, and in magazine articles bringing up topics like the perfect breast and the hottest careers. Such messages are also conveyed to us in the laws enforced by a particular province or country, in religious creeds and in cultural traditions. However, the images presented before us often are inconsistent. Men are encouraged to be sensitive and caring, and at the same time tough and independent. Women are portrayed in some mediums as self-sufficient and career oriented, while in others they are depicted as happy homemakers. Given that these ideals are incompatible, how should we determine what characteristics to admire or what kind of interpersonal relationships to emulate? What can we reasonably expect from ourselves and our potential partners? Self-help books are designed to assist us in answering these questions.

That there is a need for such literature should not be surprising. Only thirty to forty years ago ideals of gender roles were much more clearly defined. Quite simply, women stayed home and men went to work: the private realm was the domain of women while men governed the public arena. This division of labour was justified according to inherent sex differences. Women did not simply develop their culinary and parenting skills; they were born with such abilities. By nature women had an aptitude for housework and, as they were more emotional and thus more irrational, they were best suited for staying at home and caring for the family. If they did work, women could only perform jobs which were viewed as extensions of their "wifely" or "motherly" roles; they could be nurses or teachers. And these pastimes were not expected to interfere with the fulfilment of their familial duties. After working all day, there were still children to be cared for, meals to prepare and a home to keep clean.

Men likewise were born with certain innate qualities. They were born rational and ready to deal with the intricacies of public life. Men didn't succumb to their emotions or passions and as such they were better equipped to handle power and mechanics. Their duty was to "bring home the bacon." Responsibility for the financial support of the family was placed squarely upon their shoulders. They had neither the time not the aptitude for dealing with children or doing housework. Yet they were the "king of their castle;" they "ruled the roost." As women were the weaker sex, they required men's guidance and protection. In return, men expected to be treated with due respect: their superiority in both judgement and action was to be met with deference.

During this era, we might buy a self-help book to help us get rid of nasty stains, improve our manners, or help us tune up our car. But we would not buy a book to help us determine what qualities, attitudes and actions were appropriately masculine and feminine. The images of men and women endorsed through various mediums were uniform. In an attempt to discourage women who had worked in various jobs during the war from continuing to participate in the public realm, a unified effort was made to have women return to their "proper place"—to once again be happy homemakers. As such, the messages transmitted from television, advertisements, the state and the church were homogeneous. Although not all men and women ascribed to these ideals, they knew what qualities defined a "good" woman and distinguished her from a "good" man. This consistency was furthered by a veil of silence which prohibited discussions of sex and sexuality. Good "girls" and responsible men simply did not talk about their bodies or about their intimate relations. Questions about how men and women were to interact and about the nature of femininity and masculinity were not raised in the realm of public discourse. Somehow everyone just knew the answers to such questions. Consequently, there was neither a forum nor a perceived "appropriate" need for self-help books focusing on gender roles and personal relationships.

Such is not the case for us in the 1990s. Over the past thirty years dramatic changes have taken place in our ideals about what roles men and women should play and about what constitutes a "good" relationship. It is no longer apparent that sex differences are inherent. Few women would stand for being told that by nature they are irrational, emotional, and inferior to men. And how many men would agree that by nature they do not have the capacities necessary to be a primary caregiver? Differences in the attitudes, aptitudes and behaviour of men and women are viewed as the consequence of not only physiology, but also of socialization and enculturation. Consider the problems this introduced into gender relations. Gone was the theoretical basis for uniform images and ideals about masculinity and femininity. With the dissolution of belief in sex differences came the need to question the roles traditionally ascribed to each sex. This provided new opportunities and new obstacles. Public discussions of gender issues led to the advocation of diverse accounts of what men and women are and should be like and about how their relationships should be structured. The need to sort through these alternatives gave rise to the kind of self-help books that today line our bookstore and library shelves.

Until recently, books of this kind primarily have been written for women. With titles such as *Why Women Worry* and *Why Do I Feel Like I'm Nothing Without A Man*, self-help books have responded to the difficult choices women have had to make regarding careers, marriage and family. Consider, for example, the repercussions of women entering the work force on their expectations about education and employment options, marital status, childbearing, and child rearing. With the expansion of career options came the need to determine what kind of profession to pursue. Should she become a lawyer, a construction worker or a homemaker? In addition to changing social values, the financial independence of working outside the home gave many women the option of marrying later in life or of not marrying at all.

Without good quality and readily available daycare women's involvement in the work force is extremely difficult.

Reproductive technologies have given women some measure of control over when, where and if they will have children. Moreover, choosing to have children no longer necessarily required women to abandon their jobs. Indeed, this has resulted in the birth of the daycare industry. In light of the possibilities which changing social circumstances have afforded women, there are no longer any clear-cut expectations about women's place in society and about what qualities and characteristics "good" women exhibit. Self-help books are designed to assist readers sort through these difficult issues.

The same is true for men. The recent upsurge of the Men's Movement has led to the expansion of the market in men's self-help books. *Iron John* and *Fire in the Belly* are just two bestsellers that question what it means to be masculine in contemporary society. Rejecting the roles men have traditionally been required to fill, these books explore the options which men have when it comes to careers, family and personal development. Not wanting to be the stoic master-of-all nor wanting to feel that they must be sensitive, caring homemakers, an attempt is made to understand men's nature based upon ancient rituals and the notion of brotherhood. These books try to understand what men are like outside the limitation placed upon them by references to sex differences.

With both sexes trying to define for themselves what it means to be male and female, confusion about interpersonal relationships can only be expected. Titles such as *Men: A Translation for Women*, *When Love*

Goes Wrong, and *The Modern Man's Guide to Modern Women* line bookstore shelves. When the need to marry was alleviated and equality between the sexes became the goal for many, the traditional ideal of what good relationships entailed broke down. No longer willing to divide responsibilities according to the public/private distinction, it became necessary to negotiate what roles each partner will play both in the workforce and in the household. In spite of being paid only 69.6% of their male counterparts' wages, of facing sexual harassment, and of continually bumping into an artificial glass ceiling, women are entering the workforce in increasing numbers. Couples must now deal with the stress and strain of two careers. Furthermore, as women rise through occupational hierarchies, it is possible for them to make more money and have more prestige than their male partners. Consider how such social changes have upended the roles traditionally ascribed to men and women.

glass ceiling—invisible barrier to advancement.

Expectations have likewise changed with regard to the division of labour within the home. It is no longer given that women will stay home and care for their children. Nor is it the case that they are willing to work full time and take full responsibility for housekeeping and child rearing. Decisions must be made about who should wash the laundry, care for the children, tune up the car and fill out the tax forms. As noted earlier, there is no consensus on what duties each sex ought to undertake. This is the case not only in the kitchen but also in the bedroom. There are no clear cut rules about who should make the first move, when it's appropriate to initiate sexual relations, and when or if one should marry. Amidst all these arbitrations, is it any wonder that we would look to books to help us sort out gender relations?

Self-help books have played an important role in bringing issues concerning gender and interpersonal relationships into the realm of public discourse. By exploring the repercussions of the breakdown of stereotypes, these books have made possible discussions about sexuality, abuse and harassment. They have increased our awareness and tried to guide us through the myriad of alternative accounts of what it means to be male and female in the 1990s. And for this such books should be praised. However, the advice they offer needs to be carefully evaluated.

Too often books in this genre provide pat answers to complex questions. Personal experiences vary greatly yet they provide the basis for determining what we think are appropriate gender roles and relations. Our ideals about men and women are influenced by societal norms, cultural traditions and familial standards. How can self-help books contend with such diversities? Another problem with such texts is that although they often sound convincing, they cannot offer any final solutions to our gender troubles. As noted earlier, there are conflicting messages from a variety of sources about what men and women in the 1990s ought to be like. There are no standard formulas that can be applied to sort through this fluctuating mass of information. Note that resolutions to various dilemmas differ from text to text. How then should we choose which book to read? Which solution, which book is most reliable? Furthermore, gender relations continue to evolve as new pressures are placed upon them. Consider how our understanding of relationships must change in order to come to grips with AIDS, date rape, and the backlash to feminism. Is it possible for self-help books to adequately account for how such factors will influence gender roles and relationships? And can they forecast what influences will precipitate future change?

There are no short cuts in trying to understand and define one's gender role, if indeed there is such a role. And there are no ways to side step careful consideration of the nature of interpersonal relationships. We need to begin by becoming aware of the presuppositions we have about gender roles. What roles have we been socialized to believe are appropriate for men and women? Questions also need to be asked about how we define and give expression to our sexuality. From where do the ideals and the presumptions which interlay our understandings of femininity and masculinity arise? How do these ideals mould our attitudes towards our physiology? Finally, we must investigate how value has attributed to activities and attitudes which are deemed masculine and feminine. Only once we have addressed these kinds of questions can we begin to sort through the complexities of our gender relations for such considerations frame the way we perceive and respond to changes in our ideals about men and women and about relationships. While self-help books can bring our attention to specific problems and dilemmas, they lack the theoretical depth necessary to address these broader issues. So while it may be tempting to try to resolve your problems with your partner and come to have reasonable expectations of yourself by referring to *Women Who Love Too Much* or to *Why Men Are The Way They Are*, be forewarned. It is only through critical reflection that we can begin to understand what it means to be male and female in the 1990s.

UNIT 3

CONFLICT AND COOPERATION

■ **ISSUE 1:**
The Individual and the Collective

■ **ISSUE 2:**
Relations between Collectives

The Individual and the Collective

No man is an island entire of itself; every man is a piece of the continent, a part of the main. If a clod be washed away by the sea, Europe is the less, as well as if a promontory were, as well as if a manor of thy friend's or thine own were. Any man's death diminishes me, because I am involved in mankind, and therefore never send to know for whom the bell tolls; it tolls for thee.

John Donne

The worst sin towards our fellow creatures is not to hate them, but to be indifferent to them; that's the essence of inhumanity.

G. B. Shaw

Introduction

John Maxwell

Our experience tells us that human beings are social animals. We work together, play together, make war together—in fact, very few human activities are truly solitary. Human beings live in a cultural environment; that is, an environment of beliefs, values, rules, objects, and tools which they have created. Even individuals who are physically isolated from others maintain their social ties through culture.

The first reading, "The Individual and Society," presents several models of human nature and of human society. Each model can be used as a basis for deciding what view to take on issues of social importance. For example, viewing human nature as essentially selfish and always looking out for "number one" leads one to see social problems differently than if one viewed human nature as essentially social and cooperative. For instance, consider the different views one might take on the need for and value of punishment for crime.

To view society as more than the sum of its members invites the question whether the individual in a society, especially a complex one, is somewhat less than his or her constituent portion of society. Auden's poem "The Unknown Citizen" provides an unsettling view of a person's place in society.

Of course, often collective action is more effective than individual action. If my driving interest is to obtain food, I may be able to do this more effectively by hunting or farming with others. Ultimately a group may discover that a degree of specialization is required. They may also find after a period that the interests of some members become dominant or that some are getting greater benefits from group activities. At this point the group must be seen as a collection of groups rather than as a single group and we are confronted with the problem of our second issue—collectives.

The Individual and Society

John Maxwell

Human beings are social animals. This means that most of our behaviour occurs in the context of interaction with other people; very few human activities are truly solitary. In fact most of our behaviours, our attitudes, our values, and even some aspects of our personalities are learned as we interact with others. Even those characteristics which are determined by our heredity are modified to meet the demands of our social experience.

We know from our experience that society is a structure of rules (broadly defined to include traditions, customs, laws, conventions, etc.) which define the relationships between individuals and their society. Much of our behaviour is determined by the specific social institutions in which we participate. These institutions define our roles in much the same way as a script and stage directions define the roles of actors on the stage. There is certainly room for individual interpretation and expression but by and large our behaviour must fit within socially structured guidelines.

One of the tasks of social philosophers and social scientists is to explain how individuals are integrated into the social world, how they become and remain part of a society and why the society persists over generations. The answers to these types of questions are not easily derived from our immediate experience and often require that we generate speculative theories to help us make sense out of our experience. There are many theories which attempt to explain the phenomenon of society. We may prefer one theory over another simply because it provides the answers we *want* to believe. However, no single theory has answered all of our questions satisfactorily and we are constantly challenged to develop new understandings which more closely reflect social reality.

In this chapter we will briefly review four theories which purport to account for the relationship between us and our society. We will concentrate on how each of these theories deals with:

1. *Assumptions about human nature:* Are human beings basically good or basically bad? Are we governed by reason or by passion? Are we basically self-interested or altruistic?

2. *The relationship between the individual and society:* Are all people seen as being equal? What, if anything, should people have to say about the way they are governed? Why should people obey the rules? What is more important, the individual or the society?

3. *The role of "authority" within the society:* Who has the authority to make decisions? How do they get and maintain this authority? What responsibilities do the "rulers" have to the people they "rule"?

4. *The question of altruism and self-interest:* Are self-interest and altruism mutually exclusive behaviours? How do self-interest and altruism relate to such things as "good" and "evil"? Which attitude (self-interest or altruism) is better for the society at large?

First of all, we must understand what it is that we take for granted about our own society. These unquestioned beliefs about the relationship between ourselves and society colour the way we view any theory which purports to explain the relationship. Our society is built upon the principles of liberal democracy, socio-political and economic freedom, and individualism. These principles derive from the great social, political, and scientific revolutions of the 17th, 18th, and 19th centuries in Europe. For example, most North Americans are taught (and probably believe) that the best way to resolve a dispute is to vote and that the best decision is the one that gets the most votes. Most of us also are generally willing to act in accordance with a group decision and believe that the "principle of fairness" insures that we will not always be on the "losing end" of the decision.

That there is a structure of basic rules does not mean that they are always operative nor does it mean that they apply universally. One of the constant complaints in our society is that the rules which are theoretically based on the principles of democracy are not applied to everyone, at all times, or in the same way. Our system permits and even encourages us to raise questions of fairness and justice. An important question is why it is that even those people who suffer the worst injustices and benefit least from the "principle of fairness" continue to support the basic principle of the system.

Thomas Hobbes

Until the fourteenth century in Europe the dominant theory of society was tied to the religious doctrines of the Catholic Church. In short, people were taught that the social order existed because God had created it and that to question the social order was to question the will and wisdom of God. Thomas Hobbes (1588–1679) was concerned with developing a theory which would explain social order without attributing this order to a super-natural power. In his book *Leviathan*, Hobbes speculates on "The Natural Conditions of Mankind." In attempting to explain social order Hobbes makes certain assumptions about human nature and the behaviour of pre-social human beings.

Hobbes assumed that human beings in their natural state are essentially non-social and that they are driven, as are all other "wild" animals, by basic passions (lust, greed, etc.); in nature there is no morality and no system of rules to govern behaviour. These basic passions cause human beings to be suspicious and aggressive in their relations with each other. The unregulated desire for self-gratification naturally puts people into conflict with each other and leads to the situation which Hobbes described as the "warre of every man against every man," a situation in which "might is right."

Fortunately, human beings are, according to Hobbes, rational creatures and ultimately their "reason" leads them to see that ordered relationships with others are beneficial. In other words, the rational human being understands that self-interest may be advanced through cooperation with others. This cooperation can only develop if there are rules which govern the relations of people with each other. Since there is no "natural" commitment to the rules, people will only abide by them if they see the immediate satisfaction of self-interest or if there is some power strong enough to enforce the rules. Consequently, people willingly submit to the power of one person, the sovereign, who is able to impose order and, through the use of force, maintain a stable society.

Thus, social stability is a human product, a matter of a "social contract" to which all people at least tacitly submit. What we call "morality" is nothing more than a system of conventions (i.e., agreed upon rules) designed to regulate our basically self-interested behaviour. It is only through the exercise of force (or the potential use of force) that the sovereign has the authority to create and enforce a structure of rules. The sovereign invents these rules to satisfy his own needs and the needs of those whose support he seeks in order to maintain power; his only commitment to rule well relates to the fact that his self-interests are furthered if he does so. The only check on the sovereign's behaviour is the threat of organized rebellion.

"(In) this warre of every man against every man, ... nothing can be unjust. The notions of right and wrong, justice and injustice have there no place. Where there is no common power there is no law: where no law, no injustice."

Thomas Hobbes

Thomas Hobbes assumed that human beings in their natural state are essentially non-social and that they are driven, as are all other "wild" animals, by basic passions (lust, greed, etc.); in nature there is no morality and no system of rules to govern behaviour.

Life, Liberty and the Pursuit of Happiness

Declaration of Independence

The ideas behind the Declaration of Independence derive in large part from the writings of John Locke. Thomas Jefferson simply gave clear and common sense expression to ideas that were freely held by progressive thinkers in the 18th century. The appeal of the language and its expression have not diminished in over two-hundred years;

We hold these truths to be self-evident, that all men are created equal, that they are endowed by their Creator with certain unalienable Rights, that among these are Life, Liberty and the pursuit of Happiness. That to secure these rights, Governments are instituted among Men, deriving their just powers from the consent of the governed. That

whenever any Form of Government becomes destructive of these ends, it is the Right of the People to alter or abolish it, and to institute new Government ...

Hobbes's view of people and society is often described as "pessimistic" in that it is based on the assumption that the "natural" human being is at best un-social and at worst anti-social. Some two hundred years after Hobbes's death Sigmund Freud developed a theory of the personality which shares this "pessimistic" view of human nature and describes the "person" as the product of an ongoing conflict between natural self-interest and the demands of the society. This theoretical conflict is often expressed as the struggle between "good and evil" and has a long tradition in our religious thought and in our literature and clearly colours the way we see ourselves and our society and other societies.

John Locke

In his *Second Treatise on Civil Government*, John Locke (1632–1704), like Hobbes, attempted to build a theory of social behaviour based on certain assumptions about human beings in the "state of nature." Locke assumed that God created human beings to live harmoniously in the state of nature (compare this to the Garden of Eden). With few exceptions people recognized each other's "natural rights" and sought to meet their needs through cooperative action. Locke believed that people will naturally act altruistically (i.e., in the interest of the group) and it is an element of God's plan that self-interest is best achieved through cooperation.

Locke's theory is based on an "optimistic" view of human nature. "Optimistic" theorists typically believe that if people behave badly it is

John Locke (1632–1704)

not because they are "naturally bad", rather it is because the social structure is imperfect or because they are not aware of the rules of good conduct or the consequences of their actions. Locke argued that there are laws of nature which govern human behaviour. As rational creatures human beings should use their intelligence to discover what these laws are and live by them.

Government and other social organizations are created by human beings to facilitate cooperation and to exercise control over those few people who choose not to follow the laws of nature. Government (the sovereign) is obliged by the laws of nature to rule in the best interests of the society at large. If the sovereign abuses the privileges of authority then the people are authorized (by the laws of nature) to overthrow him.

> "The state of nature has a law of nature to govern it, which obliges everyone; and reason, which that law, teaches all mankind who will but consult it that, being all equal and independent, no one ought to harm another in his life, health, liberty, or possessions."
>
> *John Locke*

Karl Marx

John Locke suggested that the negative aspects of human behaviour (greed, lust, etc.) are not natural but are the products of either ignorance and error (regarding appropriate behaviour) or some minor and correctable fault in the social structure. Karl Marx (1818–1883) very definitely saw "evil" as a social product, specifically as a result of the relationships (and therefore the attitudes and values) imposed upon people by the structure of the productive system dominant in the society. In other words Marx is saying that people are victims of the social structure.

Marx argued that the system of material production in the society historically has created social structures which divide people into two types—those who own and control the basic means of production and those who actually do the labour. In the pre-industrial days the two groups were the landowners and the peasants; in industrial Europe the two groups (classes) are the capitalists and the workers. According to Marx the peasants/workers are the "slaves" and the landowners/capitalists are the masters. The two groups are in a constant state of conflict because the self-interests of each group are diametrically opposed—in other words what is "good" for the boss is "bad" for the employee and vice versa. Because it controls societal resources, the "master class" controls all the important institutions in society and it uses these institutions to further its own interests. So it is that Marx argued that the landowners/capitalists controlled organized religion and used religious institutions and beliefs to control the peasants/workers. The "authority" of the ruling class is based upon the control over the institutionalized means of force (i.e., the police and military).

Karl Marx (1818-1883) saw "evil" as a social phenomenon resulting from the relationships (and therefore the attitudes and values) imposed upon people by the structure of the economic system.

> "That the only purpose for which power can rightfully be exercised over any member of a civilized community, against his will, is to prevent harm to others. His own good, either physical or moral, is not a sufficient warrant ... Over himself, over his own body and mind, the individual is sovereign."
>
> *John Stuart Mill*

John Stuart Mill
(1806–1873) agreed with Locke that reason will over-rule the "baser" aspects of human behaviour (self-interest, greed, etc.) provided that people have sufficient information about the issue and the consequences of its various possible resolutions.

Marx believed that primitive societies operated communally—that is, the people cooperated in the attainment of common goals. In such communities self-interested behaviour is moderated because people are committed to the group and its goals. He argued that the only truly stable society must be a communal society and that the conflict of interests in other forms of society must eventually lead to open violence and revolution. Marx believed that the ultimate revolution would be a product of the conflict between the capitalists and labour in the industrial/capitalist society and that this revolution would produce a communal/industrial state in which the principle of "from each according to his ability, to each according to his needs" would apply. Of course this revolution would not occur until the oppressed masses use their natural reasoning abilities to recognize that they were being systematically exploited and to develop a systematic plan for revolutionary activity.

John Stuart Mill

Democratic theory is based on an "optimistic" view of human nature. Democracy assumes that the decisions made through the democratic process are, at least in the long run, the best decisions and that individual self-interests are best served through willing compliance with these decisions. The authority of the leaders in a democratic system is simply based on their position as agents whose task it is to act in accordance with "the will of the people."

As a democratic theorist John Stuart Mill (1806–1873) had great faith in the ability of the "common man" to participate in the democratic process and to make sound decisions based on a rational consideration of the issues and possible consequences. In other words Mill agrees with Locke that reason will over-rule the "baser" aspects of human behaviour (self-interest, greed, etc.) provided that people have sufficient information about the issue and the consequences of its various possible resolutions. Mill recognized, of course, that many issues do not have an inherently right or wrong side, that there will often be issues where all sides can be supported by sound reasoning.

Mill cautioned that the democratic system could lead to "majoritarianism," a situation where a majority shared a broad set of interests which were at odds with the interests of a minority—in such a situation the members of the minority would always be complying with the rules established by the majority.

Majoritarianism is not a threat if a society is truly "pluralistic." In a pluralistic society the social, political, and economic interest groups are continually shifting and there is no large scale control by a single interest

MENCIUS AND HSÜN TZU

References to classical Chinese philosophy, such as the ideas of Mencius and Hsun Tzu extracted below, demonstrate that fundamental ideas about human nature, justice and ethical conduct have always been global as opposed to exclusively European concerns.

MENCIUS

"All men have a mind which cannot bear to see the sufferings of others.

"The ancient kings had this commiserating mind, and they, as a matter of course, had likewise a commiserating government. When with a commiserating mind was practised a commiserating government, to rule the kingdom was as easy a matter as to make anything go round in the palm.

"When I say that all men have a mind which cannot bear to see the sufferings of others, my meaning may be illustrated thus: even now-a-days, if men suddenly see a child about to fall into a well, they will without exception experience a feeling of alarm and distress. They will feel so, not as a ground on which they may gain the favour of the child's parents, nor as a ground on which they may seek the praise of the neighbours and friends, nor from a dislike to the reputation of having been unmoved by such a thing.

"From this case we may perceive that the feeling of shame and dislike is essential to man, that the feeling of modesty and complaisance is essential to man, and that the feeling of approving and disapproving is essential to man.

"The feeling of commiseration is the principle of benevolence. The feeling of shame and dislike is the principle of righteousness. The feeling of modesty and complaisance is the principle of propriety. The feeling of approving and disapproving is the principle of knowledge."

HSÜN TZU

"The nature of man is evil; the good which it shows is factitious. There belongs to it, even at his birth, the love of gain, and as actions are in accordance with this, contentions and robberies grow up, and self-denial and yielding to others are not to be found; there belong to it envy and dislike, and as actions are in accordance with these, violence and injuries spring up, and self-devotedness and faith are not to be found; there belong to it the desires of the ears and the eyes, leading to the love of sounds and beauty, and as the actions are in accordance with these, lewdness and disorder spring up, and righteousness and propriety, with their various orderly displays, are not to be found. It thus appears, that to follow man's nature and yield obedience to its feelings will assuredly conduct to contentions and robberies, to the violation of the duties belonging to every one's lot, and the confounding of all distinctions, till the issue will be in a state of savagism; and that there must be the influence of teachers and laws, and the guidance of propriety and righteousness, from which will spring self-denial, yielding to others, and an observance of the well-ordered regulations of conduct, till the issue will be a state of good government.—From all this it is plain that the nature of man is evil; the good which it shows is factitious."

"In the name of democracy, welcome! Up to now we've had a one-party system."

group. For example, I might be a member of a minority group with reference to a particular economic issue (let us say the issue of free trade with Mexico), but my views on another issue (perhaps multi-culturalism) are those shared by a majority of Canadians. In a pluralistic society (or at least one which is believed to be pluralistic) people are willing to "go along with the majority," because they believe that in the long run they will frequently be part of the majority.

Summary

Each of us relates to society within the framework of a set of traditions, customs, laws, conventions, and beliefs. The four theorists briefly presented in this article have attempted to understand the nature of the relationship between the individual and the society.

Hobbes begins with a "pessimistic" view of human nature which says that "the baser passions" are the dominant factors in determining our behaviour. On the basis of this assumption Hobbes theorizes that society can only be maintained through the agency of a self-interested ruler whose position is ultimately dependent on the use of force. People obey the ruler because they fear his power but also because they recognize that an ordered society is in their best interests.

Marx has an "optimistic" view of human nature but a "pessimistic" view of society—it is the structure of social institutions which interfere with our natural desire to live in communal societies. Until the final revolution occurs we must live under the stress of a society in which a ruling class controls societal resources and oppresses and exploits those who are ruled.

Review

The Individual and Society

In this unit, the ideas of four philosophers concerning human nature and society are summarized, beginning with the 17th-century English writer Thomas Hobbes.

Hobbes believed that human beings are motivated chiefly by self-interest. He believed that they want to preserve their own liberty but also wish to acquire dominion over others. This perpetuates a constant state of war. However, because of the natural impulse toward self-preservation, people are also capable of living harmoniously in groups by submitting to a central authority or sovereign who is able to insure stability and peace. Self-preservation outweighs self-interest, according to Hobbes, as citizens behave as though they had a "social contract" towards their ruler and towards each other. Hobbes saw morality as a socially agreed upon convention and man as a base creature of passion, which fostered Hobbes' pessimistic view of humanity.

In contrast, John Locke, a young contemporary of Hobbes, saw human beings as peace loving and eager to cooperate with others. Within his optimistic view of mankind, wars and other evils occur not because human beings are essentially bad but rather because of flaws in the social structure.

The notion that class structure victimized whole groups of people was a key feature of the writings of Karl Marx. Marx was a 19th-century German socialist-philosopher whose ideas affected global politics in a profound way and did not diminish in influence until the late 1980s.

According to Marx, an industrial society produces inequalities among citizens. A class structure emerges with two basic categories of people, the capitalist-owners and the peasant-labourers, whose most basic interests are diametrically opposed. The result is a perpetual state of conflict that inevitably leads to violent social upheaval. Convinced that communism is the only stable form of social organization, Marx thought that the capitalists would hold power only until the oppressed masses recognized their exploitation when they would rise up and revolt.

But unlike Marx, a British contemporary by the name of John Stuart Mill saw a great deal of good in the common man. Mill was a proponent of democracy and a believer in the inherent tendency of human beings to reason. He felt that people are well disposed towards the idea of submitting themselves to the "will of the people." However, he cautioned against "majoritarianism," a situation where the intolerance found in a majority dominates and denies the rights of a minority. The risk is lessened in a "pluralistic" society containing many interest groups.

Whole shelves of books have been written about each of these major theories. They are but four of the many social theories that attempt to define the complex relationship between an individual and his or her society in a given age.

Locke holds an "optimistic" view of human nature and sees society as the means through which human endeavour is "enabled." Society provides the coordinating structures which permit us to cooperate to achieve our collective and individual goals. There are some flaws in the social structure and these may combine with human ignorance and error to create conflict and injustice but these problems can be remedied through the use of reason.

Mill's commitment to democratic theory presumes an "optimistic" view of human nature; democracy can't work unless people respond intelligently, fairly, and humanely to the challenges of living in society. Majority decisions may not always be the best but in general they reflect the collective wisdom of the people—as the people become better educated on the issues they will make better decisions. Majoritarianism is a danger in our type of democracy (based on the principle of majority rule) but this danger is minimized if the society is pluralistic and the composition of interest groups varies depending upon the issue.

QUESTIONS

1. Outline the main points of each of the models of society presented in this article.

2. Using the principles of comparison and contrast discussed in the Appendix of this book, explain the similarities and differences between Hobbes, Locke, Mill, and Marx with respect to their theories of human nature.

3. Should individuals riding in cars be required by law to wear seat belts? The harm that may come to them from being in an accident while not wearing a seat belt is primarily to themselves, though the general effect of many injuries is the raising of insurance rates to everyone. Aside from the rightness or wrongness of seat belt legislation, are seat belt laws enforceable? Analyze these questions from the point of view of each of the models in the preceding article.

4. Should all tobacco use be banned? Does the analysis of this question raise the same considerations as the seat belt issue? If so, do the conclusions implied by each of the models for the tobacco issue correspond to those for the seat belt issue, or are there different considerations? If the latter, what are they?

5. Suppose you read in the newspaper that a certain politician said that unemployment insurance benefits should never be paid to anyone who has resigned from a job voluntarily. What models of society could that politician believe in?

Gandhi

Bernadette Barber

Mohandas Karamchand Gandhi was born in 1869 in Porbander, on the west coast of India. His was a Hindu family of the Bania caste, somewhere in the upper middle level of the Hindu caste system; the men in his family had progressed from being grocers to ministers in small Indian states. Portbai, his mother, was devoutly religious and practiced constant self-discipline through fasting and prayer; Gandhi was particularly fond of her. At age thirteen Gandhi was subject to child marriage, a custom he later condemned. In 1887 he left for England to train as a lawyer in the British legal system, a pattern that many young Indian intellectuals followed. Gandhi was not an effective lawyer. He records an incident in his autobiography when, at his turn to speak before the court, he became tongue-tied and fled the court room amidst hoots of laughter. In 1893, humiliated by his failure as a practicing lawyer he left his wife and by now two children with his parents and went to practise law in Natal, a British colony in what is now known as South Africa. After twenty-two years of confronting the blight of apartheid he returned to India in 1915 with his wife and five children. The shy young lawyer had been transformed by his experiences into an internationally known leader and innovator in human rights causes. For the last thirty-three years of his life he laboured to bring about the independence of India and the unity of Hindus and Moslems within India itself. He was killed in 1948 by gun shots fired at point blank range during a prayer meeting, by a Brahmin, a Hindu of the highest caste.

The India Gandhi inherited was an important part of the British Empire. Since 1600 with the founding of the lucrative East India Company, Britain had gained economic, military and legislative control over a vast, heavily populated and intensely divided land. Gandhi was part of a Hindu majority constantly at war with the Moslem minority, but religious differences were not the only sources of division and discontent in the British colony. India was really a composite of numerous warring states and families, a country mainly populated by millions of impoverished villagers who were exploited by their own privileged classes as well as by the British.

Movements towards independence had flared up and been firmly repressed through economic, legal and military means by the British before Gandhi returned from Natal. The first meeting of the Indian National Congress, for instance, took place in 1885. Historians differ as to whether India's liberation in 1947 would have occurred with or without Gandhi's leadership. Evidence can be cited for both positions. Gandhi's legacy, however, lies not so much in his worldly successes, which were not many, but in the spiritual challenge or alternative he presented.

Influences

Gandhi was reared to know and love the Hindu scriptures; the Bhagavad Gita or "Song of God" describes the "way of love" taught by the god Sri Krishna:

> That man I love who is incapable
> Of ill will, and returns love for hatred.
> Living beyond the reach of *I* and *mine*,
> And of pain and pleasure, full of mercy,
> Contented, self-controlled, of firm resolve,
> With all his heart and all his mind given
> To Me—with such a one I am in love.
>
> Not agitating the world, or by it
> Agitated, he stands above the sway
> Of elation, competition and fear,
> Accepting life, good and bad, as it comes.
> He is pure, efficient, detached, ready
> To meet every demand I make on him
> As a humble instrument of My work ...
>
> Who serves both friend and foe with equal love,
> Not buoyed up by praise, nor cast down by blame,
> Alike in heat and cold, pleasure and pain,
> Free from selfish attachments and self-will,
> Ever full, in harmony everywhere,
> Firm in faith—such a one is dear to Me.

To understand what shaped Gandhi, it is necessary to understand that a major influence was his love of God, or Truth, as he preferred to call it, that he found in his Hindu religion. Some of his favourite non-Hindu teachings were from the Judaeo-Christian tradition: "The meek shall inherit the earth" from Jesus' Sermon on the Mount; "love

Mohandas Karamchand Gandhi

For Gandhi, the charka or spinning wheel was a powerful symbol. It typified what he called the "proletarianism of science".

your enemies, do good to those who curse you;" and, "if someone should hit you on the cheek, turn to them the other also."

However, it was not only spiritual influences that shaped Gandhi. In his 1982 film *Gandhi*, Richard Attenborough traced the beginning of Gandhi's evolution into a world figure from an experience Gandhi had in 1893 when he first arrived in South Africa at age twenty-four. He was thrown off a train for refusing to relinquish his paid-for first-class ticket and travel third class where, as he was told, all "coolies" travelled. Attenborough's choice was a biographically accurate one, for years later Gandhi commented that the incident was the "creative experience of his life." His real-life experience of being treated as a second-class citizen because of the colour of his skin and his ethnic background was as much an influence on the course of his life as any spiritual ideal. It was the combination of these things, the ideals and the experience, plus Gandhi's personal response to both, that made him who he was.

Brahmacharya and Satyagraha

In his *Autobiography*, subtitled "My Experience with Truth, All Men are Brothers", and in *Satyagraha in South Africa*, Gandhi constantly explores and explains the two courses of action to which he came to dedicate his life and for which he became both famous and notorious; namely, "brahmacharya" and "satyagraha."

"Brahmacharya" literally means "the course of conduct to be followed in pursuit of Brahman or Truth." It is the way to realize the ideal of ahimsa (non-violence) and it involves "complete control of the senses at all times and in all places; in thought and deed." The value of self-control and self-denial is not a uniquely Hindu teaching; all religions advocate brahmacharya in some form or other. The painful practices of brahmacharya, which horrified the secular West, include fasting regularly, abstaining from non-procreative sex, and a vegetarian diet (so as to reduce the amount of violence needed to survive). The purpose of such self-denial is the control of natural desires so as to be better able to listen to the spirit, to the "small voice" of Truth within.

His practise of brahmacharya, it should be noted, was one of the main sources of Gandhi's attraction for the millions of Indian villagers he inspired. They saw an upper-class Indian divest himself of all wealth and privileges and voluntarily live the poor and simple life they were condemned to live. Through his spinning wheel program he made the ideals of liberation from foreign and domestic exploitation tangible; in his lifestyle he made his love and commitment to the Indian populace visible.

Alongside his awareness of the importance of brahmacharya in personal life grew Gandhi's other and best-known course of conduct; namely, satyagraha.

"Civil disobedience" was the label given by the West to the movement called "satyagraha" by Gandhi. It is a far more complex and demanding course of conduct than that suggested by the western label of "passive civil disobedience," a label that Gandhi himself rejected because it did not capture the essence of what he believed satyagraha was all about. The term "civil disobedience" conjures up images of youths being dragged from driveways of nuclear missile-building plants by police, or it may evoke images of strikes, marches, peaceful demonstrations. These images only partly describe Gandhi's principle of satyagraha which literally translates into "holding fast to truth" or "soul force."

Satyagraha was fully born according to Gandhi in the years 1906 to 1908, during the passing and enforcement of the pass book law in South Africa. This piece of anti-Indian legislation was part of the beginning of apartheid and required Indians to carry a pass book on pain of fines, imprisonment and deportation. Gandhi and a number of Indians, Hindu and Moslem alike, swore to disobey the law unto death. In a public gesture faithfully reported by the press that stirred the consciences of the liberal establishment back in Britain, Gandhi burned hundreds of the pass books before he was beaten into unconsciousness by the South African police. He had gauged his opponent well and knew that the obvious moral inferiority of violence or "body force" would shame the British.

Satyagraha is a non-violent action aimed at converting one's opponent to Truth through self-suffering. It is imperative that only the satyagrahi suffer, according to Gandhi, in case his or her cause is not just, so that no harm is done to others. Non-violent action meant far more than physical passivity, for Gandhi. The perfect act of satyagraha meant non-violence in thought and emotion. Through training in brahmacharya and satyagraha, Gandhi thought that people could be weaned from hatred of others to hatred of evil.

The satyagrahi worked only to eliminate the unjust law or the violence, not the aggressor, since violence, even in a good cause, merely continued the hold evil has over human nature:

> I am more concerned in preventing the brutalization of human nature than in the prevention of the sufferings of my own people. I know that people who voluntarily undergo a course of suffering raise themselves and the whole of humanity; but I also know that people who become brutalized in their desperate efforts to get victory over their opponents or to exploit weaker nations or weaker men, not only drag down themselves but mankind also.

When confronted with injustice the satyagrahi studied how not to co-operate with the injustice and how best to defy the law. This is why Gandhi disliked the term "passive" civil disobedience. In his satyagraha, the satyagrahi took the initiative and actually provoked the authorities by breaking the law; it was an active form of disobedience.

Finally, Gandhi taught that non-violence was a universal principle, that it was a deeper or more fundamental principle than violence, and that in the long run, it would triumph over evil.

One of the best examples of satyagraha in action is the Salt March. Here, Gandhi set off on a two-hundred-mile walk accompanied by thousands of Indians. He marched down to the Indian Ocean and seized a handful of salt. Big deal? In seizing the salt Gandhi was breaking British law which maintained a monopoly on the refining of salt which was a vital necessity in Indian life. Gandhi went further. He encouraged Indians to manufacture their own salt and attempt to take back the salt mines. While Gandhi was in prison for his leadership role, hundreds of Indians voluntarily endured the beatings of the British army in the attempt to regain control over Indian salt. Again the press reports played an important role in showing the morally superior tactics of the Indians in this case.

"Generations to come will scarce believe that such a one as this in flesh and blood walked upon this earth."

Albert Einstein

Nonviolence as a Universal Principle

Non-violence or ahimsa is central to Gandhi's concept of human nature. It is a universal spiritual force that "resides in everybody, man, woman, and child, irrespective of the colour of the skin … In many it lies dormant, but it is capable of being awakened by judicial training."

Animals operate according to "the law of the jungle," Gandhi said, but human beings are made to operate according to the principle of ahimsa written, encoded as it were, into our deepest nature. "I see that there is an instinctive horror of killing living beings under any circumstances whatever," Gandhi wrote. Ahimsa then, is a universal principle derived from the observation both of the external world and of his own interior landscape. It is also a principle, as mentioned earlier, derived from Gandhi's religious influences.

But the fact that ahimsa is a universal principle of human nature and conduct does not mean that physical force, for instance, should never be used. Gandhi's challenge to us is not as simple as "never take a life." He essentially throws each of us back upon our own conscience:

> For, although, essentially the principle is the same, yet everyone applies it in his or her own way … Meat-eating is a sin for me. Yet, for another person, who has always lived on meat and never seen anything wrong in it, to give it up, simply in order to copy me, will be a sin.

The universal principle of ahimsa is not a law so much as an attitude or a standard that informs our deliberated choices. "Taking life may be a duty," Gandhi says:

> Suppose a man runs amuck and goes furiously about, sword in hand, and killing anyone that comes in his way, and no one dares to capture him alive. Anyone who despatches this lunatic will earn the gratitude of the community and be regarded as a benevolent man.

Nevertheless, for those of us who sigh with relief at such a loophole, and immediately plan to justify all our decisions through it, Gandhi reminds us that ahimsa is "the better way" that we are to discern according to our conscience, according to the voice of Truth present in every human being. This is at once Gandhi the existentialist and Gandhi the moralist speaking—we are free to choose and shape our lives by our choices, but our choices are measured by the ultimate principle of ahimsa written into our nature and existing objectively or independently of us.

Soul Force vs. Brute Force

Gandhi on Non-Violence

The first important work written by Gandi was a pamphlet entitled Indian Home Rule, *which was composed in 1909.*

In his introduction, prepared in 1921, Gandi writes: "I felt that violence was no remedy for India's ills, and that her civilization required the use of a different and higher weapon for self-protection.... In my opinion it is a book which can be put into the hands of a child. It teaches the gospel of love in place of that of hate. It replaces violence with self-sacrifice. It pits soul force against brute force ... My conviction is deeper today than ever. I feel that if India will discard 'modern civilization' she can only gain by doing so."

The pamphlet has twenty chapters. Selections on non-violent protest are provided below. The presentation is in the form of questions and answers. In what follows, the READER *is a hypothetical questioner, the* EDITOR *is Gandhi.*

READER: From what you say I deduce that passive resistance is a splendid weapon of the weak, but that when they are strong they may take up arms.

EDITOR: This is a gross ignorance. Passive resistance, that is, soul-force, is matchless. It is superior to the force of arms. How, then, can it be considered only a weapon of the weak? Physical-force men are

strangers to the courage that is requisite in a passive resister. Do you believe that a coward can ever disobey a law that he dislikes? Extremists are considered to be advocates of brute force. Why do they, then, talk about obeying laws? I do not blame them. They can say nothing else. When they succeed in driving out the English and they themselves become governors, they will want you and me to obey their laws. And that is a fitting thing for their constitution. But a passive resister will say he will not obey a law that is against his conscience, even though he may be blown to pieces at the mouth of a cannon.

What do you think? Wherein is courage required—in blowing others to pieces from behind a cannon, or with a smiling face to approach a cannon and be blown to pieces! Who is the true warrior—he who keeps death

always as a bosom-friend, or he who controls the death of others? Believe me that a man devoid of courage and manhood can never be a passive resister.

This, however, I will admit: that even a man weak in body is capable of offering this resistance. One man can offer it just as well as millions. Both men and women can indulge in it. It does not require the training of an army; it needs no jiu-jitsu. Control over the mind is alone necessary, and when that is attained, man is free like the king of the forest and his very glance withers the enemy,

Passive resistance is an all-sided sword, it can be used anyhow; it blesses him who uses it and him against whom it is used. Without drawing a drop of blood it produces far-reaching results.

It never rusts and cannot be stolen. Competition between passive resisters does not exhaust. The sword of passive resistance does not require a scabbard. It is strange indeed that you should consider such a weapon to be a weapon merely of the weak.

Criticisms and Objections

The main objection that has been levelled against Gandhi's philosophy is that ahimsa is not the underlying and fundamental principle of human nature. Rather, self-preservation, self-interest, the Darwinian law of survival of the fittest, is the code written into human nature. Gandhi's expectation that people could be taught to respond non-violently to aggression is an unrealistic one according to his critics.

The piece of evidence considered to be most damning in the case against Gandhi's ideas is Hitlerism. Gandhi seems not to have seen Hitler as a lunatic who should simply be stopped by physical force. He praised France for surrendering to the Nazis and advised the British government and its allies to use non-violent non-co-operation—satyagraha:

> I venture to present you with a nobler and braver way.... I want you to fight Nazism without arms, or ... with non-violent arms.... You will invite Herr Hitler and Signor Mussolini to take what they want of the countries you call your possessions. Let them take possession of your beautiful island, with your many beautiful buildings. You will give all these but neither your souls, nor your minds.

Winston Churchill was not prepared for such detachment from worldly concerns, however, and most if not all of the other allied nations agreed with him. The Jewish people, especially, were baffled and outraged by Gandhi's position. Satyagraha or ahimsa was not a universal principle for response to aggression; it could work in certain situations like India. But in the case of a Hitler, violence was the best response. Gandhi may say "I would rather be killed than kill" but others would say the reverse. Gandhi was trying to eradicate violence from the human heart; the allies were trying to put a (violent) end to World War Two.

Conclusion

panacea—a remedy or cure-all.

What can we write of Gandhi's legacy? Was he, as Arthur Koestler, one of his fiercest critics argued, an irresponsible idealist pushing non-violence as a "universal panacea"? Or, was he "the man of infinite goodness, a seeker all his life of Truth, which he equated with God, a pilgrim who believed that love was the greatest gift of man and that love and understanding and tolerance and compassion and non-violence, if they were only practiced, would liberate mankind from much of the burden, oppression and evil of life," as the American journalist, William Shirer reported at the time?

Most of Gandhi's admirers and critics agree that Gandhi's contribution to subsequent generations is that he made a world caught in the vicious circle of violence aware of the alternative methods of non-violence. Even those who argue that only under certain conditions could non-violent methods be used are in fundamental agreement as to Gandhi's contribution to the non-violent resolution of conflict.

Indeed, if we study our own Western attitudes towards strikes, demonstrations, picket lines, and various other manifestations of civil unrest and disobedience, we find that Gandhi's ideal of non-violence has become the unwritten moral code, the standard by which we measure the validity of an issue. Peaceful protests are taken far more seriously than violent ones. Non-violence as Gandhi taught, is recognized as morally superior to violence, in achieving political goals. Machiavellian tactics may still be publicly practiced by those in power, but Gandhian tactics are still expected from the less powerful. Gandhian tactics were born from a position of complete powerlessness; the one resource left to the powerless to prove the justice of their cause, Gandhi believed, was the appeal to the opponent's conscience. Martin Luther King, the crusader for black civil rights, called himself a disciple of Gandhi, recognizing that only by showing themselves morally superior to the brutality of the racist community could his people show themselves deserving of the civil rights withheld from them.

In the long run, Gandhi taught that only non-violence had the power to break the chain of human destructiveness.

I Have A Dream …

Dr. Martin Luther King, Jr.

I am happy to join with you today in what will go down in history as the greatest demonstration for freedom in the history of our nation.

Five score years ago, a great American, in whose symbolic shadow we stand today, signed the Emancipation Proclamation. This momentous decree came as a great beacon light of hope to millions of Negro slaves, who had been seared in the flames of withering in justice. It came as a joyous daybreak to end the long night of their captivity.

But one hundred years later the Negro still is not free. One hundred years later the life of the Negro is still sadly crippled by the manacles of segregation and the chains of discrimination.

One hundred years later the Negro lives on a lonely island of poverty in the midst of a vast ocean of material prosperity. One hundred years later, the Negro is still languishing in the corners of American society and finds himself an exile in his own land. So we have come here today to dramatize a shameful condition.

In a sense we have come to our nation's capital to cash a cheque. When the architects of our great republic wrote the magnificent words of the Constitution and the Declaration of Independence, they were signing a promissory note to which every American was to fall heir.

This note was a promise that all men, yes, black men as well as white men, would be guaranteed the inalienable rights of life, liberty, and the pursuit of happiness.

It is obvious today that America has defaulted on this promissory note in so far as her citizens of color are concerned. Instead of honouring this sacred obligation, America has given the Negro people a bad cheque, a cheque which has come back marked "insufficient funds."

But we refuse to believe that the bank of justice is bankrupt. We refuse to believe that there are insufficient funds in the great vaults of opportunity of this nation. So we have come to cash this cheque, a cheque that will give us upon demand the riches of freedom and the security of justice.

The civil rights movement in the USA, like Gandhi's earlier campaigns in India, advocated non-violence. The response of the authorities, however, was frequently a violent one.

We have also come to this hallowed spot to remind America of the fierce urgency of now. This is no time to engage in the luxury of cooling off or to take the tranquillizing drug of gradualism.

Now is the time to make real the promise of democracy.

Now is the time to rise from the dark and desolate valley of segregation to the sunlit path of racial justice.

Now is the time to lift our nation from the quicksands of racial injustice to the solid rock of brotherhood.

Now is the time to make justice a reality to all of God's children.

It would be fatal for the nation to overlook the urgency of the moment. This sweltering summer of the Negro's legitimate discontent will not pass until there is an invigorating autumn of freedom and equality. Nineteen sixty-three is not an end but a beginning. Those who hope that the Negro needed to blow off steam and will now be content, will have a rude awakening if the nation returns to business as usual.

There will be neither rest nor tranquillity in America until the Negro is granted his citizenship rights. The whirlwinds of revolt will continue to shake the foundations of our nation until the bright day of justice emerges.

But there is something that I must say to my people who stand on the warm threshold which leads into the palace of justice. In the process of gaining our rightful place we must not be guilty of wrongful deeds. Let us not seek to satisfy our thirst for freedom by drinking from the cup of bitterness and hatred.

Dr. Martin Luther King, Jr.

The World House

Some years ago a famous novelist died. Among his papers was found a list of suggested plots for future stories, the most prominently underscored being this one: "A widely separated family inherits a house in which they have to live together." This is the great new problem of mankind. We have inherited a large house, a great "world house" in which we have to live together—black and white, Easterner and Westerner, Gentile and Jew, Catholic and Protestant, Moslem and Hindu—a family unduly separated in ideas, culture and interest, who, because we can never again live apart, must learn somehow to live with each other in peace.

One of the great liabilities of history is that all too many people fail to remain awake through great periods of social change. Every society has its protectors of the status quo and its fraternities of the indifferent who are notorious for sleeping through revolutions. But today our very survival depends on our ability to stay awake, to adjust to new ideas, to remain vigilant and to face the challenge of change. The large house in which we live demands that we transform this world-wide neighbourhood into a world-wide brotherhood. Together we must learn to live as brothers or together we will be forced to perish as fools.

We must forever conduct our struggle on the high plane of dignity and discipline. We must not allow our creative protest to degenerate into physical violence.

Again and again we must rise to the majestic heights of meeting physical force with soul force. The marvellous new militancy which has engulfed the Negro community must not lead us to a distrust of all white people, for many of our white brothers, evidenced by their presence here today, have come to realize that their destiny is tied up with our destiny and their freedom is inextricably bound to our freedom.

We cannot walk alone.

As we walk, we must make the pledge that we shall always march ahead. We cannot turn back. There are those who are asking the devotees of civil rights, "When will you be satisfied?"

We can never be satisfied as long as the Negro is the victim of the unspeakable horrors of police brutality.

We can never be satisfied as long as our bodies, heavy with the fatigue of travel, cannot gain lodging in the motels of the highways and the hotels of the cities.

We cannot be satisfied as long as the colored person's basic mobility is from a smaller ghetto to a larger one.

We can never be satisfied as long as our children are stripped of their selfhood and robbed of their dignity by signs stating "For Whites Only."

We cannot be satisfied as long as the Negro in Mississippi cannot vote and a Negro in New York believes he has nothing for which to vote.

No, no we are not satisfied and we will not be satisfied until justice rolls down like waters and righteousness like a mighty stream.

I am not unmindful that some of you have come here out of great trials and tribulations. Some of you have come fresh from narrow jail cells. Some of you have come from areas where your quest for freedom left you battered by the storms of persecutions and staggered by the winds of police brutality.

You have been the veterans of creative suffering. Continue to work with the faith that unearned suffering is redemptive.

Go back to Mississippi, go back to Alabama, go back to South Carolina, go back to Georgia, go back to Louisiana, go back to the slums and ghettos of our northern cities, knowing that somehow this situation can and will be changed.

Let us not wallow in the valley of despair. I say to you today, my friends, so even though we face the difficulties of today and tomorrow....

... I still have a dream. It is a dream deeply rooted in the American dream.

I have a dream that one day this nation will rise up and live out the true meaning of its creed. We hold these truths to be self-evident that all men are created equal.

I have a dream that one day out in the red hills of Georgia the sons of former slaves and the sons of former slave owners will be able to sit down together at the table of brotherhood.

I have a dream that one day even the state of Mississippi, a state sweltering with the heat of injustice, sweltering with the heat of oppression, will be transformed into an oasis of freedom and justice.

I have a dream that my four little children will one day live in a nation where they will not be judged by the color of their skin but by the content of their character.

I have a dream today.

I have a dream that one day down in Alabama, with its vicious racists, with its governor having his lips dripping with the words of interposition and nullification; one day right there in Alabama little black boys and black girls will be able to join hands with little white boys and white girls as sisters and brothers.

I have a dream today.

The Views of Malcolm X

Malcolm X

Malcolm X

Malcolm X was born Malcolm Little in Omaha, Nebraska. He was assassinated in 1965. His life has recently been portrayed in the film *Malcolm X*.

While in prison, Malcolm X joined the Nation of Islam. He took on the surname "X" to signify that, like most descendants of the slaves forcibly brought to the United States from Africa, he had lost his ancestral name. He joined the Nation of Islam in prison and became a devoted follower of the Islamic religion. The Nation of Islam maintained that the solution for black people in the United States was complete separation for blacks.

Malcolm X's views underwent a radical change in 1964. During a series of religious trips to Mecca and the newly independent African states, he encountered good people of all races. His views began to change accordingly. He came to the conclusion that he had yet to discover true Islam. He came to regard not all whites as racists, and saw the struggle of black people as part of a wider freedom struggle. He established his own religious group and a political organization, the Organization for Afro-American Unity.

Along with Martin Luther King, Malcolm X symbolized the civil rights movement in the United States during the 1960s.

Before Going to Mecca

"No *sane* black man really wants integration! No *sane* white man really wants integration. No sane black man really believes that the white man ever will give the black man anything more than token integration. No! The Honorable Elijah Muhammad teaches that for the black man in America the only solution is complete *separation* from the white man!"
The Autobiography of Malcolm X, p.248.

"And this is one thing that whites—whether you call yourselves liberals or conservatives or racists or whatever else you might choose to be—one thing that you have to realize is, where the black community is concerned, although the large majority you come in contact with may impress you as being moderate and patient and loving and long-suffering and all that kind of stuff, the minority who you consider to be Muslims or nationalists happen to be made of the type of ingredient that can easily spark the black community. This should be understood. Because to me a powder keg is nothing without a fuse." *Malcolm X Speaks*, p.48.

After Going to Mecca

"Never have I witnessed such sincere hospitality and the overwhelming spirit of true brotherhood as is practiced by people of all colors and races here in this Ancient Holy Land, the home of Abraham, Muhammad, and all the other prophets of the Holy Scriptures. For the past week, I have been utterly speechless and spellbound by the graciousness I see displayed all around me by people of *all colors*."
The Autobiography of Malcolm X, p.344.

"My pilgrimage broadened my scope. It blessed me with a new insight. In two weeks in the Holy Land, I saw what I never had seen in thirty-nine years here in America. I saw all *races*, all *colors*,—blue-eyed blonds to black-skinned Africans—in *true* brotherhood! In unity! Living as one! Worshipping as one! No segregationists—no liberals; they would not have known how to interpret the meaning of those words.

"In the past, yes, I have made sweeping indictments of *all* white people. I never will be guilty of that again—as I know now that some white people *are* truly sincere, that some truly are capable of being brotherly toward a black man. The true Islam has shown me that a blanket indictment of all white people is as wrong as when whites make blanket indictments against blacks.

"Yes, I have been convinced that *some* American whites do want to help cure the rampant racism which is on the path to *destroying* this country!"
The Autobiography of Malcolm X, p.366.

I have a dream that one day every valley shall be exalted, and every hill and mountain shall be made low, the rough places will be made plane and the crooked places will be made straight, and the glory of the Lord shall be revealed and all flesh shall see it together.

This is our hope. This is the faith that I will go back to the South with. With this faith we will be able to hew out of the mountain of despair a stone of hope.

With this faith we will be able to work together, to pray together, to struggle together, to go to jail together, to stand up for freedom together, knowing that we will be free one day. With this faith we will be able to transform the jangling discourse of our nation into a beautiful symphony of brotherhood.

This will be the day when all of God's children will be able to sing with new meaning "My country 'tis of thee, sweet land of liberty, of thee I sing. Land where my fathers died, land of the Pilgrim's pride, from every mountainside, let freedom ring!"

And if America is to be a great nation, this must become true. So, let freedom ring from the prodigious hilltops of New Hampshire. Let freedom ring from the mighty mountains of New York.

Let freedom ring from the heightening Alleghenies of Pennsylvania.

Let freedom ring from the snow-capped Rockies of Colorado.

Let freedom ring from the curvaceous slopes of California.

But not only that, let freedom ring from Stone Mountain of Georgia.

Let freedom ring from Lookout Mountain of Tennessee.

Let freedom ring from every hill and molehill of Mississippi, from every mountainside.

Let freedom ring and when this happens, when we allow freedom to ring, when we let it ring from every village and every hamlet, from every state and every city, we will be able to speed up that day when all of God's children, black men and white men, Jews and Gentiles, Protestants and Catholics, will be able to join hands and sing in the words of the old Negro spiritual, "Free at last, free at last. Thank God Almighty, we are free at last."

Delivered at the Lincoln Memorial, Wednesday, August 28, 1963.

The Unknown Citizen

W.H. Auden

(To JS/07/M/378
This Marble Monument
Is Erected by the State)

He was found by the Bureau of Statistics to be
One against whom there was no official complaint,
And all the reports on his conduct agree
That, in the modern sense of an old-fashioned word, he was a saint,
For in everything he did he served the Greater Community.
Except for the War till the day he retired
He worked in a factory and never got fired,
But satisfied his employers, Fudge Motors Inc.
Yet he wasn't a scab or odd in his views,
For his Union reports that he paid his dues,
(Our report on his Union shows it was sound)
And our Social Psychology workers found
That he was popular with his mates and liked a drink.
The Press are convinced that he bought a paper every day
And that his reactions to advertisements were normal in every way.

Policies taken out in his name prove that he was fully insured,
And his Health-card shows he was once in hospital but left it cured.
Both Producers Research and High-Grade Living declare
He was fully sensible to the advantages of the Instalment Plan
And had everything necessary to the Modern Man,
A phonograph, a radio, a car and a frigidaire.
Our researchers into Public Opinion are content
That he held the proper opinions for the time of year;
When there was peace, he was for peace; when there was war, he went.
He was married and added five children to the population,
Which our Eugenist says was the right number for a parent of his generation,
And our teachers report that he never interfered with their education.
Was he free? Was he happy? The question is absurd:
Had anything been wrong, we should certainly have heard.

Review

The Unknown Citizen by W.H. Auden

The "Unknown Citizen" in Auden's poem of the same name does not seem like a particularly noble hero, does he? In fact, his primary quality is that he has managed to keep himself entirely out of trouble.

A competent worker and a good consumer, he led a statistically "normal" life—neither complaining nor arousing complaints from others. He had few positive attributes to speak of. He was just a small voiceless cog in a big machine. What kind of state might erect a marble monument to honour a person like that?

In many respects, this state has much in common with contemporary Western society, especially the America of several decades ago, when the poem was written. It is a nation of automobiles, phonographs, radios, refrigerators, unions, factories—and a highly compartmentalized government bureaucracy that pervasively keeps a close (and not entirely innocent) watch on its citizens.

This poem is an ironic view of a society that sees itself as an ideal place to live, a Utopia, but one that is actually highly intolerant of individuality and free expression. The Unknown Citizen complacently accepts the status quo (and the irony) without protest. Now a monument has been erected to remember his name—even as that name is forgotten for all time.

Relations Between Collectives

Out of timber so crooked as that from which man is made nothing entirely straight can be built.

Immanuel Kant

Niccolo Machiavelli

Antanas Sileika

Niccolo Machiavelli was a statesman and diplomat who lived in Florence from 1469–1527, and it is important to understand the world that he came from before going over a few of his ideas. At the time Machiavelli lived, Italy was a collection of city states that were perpetually jockeying with one another for advantage. They formed complicated, shifting alliances and in addition foreign countries often looked upon the Italian peninsula as ripe for occupation.

Machiavelli became a victim of this complicated, cut-throat world, when new rulers, the Medicis, took control of Florence. They first tortured him and then banished him to a small family estate. Machiavelli was desperate for new employment, so he wrote a kind of political handbook called The Prince and dedicated it to the Medicis in attempt to gain their favour.

Both Machiavelli and his book have been attacked ever since because Machiavelli was so unsentimental that he sounded perfectly wicked. His premise was that the world was a very dangerous place for a prince, and the book was supposed to be a guide to survival. Machiavelli called his ruler a "prince," but today we would call a person who has just come to power by force of arms or scheming, a dictator. Machiavelli's book told a dictator how to take power and how to hold on to it.

To this day, a ruthless political schemer is called "Machiavellian."

Do 400 year-old ideas have any relevance today? Let's take a look at some of the principles Machiavelli advocated, and then see if we can find any examples of modern Machiavellian behaviour in politics.

Some of Machiavelli's Ideas from The Prince

How to Keep a Principality One Has Conquered

A prince who has just taken power by force of arms or scheming is in a dangerous position. He may still have many hidden enemies and he must make himself safe from them. Machiavelli suggested that most of the population in a newly taken country should be left in peace. They should be allowed to keep their taxes, languages, and customs

Countries do not have friends. They have interests.

Charles De Gaulle

because they are familiar with them. After all, a new prince can not afford to antagonize everyone. However, the members of the former ruling family must be eliminated entirely—elimination, of course, means murder. Machiavelli said that as long as any members of the ruling family remained, there was a danger they might surround themselves with followers and overthrow the new prince. To protect against this, they must all be murdered.

With pointers such as this, one can see how Machiavelli gained his reputation for wickedness. And yet, this barbaric principle was followed in the recent past. Let us consider the fate of the Romanovs, the ruling Czars of Russia who lost power to the Communists in 1917. To consolidate their power, the Communists had the Czar, his wife, and all their children murdered. The Communists feared that if any Romanovs lived, they might yet return to power. Almost four hundred years after his death, Machiavelli's principle was being applied.

"My people! The hated dictatorship is over! From now on, you will elect me democratically!"

The Nature of Human Beings

The wish to acquire, says Machiavelli, is a normal part of human nature. We all want things, and when we have them, we want more. The same is true of countries. Furthermore, we tend to admire countries and rulers that are rich and powerful, and tend to despise those that are poor. Machiavelli suggests that it is worth trying to become as powerful as possible by virtually any means because people admire the rich. People may not actually despise the poor, but no one looks up to them.

It cannot be denied that people admire "winners." Even though Canada and many other countries could be placed on almost the same pedestal, let us restrict our attention for a moment to the USA, perhaps the richest of Western countries. The United States is certainly admired by many, and the admiration is not always for the democracy and freedom enjoyed by Americans. More precisely, poorer foreigners admire the United States because it is a rich country. At the very moment when many Eastern European countries are becoming politically free, thousands of emigrants want to leave those nations for the USA. Why should this be so when the citizens of East European countries either enjoy the same freedoms as Americans or will do so very soon? It is because they admire success, and in this case success means money.

How to Keep Vices from Affecting One's Hold on Power

Machiavelli believed that most people could not be free of all vices. By vices, we mean character flaws that lead to extravagance, violence, sexual perversity, etc. He believed it was natural for people to have weaknesses. A prince had to be very careful about vices, though, because certain of them could cost him his principality. A prince who had a weakness for spending money might no longer be able to pay an army, for example, and therefore leave his country open to attack. Machiavelli suggested that a prince might allow himself certain vices, as long as they did not weaken his hold on the state. In other words, it may be good to be virtuous, but virtue is not possible for most people to attain.

In modern times, we like our politicians to be squeaky clean, but Machiavelli would say that this is impossible. John F. Kennedy is remembered as a remarkably appealing president of the United States. Many think of his time as one of great hope. Thirty years after John F. Kennedy's death, we have learned that the man had a weakness for women that led him into numerous affairs, among them an affair with Marilyn Monroe. For some people, this knowledge lowered Kennedy's appeal. It was disappointing to learn that such a seemingly upright man repeatedly betrayed his wife. Machiavelli would not have been surprised, though, because he would have said that the vice was not important. After all, it did not affect Kennedy's ability to rule.

How to Hold a Newly Acquired Country

The problem with holding a country that is far away is that armies of occupation cost a great deal, and one can beggar oneself by maintaining large numbers of soldiers. Machiavelli suggested that a cheaper method is to confiscate the land of a small number of local people and to send colonists to occupy that land. The colonists will be grateful to the prince for their new land, and help him hold it against the hostile locals.

We don't think of colonies very much in modern times, but we should remember that North and South America were colonies of various European powers. It would have been very expensive to force the native peoples into submission using only paid soldiers. It was far cheaper to give land to people, colonists, and to have them dominate the local inhabitants. The native people of North America were forced into submission by a distant power not merely because the power was more technologically advanced, but because emigrants were sent to this continent to establish the rule of the distant powers.

Is It Better to Be Loved or Feared?

Most individuals would of course prefer to be loved, but Machiavelli says that this is not easy for a prince because it is difficult to make the majority of people love you. People will only obey you if they love you or fear you, and since the former is impossible to achieve, it is better to have people fear you.

Again, an attempt to strike fear into the hearts of one's subjects may sound horrible, but let us consider just one of this century's dictators. Joseph Stalin ruled the Soviet Union for almost thirty years, and in his time he was responsible for the deaths of millions and the imprisonment of many more. His secret police were feared, and several million Ukrainians were starved into submission to his policies. Machiavelli would say that Stalin understood how to stay in power.

On the Nature of War

Machiavelli believed that wars were an expression of humanity and were therefore impossible to avoid. Admittedly, Machiavelli lived in a time when the most powerful weapons were cannons, and so the danger of fighting a nuclear war could never have occurred to him. If we restrict our argument to conventional wars, of which there have been over 150 since 1945, we might agree that there is no use in saying there *should not* be wars if they continue to happen. Machiavelli said wars would always happen, and therefore one should never try to avoid war. Instead, the prince should always choose to fight a war when it is to his advantage.

Should a country only fight when it is attacked? This sounds like a very noble sentiment, but countries that live in dangerous circumstances can not afford to be sentimental. In the late 1970s, it became clear that Iraq was preparing to build nuclear arms. The laboratories for research and the plants for construction were already largely in place. The state of Israel could not afford to allow Iraq to become a nuclear-equipped country because Israel and many of its neighbours were in a perpetual state of tension. Therefore, the Israeli government decided to launch a pre-emptive strike. Using its air force, and without an explicit declaration of war, Israel destroyed the labs and plants that would have given Iraq the ability to build nuclear weapons. Machiavelli would have nodded approvingly at Israel's application of his principles.

Realpolitik—A Modern Extension of Machiavelli's Ideas

We have looked at a few paraphrased examples from Machiavelli's book of thirty-six chapters. Now let us get a little closer to modern times.

The German term "realpolitik" was coined to describe the policies of Otto von Bismarck, the nineteenth-century German chancellor who said that he recognized the right of no other nation when it came to foreign policy. "Realpolitik" refers to an unsentimental attempt to

Review

Niccolo Machiavelli

This article is a summary of some of the pragmatic and often shocking ideas about how to run a state as advocated by Niccolo Machiavelli, a Renaissance-era Florentine statesman and political analyst. His handbook on the subject, written in 1513, is entitled *The Prince*.

Italy in the 15th-century was a patchwork quilt of frequently battling principalities with constantly shifting loyalties. A close observer of this frenzied political scene, Machiavelli, a ruthless political schemer, believed that "might makes right." A ruler must do whatever must be done to cement their hold on power. Ethics do not enter the picture. Political foes must be murdered; no amount of lying, cheating and treachery was beneath the political leader whose object was to subjugate another people or state. "Such intellectual honesty about political dishonesty would have been hardly possible at any other time or in any other country ... " Bertrand Russell writes in his *History of Western Civilization*.

One of Machiavelli's dictums for rulers is that "it is better to be feared than loved," and many 20th-century tyrants from Joseph Stalin to Saddam Hussein, seem to have modeled themselves on this advice. Many modern leaders also seem to share Machiavelli's belief that treachery was inevitable, even advantageous under certain circumstances. The 19th-century German notion of "realpolitik" which rationalizes unethical conduct if it advances the national interest, seems based on Machiavelli's bleak perception of politics.

Despite, or perhaps because of, his pessimistic vision of humanity, Machiavelli's name has entered the English language. Underhanded and manipulative political leaders are still commonly referred to as "Machiavellian."

further the policies of one's country, specifically, to gain material or political advantage.

A believer in realpolitik would say that there is no use talking about high moral standards. People *should* not steal, but many do. People *should* be more easily satisfied with what they have, but they are not. Countries *should* respect other countries and co-operate with them, but they do not. In other words, in a world dominated by national self-interest, only the self-interested can survive.

A Comparison of Two Articles

While we are on the subject of *should,* this might be a good moment to discuss the ideas of both Toby Fletcher and Niccolo Machiavelli.

Toby Fletcher's article, "The Future of Sovereignty," calls for a new world order, a loose federation of states that could deal better with problems such as war, pollution, and hunger. This type of call for a new world order has become increasingly popular since World War II. Decolonized states and developing countries have called for changes in the economic system we live in, as they see this economic system favouring the Western countries, mainly Europe and North America. Also, Fletcher points out, pollution, hunger, and war are international problems, and we need international bodies to control them.

A critic of Toby Fletcher might say, however, that he describes the world as it should be, and not the world as it really is. A critic might therefore say that Fletcher's ideas are idealistic and have little chance of being implemented, for no nation will ever give up sovereignty unless it is forced to do so or sees some overwhelming advantage. Certainly, economic and political union is moving forward in Europe, but the opposite is happening in the Soviet Union and Yugoslavia, and the very idea of centralization, at least in economic terms, has fallen out of favour as Eastern European economies begin the route to reforms. In short, there is no clear and definite move towards world political union, but a kind of tension exits between centrifugal (away from the centre) and centripetal (towards the centre) forces.

Fletcher's assumption that people like orderliness in line-ups is certainly not true for most of the world. Anyone who has waited for a bus in France, Italy, or Egypt knows the type of jockeying that happens when the bus arrives.

Can one therefore say that Fletcher is wrong and Machiavelli is right? The problem that most people have with Machiavelli's ideas is that they paint a picture of a world that functions purely out of motives of self-interest. Many of us would like to believe that the world is not really so amoral.

This leaves us with a fundamental dilemma. In international political terms, we can imagine a far better world, but what is the use of imagining a better world if it cannot be achieved? Machiavelli might have said that we can imagine a "kinder, gentler" world all we want, as long as we do not delude ourselves into believing it is really possible to achieve.

The Future of Sovereignty

Toby Fletcher

Much of our every day life is guided by widely-accepted, but unwritten rules of conduct called manners. For instance, many of us try to get a cup of coffee in the cafeteria before that first class in the morning. Although we may be late, we will line up and wait patiently, as long as it's clear that we are served in the order we arrived. But that quiet patience can quickly turn to anger as we see a late arrival butt into the line ahead of us. Why? What rule or tradition or custom has been broken? There is no sign which states "Line up or else." Who said a bunch of strangers are supposed to line up? Why do we feel this deep sense of injustice, even outrage, when someone is rude or impolite?

Our favourite teachers are often the ones who clearly describe a reasonable set of rules governing how classes will be managed and especially how course work will be evaluated. If the rules are clear, fair, and consistently applied, we usually accept the results of those rules. If it is clear how a paper is to be marked, we usually accept the grade we get because it is clear how the grade was determined. We keenly feel a sense of injustice if we get an unjustified low grade and we often feel a sense of being devalued if we get an unjustified high grade. Teachers and students are happier with clear and fair rules in the classroom.

The principles of proper manners and academic regulations can be generalized from the relationships among individuals to the interactions among nation states. The peoples and nations of the world have been merging more and more into an interdependent global society. Advances in technology have improved communications around the world to the point where "spaceship earth" is a concept most people can readily accept. Supersonic jet travel, live rock concerts played and televised simultaneously on two continents, instantaneous transfers of huge sums of money from Hong Kong to London to New York to Los Angeles to Tokyo, timely news and information reports from anywhere

This graffiti on a Toronto wall suggests that some, at least, are passionate about Canadian politics.

to anywhere—all of these technological applications have clarified that we live on a small, finite planet. Countries rely on each other for trade and economic stability, for security and peace, and for help and friendship when disasters strike. Unfortunately, world politics have not kept pace with world problems. Only forty years ago, the world and its resources seemed limitless, inexhaustible, yet we had just developed the means to annihilate it. Commenting on the nuclear bomb, Albert Einstein said: "It has changed everything except our way of thinking, and so we drift toward unparalleled catastrophe." We are technically quick and politically slow, with the result that our technology has far exceeded our social and spiritual development.

Our biggest problem is that while the world has become a finite, integrated whole, we continue to think that all political power should be kept at the level of the nation. Global politics are still dominated by a view of the world that prevailed before growth and technology made us so interdependent. In this view, the world is an aggregate of sovereign nations having neither rights nor obligations toward each other. Sovereign-nation thinking relies on "might makes right" and divides the world into East and West, North and South, "us" and "them." People are citizens of the country to which they owe their highest loyalty. We support two standards for humanity—we look after the welfare of our own citizens, but disclaim any political or ethical responsibility for the plight of people in other countries. Just as sovereign-nation thinking sets up boundaries to compassion and responsibility, so it sets up barriers to cooperation around the vital interests which all people, all nations have in common. An intolerable irony: each nation trying to put its immediate interests ahead of the overall interests of the world worsens the global crisis and no one's interests are truly served. Everyone who has a television has seen the images of starving children in Ethiopia. We know there is a problem of properly distributing the food we produce to ensure that everyone is fed. Last year, the world's military expenditures totalled $1,000 billion spent to buy weapons to hurt others and protect ourselves. Imagine potential changes, if even half of those dollars went to help feed the hungry or to improve agricultural methods and technology.

Millions of young people have been killed or maimed in over 150 wars fought since 1945. We are poisoning our air, our water and destroying our habitats. Our situation begs us to change, begs us to rethink our assumptions, to go beyond the sovereign-nation system to conceive a new world order.

Humans are social and cooperative. We are born into groups, nurtured by groups, socialized by groups, and very early on in our lives we begin to influence, create, and develop groups. We form groups for many reasons: to protect ourselves, to gather food, to teach the young, to have fun, to solve problems, to do things. We form families, clans, tribes, churches, nations, provinces, states, countries, empires, dynasties, teams, associations, leagues, companies, corporations, and conglomerates.

If we want the nations and peoples of the world to live together as a peaceful, interactive community, then we need some form of government. Most people, even those who don't like government, accept that to be able to live together socially, we must have a way to make decisions and take action on matters affecting the community as a whole. Many people resent government for being restrictive, cumbersome, and expensive, yet ignore the freedoms and benefits provided.

Metropolitan Toronto is a very complex operation. We have developed a structure where elected officials draft by-laws which greatly influence our urban behaviour—how fast we drive, where we can park our cars, how many dogs and cats we can own, how high fences can be between neighbours, and now even where we can smoke.

Most of us comply with these by-laws most of the time and we know the consequences of breaking them. Disagreements are settled at City Hall.

We rely on our cities to provide us with water, electricity, sewers, police and fire protection, and garbage removal. For bigger issues such as education, health care, highway safety, and liquor control, we turn to our provincial government.

In order to balance the potentially conflicting regional interests among provinces, we have a national government which attempts to address issues such as monetary policy, taxation, postal service, defence and trade.

We create organizations to accomplish things, but very often our organizations are not as efficient nor as effective as we would like them to be. Describing problems, then explaining possible solutions can be very frustrating, and there is always the terrible temptation for those in power to dictate to the powerless. But the best solutions invariably result when everyone who has an interest or will be affected has some influence on the outcome. Giving people a voice, consulting, and consensus-building, take time. Sharing power and giving up authority are extremely difficult to do.

More and more now we are confronted by problems that threaten all humans, problems which transcend city and state boundaries, problems which require national governments to cooperate and collaborate—two activities which many governments are reluctant to do.

Canadian values of regionalism, interdependence, multiculturalism, and national problem-solving could provide the foundation for a global political framework. Newfoundland, Quebec, Ontario, and British Columbia are very different and distinct components of Canada.

Like many places in the world today, Bosnia's tragedy derives from seemingly insoluble ancient differences between ethnic groups within its borders, compounded by super-power relations and global politics.

Disputes among them are settled at conferences, in the courts, or in their legislatures. It is extremely unlikely that citizens of one province would actually go to war against citizens of another province. It is not that there is no conflict; it is that the conflict is appropriately managed.

Federalism is a system of government in which a number of states form a union but remain independent (or sovereign) in their internal affairs. A federal government can be weak or strong, depending on how responsibilities are divided between central authority and the component states.

The United States of America is an example of a strong central government with fifty relatively weak states. The European Community is an excellent example of twelve sovereign, diverse states joining together to form a remarkably effective and powerful federal union. Canada's federal system lies somewhere in between.

Countries have associated with each other for a variety of reasons:

1. *geographic*, such as the Organization of American States (OAS), the Organization for African Unity, the Pacific Rim, the Arctic Nations;

2. *colonial*, e.g., the Commonwealth, the Francophonie;

3. *military*, e.g., the North Atlantic Treaty Organization (NATO);

4. *political*, e.g., the Western democracies, the Communist Bloc, the nonaligned countries;

5. *religious*, e.g., Arab League;

6. *economic*, e.g., the Organization of Petroleum Exporting Countries (OPEC), the Group of Seven, the European Community (EC).

Economic partnerships seem to be the most enduring, egalitarian, and effective. Countries seem to be much more willing to surrender certain sovereignty rights for economic gain. The best example of this is the European Community. The EC has become a single market of 325 million consumers—far greater than the U.S.-Canada free trade zone of 265 million. The EC comprises twelve remarkable nations: Belgium, Britain, Denmark, France, Greece, Ireland, Italy, Luxembourg, Netherlands, Portugal, Spain and West Germany. Remarkable because of their ethnic, cultural, political, and historical diversity. Many of these countries have been at war with each other and are still intensely nationalistic, yet they will share a common currency and passport; they will recognize common patents and professional designations; citizens can live, work and move freely anywhere within the community. These countries have established a democratically-elected parliament to pass

Review

The Future of Sovereignty

The principles that govern good behaviour among individuals should also be applied to govern the conduct among modern states, Toby Fletcher writes in this essay.

Technological changes have advanced communications and travel so rapidly that it is possible to perceive the world not just as a conglomeration of nations but as a unified "spaceship earth." In this modern world, Fletcher writes, the concept of "nationhood" is old and divisive; people need to put the global agenda ahead of nationalistic goals.

The author proposes that nations should invest in agricultural technology, not weapons, and co-operate to find fair solutions to a host of global problems such as food shortages and starvation, pollution, exploitation of resources and war. As there is government on the municipal, provincial, and federal levels, so too the nations of the earth ought jointly to establish a world government.

According to Fletcher, the global government would be composed of a democratic legislature and a justice system, and impose sanctions against transgressors of international law. A global police force would also be necessary to enforce compliance.

legislation to deal with common problems—for example, their environmental challenges. But each country retains a distinct identity and internal control over social policies, language, culture, and internal security. Together, they are the strongest economic union in the world. Each member nation has sacrificed some sovereignty to the centre of European power, Brussels. But this surrender has nothing to do with altruism or high-minded idealism, but everything to do with a practical re-definition of self-interest, involving a redrawing of the boundaries of identification to include not only a sense of being French or German or Italian but also a sense of being a member of a united Europe. With this membership comes, of course, much greater clout in the world.

But even with this greater clout, the EC has not been able to do much to stop the savage wars and ethnic rivalry that have torn Yugoslavia apart. At the same time as many countries wish to put aside old grievances and integrate into larger units such as the EC, NAFTA and the Pacific Rim, it is also apparent that many people do not seem to be able to surrender old hatreds. This ethnic nationalism threatens the peace of vast areas, and may yet prove to be a stumbling block to creating a working model of "harmonious diversity."

The EC may not yet speak with a united political voice capable of imposing order on other nations, but its economic achievements have been a magnet that pulls other countries into wanting to join. Countries such as Sweden, Norway and Austria are lining up to get into the club. With the remarkable changes that have taken place in Eastern and Central Europe since the collapse of the Berlin Wall, the EC may well expand to include the former East Bloc economies and provide "associate" status to the newly-emerging Baltic nations. The economic incentive has compelled nations to rid themselves of outmoded political organizations and search for new ones.

The success of the EC means that the relative power of the U.S. is declining, although the U.S. still retains enormous economic strength and will remain powerful throughout the 90s. The contest between the old "superpowers" is over but that does not mean that we do not face many multi-lateral, global concerns for which we need global cooperation:

- reducing armed conflict

- managing population growth

- reducing defence budgets

- distributing food

- reducing debt

- disposing of hazardous waste

- protecting the environment

- establishing human rights

- accommodating refugees.

To face these problems, we need world institutions. Although we are a long way from a federated world community of nations, we do have a number of global organizations, e.g., The United Nations, The World Court, The World Bank, The International Monetary Fund (IMF). The U.N. is constantly criticized for being weak and ineffective, yet its strength is in being a forum for even the weakest nation to voice its concerns. The U.N. has survived since 1945 precisely because it relies on consensus, the lowest common denominator, and the single veto. From tribe to feudal kingdom to nation-state, from town to city to metropolitan area, there has been an historical trend to ever larger social groupings. When we transcend sovereign-nation thinking, we become citizens of the world. Global interdependence requires new definitions. Our personal and national interests can only be served through a more sophisticated, cooperative and collaborative relationship among nations.

World federation will not be cheaper nor necessarily more efficient as a bureaucracy, but if we create a world order in which every individual and every nation assumes certain global responsibilities in exchange for certain guaranteed rights, then world federation will be more effective in dealing with our global challenges. Strong economically based associations of nations would reduce the need for elaborate defense systems and free up huge amounts of money which could be used to eliminate hunger, promote health and education. Open, unrestricted communications and news services would reduce totalitarian oppression and provide the opportunity for global human rights.

Minimal world governance means establishing at the global level the principles and institutions we already recognize as fundamental to our social order at the civic, provincial, and national levels. These include:

1. A democratic legislature to develop a body of world law setting out basic rights and obligations;

2. A system of world courts for interpreting those laws in cases of dispute;

3. A set of sanctions to motivate compliance with the laws; and

4. A recognized, fully-resourced and effective global police force.

These principles are familiar to everyone and are as relevant on a global scale as on a local one. International trading partnerships, associations, and communities seem to be the best way of establishing collaborative, productive relationships among nations. Clear, just rules of international behaviour are simply our best hope for a peaceful, prosperous future.

WHERE THE PEOPLE LIVE

The poorest 20 percent of the world's population shares 1.4 percent of the world's money

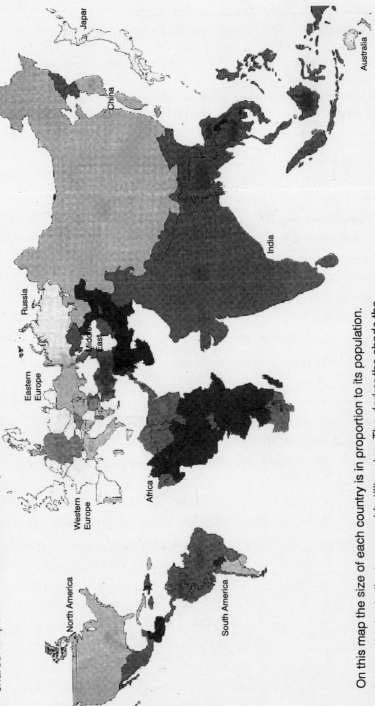

Map adapted from COLORS Magazine.
Courtesy of COLORS Magazine.

On this map the size of each country is in proportion to its population.

Darker shades indicate general fertility rates. The darker the shade the more quickly will the population of that country double.

WHERE THE MONEY LIVES

The richest 20 percent of the world's population
has 82.7 percent of the world's money

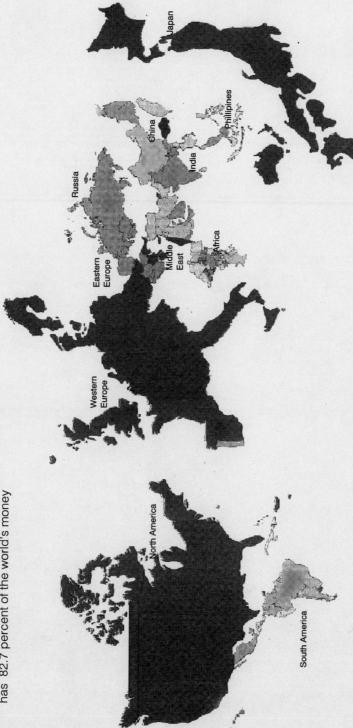

On this map the size of each country is in proportion to its wealth.
Darker shades indicate a higher quality of life in terms of literacy,
life expectancy and income, based on the UN Human Development Index.

Map adapted from COLORS Magazine.
Courtesy of COLORS Magazine.

UNIT 4

PERCEPTIONS OF THE NATURAL WORLD

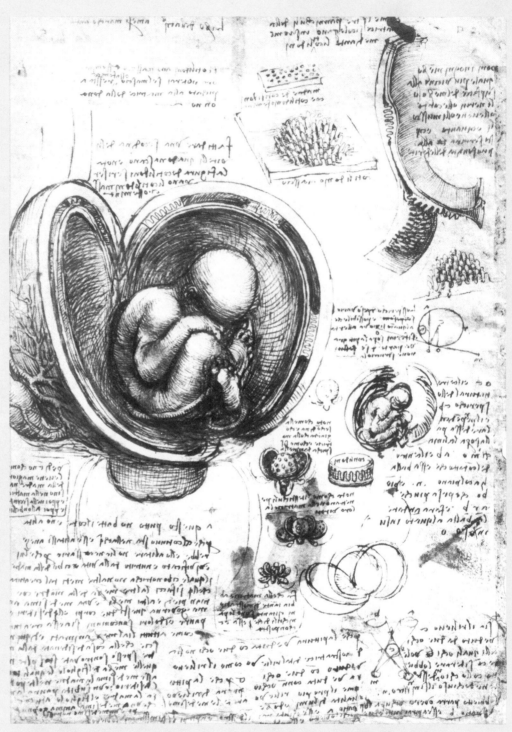

The breadth of Leonardo Da Vinci's curiosity is revealed by the enormously detailed drawings that we have of his investigations into such things as the principles of flight or human embryos, shown here.

Science and the Natural World

It seems to me that those sciences are vain and full of error which do not spring from experiment, the source of all certainty.

Leonardo da Vinci

I cannot believe that God plays dice with the cosmos.

Albert Einstein

Science may have found a cure for most evils; but it has found no remedy for the worst of them—the apathy of human beings.

Helen Keller

Curiosity and Discovery

Michael Badyk

I don't think that it really matters where or how we got it, but we have it—curiosity. All you have to do is look at children. Every day and moment is full of curiosity and discovery. Watch toddlers entering a room. Their heads will go from side to side as they look around and take it all in. The next thing they do is find things that they can reach. They'll explore and touch and look at everything they can. Anything that produces a reaction when touched will be a special delight for children.

If necessary, children will put something that they find curious into their mouths. I remember being with a friend of mine and her son when her son was about 16 months old. The little guy came into my living room, wandered over and grabbed a large rock that was on top of a stereo speaker. He then shoved half of it into his mouth. He wanted to see what it tasted like. That is probably a legitimate use for the sense of taste. As adults we suppress that sense, except for food. But people like geologists often taste rocks to test for salts and other minerals, so we can use it for more than food.

I've always liked to watch kids around Christmas time or on birthdays. Just put a present down in front of them, but tell them that they can't open it yet. They go crazy. They'll whine or plead and when they finally realize that you won't give in, they will know that they can't take the easy way out by coercing you and then their senses will start to kick in.

They'll look at it first. This might supply a clue. That's one sense. Then they'll touch it. That will give them a better sense of size and shape, building on what their eyes told them first. That's two senses that have kicked in. They'll also probably pick it up. More information. Weight. Density. They will probably also shake the box, and see what sound it will make. Hearing: sense number three. While they're this close they'll also check the box for any odours. Sense number four. Not much luck there under most circumstances. The same with taste. Kids tell me that wrapping paper tastes awful. Sense number five. All engaged. Most children may now try to guess what's in there, and they'll probably question you as to the success of their guess. Adults usually give in at this point and let the gift be opened.

If your senses allow your curiosity to be satisfied then you have made something that in general you can call a *discovery*. That's the best part about being young. Almost everything is a discovery. This curiosity/discovery cycle is precious and it must be fed and nurtured throughout a person's life. There are trails to walk, mountains to climb, books to read and many moments to savour.

Curiosity and Science

Many people have misconceptions about what science is and what it does. A dictionary will say that "science is a branch of knowledge." Perhaps a better way to put it is that science is a tool or an aid to help us explore our universe, under the influence of our curiosity. It's not as concise as the dictionary definition, but explains things a little bit more clearly. If we had that gift-wrapped present in our hands and we couldn't open it, then maybe we'd invent the X-Ray to check inside. That to me is science—exploring the small and the large.

We have done a reasonable job at explaining many facets of life on earth, but there is still a great deal to learn. The question remains "How did we as humans and our universe come to be?" This ancient question is not going to be solved soon. It might never be. There is plenty to explore and discover and to stimulate our human curiosity.

What carries us forward to acquire new knowledge is the **scientific method**—a series of logical steps that we have developed to get to the truth or the solution in the most economical way. This series of steps works quite well, but there are some underlying points that must be kept in mind.

Tentativeness. The first is that scientists must be *tentative* about conclusions. They are rarely 100% positive that what they have established is the truth. They might have made a mistake somewhere that has given them a false impression that they have uncovered the truth or solved the problem. "Good" science will never state a result to be an absolute. Words such as "maybe" or "perhaps" are the correct terms that should be used.

Verifiability. Another underlying point is something called *verifiability*. This means that the way in which scientists get their results can be repeated by others, and they will get exactly the same results. If they don't, then either their experiment was done incorrectly, or the experiment is wrong in the first place. If a number of people can obtain the same results independently then the results must be reasonable. It's simply a way of checking.

THE SCIENTIFIC METHOD

The scientific method is a series of logical steps that we have developed to get to the truth or the solution in the most economical way possible.

The Scientific Method

The steps leading to a solution in science can be broken down as follows:

STEP 1:   State the nature of the problem.

STEP 2:   What is a possible solution or the truth in this case? *(Developing an hypothesis.)*

STEP 3:   Come up with a way to test your solution. *(Designing an experiment.)*

STEP 4:   What results does your test provide? *(Collecting the data or observations.)*

STEP 5:   What is your conclusion? *(Producing an interpretation of the data or observations that you collected.)*

(measurable)

Empirical Observations. The final point is that you must have results that include *empirical observation*. These are observations that you can detect with your senses. If it is a problem that you can only think about, but not really test or produce results that you can sense, then the results will largely remain unproven or inconclusive.

Laws and Theories. The whole process that we just went through points to solving a problem and establishing the truth. If you can conclusively say that what you have discovered is the truth and it will stay that way wherever you go in the universe, and under any possible condition, then you can call your result *a law*. These are exceedingly rare commodities.

Usually, we only manage to come up with a possible explanation and these are called *theories*. They will remain only an explanation until we gather more information or come up with another explanation to establish the truth.

Theories and laws extend far beyond just the realm of science. So far in the *Humanities* text we have examined many theories. In psychology, the "four schools of thought" discussed earlier are really theories. More work needs to be conducted before any of these could be accepted as a law. If a law is developed it most likely will combine aspects of some or all the existing theories as well as new, yet-to-be-discovered information. For aspects of society it may be ludicrous even to try to establish sociological laws. Will it ever be possible to devise a law that explains how we select a mate? There are some well-known and understood factors, but the elements of chance always make it difficult to come up with a universal rule (a law).

Later in the text when we deal with the role of art we will see the attempt that has been made to develop explanations as to why people like certain works of art, or why some works can be termed "good." The complexity of variables here is such that the rational side (objectivity) may never be able to eliminate the need for the emotional (subjectivity). It would be a shame if artistic laws became "carved in stone" or captured in some formula. One of the pleasures of the arts is the surprise of something really new.

Unlike the subjects just described, we do have laws in the natural sciences. They are great and important discoveries, and nowadays we take them for granted. This can lead to the false conclusion that we know everything about the natural world, but there is an immense quantity of work still to be done. Even our understanding of something basic like light is still theoretical (either it's a particle or wave depending upon the situation).

There is enough in our existence (and even the origin of our existence) to keep our curiosity fuelled for a long time. Science and curiosity will continue to work together and we will continue to experience the joy of discovery. Thomas Huxley stated it very poignantly at the turn of the century: "It's not that the universe will live up to our imagination, it's whether our imagination will live up to the universe." These are words that have been pondered for many years, and ones that will continue to be discussed for ages to come.

> "It's not that the universe will live up to our imagination, it's whether our imagination will live up to the universe."
>
> *Thomas Huxley*

The Path of Scientific Development

Tom Olien

The three primary activities involved in scientific development are: **(1)** observing; **(2)** structuring the information; and **(3)** discovering or creating an underlying mechanism.

Inherent in each activity is a relentless (or an on-going) process of reflection, checking equipment, correcting observations, updating technique, confirming speculation and questioning theory. The result is the process shown in the chart on the next page. This process parallels the steps of the scientific method, the discipline of curiosity used by individual scientists as described in the previous article.

Observing

Scientific activity starts with observation. Initially, observations were limited to the five human senses. We now live in a world with powerful extensions to our primary senses. A simple set of binoculars drastically changes our ability to identify a bird in the woods or to see the stars and planets with a clarity that the most astute astronomer of four hundred years ago could not imagine.

Many instruments measure features of the universe that go beyond our senses. A voltameter measures electrical potential, a feature of an electric circuit unseen by human eyes except in the high values that produce a dangerous shock. A compass can detect the direction of the earth's "invisible" magnetic field, while other instruments measure its strength. The Herculean forces between the rock faces of sliding continental plates can now be measured, as can the temperatures of outer space or the heat in the core of a nuclear reactor. Today, in most industrialized countries there is a significant industry associated with the development, manufacture, sales and operation of scientific instrumentation.

Every area of scientific observation requires a unique "objectivity." Scientific "objectivity" should allow one to "see" what is really there and not what one hopes to "see." The ability to achieve this ultimate

The Path of Scientific Development

The Process

OBSERVING

- instrumentation that extends our senses
- skill in specific techniques
- patience and "objectivity"

STRUCTURING AND USING THE INFORMATION

- patterns and laws
- applied mathematical tools of analysis
- empirical rules for design and extension

DISCOVERING/CREATING AN UNDERLYING MECHANISM

- a creative leap beyond reasoning
- a simple, elegant unifying principle
- constantly creating new possibilities and being tested against new observations

abstract objectivity is at best tainted by human frailty and at worst perverted by the massive personal, social, economic or ideological consequences of the impact of a given observation. In spite of these complications, the process of scientific observation usually converges to the point where all competent observers agree that they "see" the same thing in the same set of circumstances.

Structuring the Information

Once a body of data has been accumulated from reliable observation, the next task is to attempt to make some sense and order out of the data. Science assumes that every action follows some pattern, usually some cause and effect connection. Sometimes the connections are fairly simple and obvious. Two of you may just manage to push a stalled car out of an intersection, but six of you could move it much more easily and quickly. The connection between force and motion is fairly obvious.

THE DEVELOPMENT OF SCIENCE

The three primary activities involved in scientific development are:

(1) observing;

(2) structuring the information; and

(3) discovering or creating an underlying mechanism.

The search for patterns or laws is a long-term goal of science. The methods include cataloguing samples, making diagrams, lists and graphs. Statistical analysis and other powerful mathematical tools are also used. The details of a discovery may be tucked away in seemingly random data or "noise." Finding patterns in such circumstances is not unlike the capacity of the human ear to pick out a faint cry for help in the midst of the roar of a hurricane.

At this stage of observation we may have some very useful rules for how things work, but we do not know why they work as they do. There is no obvious fundamental mechanism, only rules, often very complex and arbitrary ones connecting certain facts and events. There is still a need for a unifying principle to simplify and make sense of the regulations.

Discovering or Creating an Underlying Mechanism

The discovery of grand themes and fundamental theories is the crowning achievement of the creative human mind in the arena of science. The theories of universal gravitation, relativity, evolution, continental drift and the role of DNA in genetics are examples of underlying mechanisms.

These themes did not emerge from reason alone. Like an artist, scientists must step beyond the structured data and rules. Typically a person or a group makes an educated guess, an intuitive leap, that opens a new possibility and a new way of thinking. The genius of the process of science is that it doesn't stop with a good guess, but sets to testing it thoroughly. The creative guesses that were wrong have long since disappeared leaving us only the heroic tales and legacies of the ones that worked.

A fundamental theory (such as gravity) is often simple. It is seen as an elegant and aesthetically pleasing unifying principle. Looking back, most people would say it is obvious; it looks so right and natural. From examples in celestial mechanics, genetics and neurology we can see how these three stages develop.

The Path to an Underlying Mechanism in Celestial Mechanics

Global navigation in the fifteenth century revived interest in the stars and planets. Little change had been made to the Ptolemaic system of the universe from second-century Rome. The Ptolemaic theory held that the earth was the center of the universe and that the earth was at rest with no rotation or motion. The sun, the stars and the planets rotated around the earth. The system was adequate for the needs of the time (it worked as a system of navigation) but was very complex.

Nicholas Copernicus
(1473-1543).

The Path of Scientific Development

Celestial Mechanics

OBSERVING

- **Copernicus** (1473-1543): an idea—earth not the centre .
- **Tycho Brahe** (1546-1601): an observatory —new precision of information about planets.
- **Galileo** (1564-1642): used telescope to observe rotation of sun and the revolution of the moons of Jupiter.

STRUCTURING AND USING THE INFORMATION

- **Kepler** (1571-1630): develops three laws of planetary motion. (1) the orbits of the planets around the sun are elliptical, with the sun at one focus; (2) the line drawn from the sun to a planet sweeps out equal areas in equal times; (3) the square of the period of the planet is proportional to the cube of the radius.

de
* de.cret*
(take back)

DISCOVERING/CREATING AN UNDERLYING MECHANISM

- **Newton** (1642-1727): the law of universal gravitation. All objects in the universe attract each other. The force increases with the product of their masses and decreases with their distance apart.

$$F = \frac{G m_1 m_2}{r^2}$$

Copernicus suggested that the system would be simpler if we treated the sun as the centre of the system of planets and rotated the earth daily to allow for the rising and setting of the sun and moon and stars. It seems obvious now, but was not in the context of his time. Religious dogma and our own ego demanded that we see ourselves and our earth as the pinnacle of God's Creation, and thus the centre of it all. But the simplicity and elegance of the Copernican suggestion was convincing and encouraged a new wave of thinking.

Galileo made use of the newly developed optical lenses to make a telescope. His observations of the rotation of the sun and of moons revolving around the planet Jupiter did much to challenge the dogma

hedesy
hereticel

(a scientist excepted
charah tehory)

Galileo (1564-1642) presenting his telescope to the muses and pointing out a heliocentric system.

that had kept a static world view dominant for so many centuries. He was also instrumental in developing the experimental method and theories of terrestrial mechanics that would be vital for the next leap.

In the meantime, Tycho Brahe, a Danish astronomer, had made meticulous observations of the heavens. His observations were extensive and some one hundred times more accurate than previous observations, pushing the very limits of accuracy of the unaided eye. Johann Kepler, a German mathematician and astronomer, applied his skills to this new accurate data to develop the three laws of planetary motion. These laws correctly described and predicted the motion of the earth, moon and planets about the sun, but lacked any explanation of why they should be so.

The explanation came from the leap made by Isaac Newton. Galileo had described the action of gravity for earthbound objects such as stones and cannon balls. The leap that Newton made was to ask if gravity actually extended to the moon. Again, it may seem obvious, but it represented radical new thinking at the time, and only a few decades earlier would have been ruled out as heresy by both church and science. Newton calculated and found it worked for the moon. In fact, it worked for all the planets, with the sun as the gravitational centre of the solar system. Kepler's laws could then be deduced as a consequence of universal gravitation rather than as a separate set of rules for our planetary system.

The mechanism of universal gravitation could be applied to all objects on the surface of the earth and beyond. It explained the pattern of the tides and allowed for accurate predictions, such as the date of return of Halley's comet and the existence of the planet Neptune, finally observed in 1846.

The Path to an Underlying Mechanism in Genetics

Isaac Newton (1642-1727) described mathematically the law of gravity in its application to the whole cosmos—the mutual attraction of two masses varies inversely with the square of the distance between them.

Genetics presents a current example of the path of scientific development. Mendel is credited as the father of genetics based on his systematic observation and explanation of the patterns of genetic inheritance. The physical location of the "inheritance material" was found in the chromosomes. These appear under a microscope as small sausage-like objects within the nucleus of the cells of an organism. But there are a small number of chromosomes and a very large number of genetic features for even the simplest organism. The gene is the package of information coded for a particular characteristic. The sense of what form this "gene" could take was unknown.

The Path of Scientific Development

Genetics

IDEA — organisms "inherit" characteristics of the parent

OBSERVING

- **Mendel** (1822-1884)—observed the inheritance pattern in peas

STRUCTURING AND USING THE INFORMATION

- introduced the basic form of the laws of genetics many people use the laws of genetics to improve grains and livestock and to understand and control some genetic diseases

DISCOVERING/CREATING AN UNDERLYING MECHANISM

- **Watson and Crick** —the DNA molecule reveals the code that governs all genetics

For over half a century increasingly complex rules of genetics were developed and applied to improvements of grains and livestock and to an understanding of hereditary diseases. But the gene itself remained a mystery. The fundamental mechanism driving genetics was an illusory black box with many patterns of input and output understood, many more not understood and the action within the black box unknown. It was the study of nucleic acids, culminating in the illumination of the structure of the DNA molecule by Watson and Crick in 1953, that opened the black box and caused the revolution in genetics. Just as mechanical engineers, armed with the foundations of mechanics, generated the industrial revolution in a previous era, now genetic engineers equipped with an understanding of the fundamental genetic structure are developing tools and techniques that can systematically control the features of plants, animals and human beings. The implications are exciting and frightening but with the basic mechanism understood there is no turning back the exploration.

Black box—a term scientists use to describe a situation in which we know essentially what something does, but we don't yet comprehend how it operates (like machinery covered up by a black box).

The Path of Scientific Development

Neurology

IDEA—the basis of perception and consciousness is associated with the electrical activity of the brain

OBSERVING

- **Eccles**—physiology of individual neurons - the action potential
- **Sherrington**—physiology of nerve sequences involved in reflexes

STRUCTURING AND USING THE INFORMATION

- **Penfield**—memory triggered at specific sites within the brain
- **Edelman**—groups of neurons form the basis of perception

DISCOVERING/CREATING AN UNDERLYING MECHANISM

- no single simple process is able to present itself as the fundamental structure and operating mechanism of the brain

The Path to an Underlying Mechanism in Neurology

Neurology is the study of the nervous system and encompasses many domains of study: anatomy, physiology of the neuron, psychology, psychiatry, neural pathology. Each area has many rules and laws that can be used to predict actions in response to specific causes or stimuli. The drug *curare* was used by South American Natives on poisoned arrows. We now know that this drug blocks the transmission of nerve impulses to muscles and thus leads to paralysis. Our clear understanding of its action allows us to use curare in controlled ways during major surgery to avoid muscle reflex. Psychiatry has used electro-shock and drugs to control certain extreme psychiatric illnesses and has models of the actions of the brain that suggest why these methods are effective.

But the field of neurology is full of seeming contradictions. Wilder Penfield in working with epileptic patients was able to stimulate specific points in the brain and have memories brought to consciousness. Thus, specific memories seem to be located in a specific place in the brain. But it is also known that brain injuries to these areas do not necessarily remove the memory, but rather it seems to be stored like a hologram within a large domain of the brain.

In spite of all we know about the brain, all the rules and patterns we have sorted out so far, we do not have a clue about the fundamental mechanism of the brain. From the neck up we are wrapped in mystery. And so we stumble along, making the best we can with the rules we have obtained so far, and looking enthusiastically to the time we will break-through to a clear view of this most intriguing of all fundamental mechanisms.

Albert Einstein

The Illusion of Fundamental Mechanisms

The illusion that the power of a few fundamental mechanisms holds out to us is that we will be able to explain the universe fully. But again we are forced to let in newer and grander theories that reject previous notions or treat previous theories as a subset of a larger picture.

Only a century ago it was suggested that the physics of the day could explain all basic physical phenomena. Within twenty years, the discovery of features within the atom itself and the observance of activities taking place at close to the speed of light showed that classical mechanics and electromagnetism did not apply at the atomic level or at very high speeds. Einstein's Special Theory of Relativity thus superseded Newtonian Mechanics, not making it wrong, but limiting it to objects of ordinary size and speeds. Fundamental mechanisms still beg the question of why they are there in the first place. Newton's law of universal gravitation does not really explain what gravity is but just how it acts.

An even more subtle illusion is hidden in the almost religious belief that the methods of science will answer all life's questions and eventually allow for a more stable and satisfying life on the planet. Many of the noted physicists of the twentieth century were essentially mystics. They allowed the possibility of a dimension to human life experience that was not accessible by the methods of their science. That doesn't mean they invoked God or some outside mystical force to explain the problems of their science. But neither did they expect science to explain the mystical elements of their unique life experience. Science seeks only to illuminate the mechanisms of repeatable phenomena in all domains of our universe. As for ultimate questions about the meaning of life, science may provide clues but no answers.

The Matter Myth

Paul Davies

Scientists are really quite nice people. Unfortunately science, and its practitioners, have a rather bad public image. Partly this stems from the problems of sinister science—weapons of mass destruction, polluting technology, unethical medicine, and so on. But there is a deeper reason for the widespread antipathy. It is connected with the underlying philosophy of science itself.

mechanistic—machine-like.

For three hundred years science has been dominated by extremely mechanistic thinking. According to this view of the world, all physical systems are regarded as basically machines. Whether we are talking about the solar system, the planet's ecology or the behaviour of a human being, the machine image is usually seized upon as the appropriate paradigm. By studying the components of these machines, scientists aim to understand how they work. Central to this philosophy is the belief that complicated physical systems are merely the sum of their parts, so that understanding the parts serves to explain the whole. This is known as reductionism, and has been popular for two and a half millennia, since the Greek philosopher Democritus proclaimed that the world consisted of nothing but atoms moving in a void.

paradigm—framework or model.

The dominance of the mechanistic view of nature has provoked a sharp backlash from nonscientists, who regard science as a threatening and alienating activity. Not only does it rob the universe of its essential mystery, it seems to reduce people to mere automata, and nature to a set of mathematical rules. The scientist is portrayed as power-crazy, seeking to gain control over nature through the manipulation of these "machines."

During the last few years, however, mechanistic thinking has attracted some bitter criticism from within the scientific community itself. This is largely a result of advances in the physical sciences, such as chaos theory and information technology, that paint a very different picture of physical reality. To understand these significant developments, it is first necessary to know something of the history of the ideas involved.

"Look, an apple is about to land on him—he's got a great future ahead of him in physics!"

The triumph of mechanistic thought was achieved in the early nineteenth century, with an astonishing statement by the French mathematician Pierre Laplace. (It was Laplace who responded to Napoleon's famous query about the role of God in nature with the dismissive phrase, "I have no need of this hypothesis.") Imagine, wrote Laplace, a superbeing who could know the exact state of the universe in complete detail at some instant of time. Assuming the superbeing is capable of unlimited computing power, it could use this knowledge to calculate the entire future of the universe, and also infer its past, in every intricate detail.

Laplace arrived at his startling conclusion by appealing to the laws of mechanics formulated over a century before by Isaac Newton. The form of these laws is such that, given the position and motion of a particle of matter at some initial moment, its future motion is uniquely determined, and therefore computable, at least in principle. This unswerving faith in determinism—the belief that the future is contained in the present, and so can be figured out from a careful analysis of the present—underlies a key element of the scientific enterprise, which is prediction. The power of prediction is immense: astronomers can predict future eclipses, artillery officers can predict the point of impact of a shell, and so on.

Newton's own image of the universe was that of a gigantic precision clockwork mechanism, with each material body faithfully conforming to eternal mathematical laws. Laplace extended this idea to encompass

... secrecy strikes at the very root of what science is, and what it is for. It is not possible to be a scientist unless you believe that it is good to learn. It is not good to be a scientist, and it is not possible, unless you think that it is of the highest value to share your knowledge, to share it with anyone who is interested. It is not possible to be a scientist unless you believe that the knowledge of the world, and the power which this gives, is a thing which is of intrinsic value to humanitiy, and are willing to take the consequences.

J. Robert Oppenheimer

every atom in the universe. He concluded that if each tiny particle was locked in the deterministic embrace of a vast and lumbering cosmic clockwork, then everything that ever happened, that is happening now, and that ever will happen, is fixed since time immemorial by Newton's laws. The entire cosmos, he was convinced, slavishly follows a pre-ordained pathway of evolution to a unique destiny already written into its component parts.

Esoteric—intended or understood by only a small group.

Esoteric though they may seem, such topics were not confined to the rarefied strata of philosophical debate. It was from the doctrine of mechanistic thought so starkly expressed by Laplace that the European Industrial Revolution sprang. The view that the world is a machine ruled by mathematical certainty encouraged the belief that nature could be controlled and manipulated by understanding the laws of mechanics. And by focusing on the mechanistic aspect of physical systems, the Victorian industrialists elevated the value of material substance. Mechanistic thinking led inevitably to materialistic thinking: matter was all. Real value was that which attached to material stuff. Thus wealth was measured in bars of gold, tons of coal or acres of land.

The legacy of materialism and mechanism still permeate our society. The machine image is everywhere: the political machine, the economic machine, the weather machine. Even life itself has been mechanized. Richard Dawkins, the eloquent biologist, likes to refer to people as "gene machines." In the 1930s the Oxford philosopher Gilbert Ryle coined the phrase "the ghost in the machine" to reflect our impression that we possess nonmaterial minds that infuse our mechanistic bodies with the spark of free will. But generations of psychologists have sought to exorcise that unruly ghost. The title of a recent British television documentary about behaviour says it all: it was called *The Mind Machine*.

I have little doubt that much of the alienation and demoralization that people feel in our so-called scientific age stems from the bleak sterility of mechanistic thought. How often does one hear the plaintive cry: "We can do nothing, we are only cogs in a machine!"?

But how secure is the mechanistic paradigm? Physics, the science from which the philosophies of mechanism and materialism have sprung, has undergone some convulsive transformations in the past few decades. Einstein's theory of relativity undermined Newton's picture of space and time, while quantum mechanics has dramatically affected our view of the nature of matter. No longer can atoms be viewed as tiny billiard balls with well-defined locations and paths in space. The emerging picture of the microcosms is an Alice-in-Wonderland realm populated by fleeting, nebulous entities and ghostly patterns of pulsating energy. Crucially, quantum physics has uncovered a world

nebulous—vague.

In some ways the physical world more closely resembles a living organism than a machine.

that is fundamentally indeterministic and unpredictable. Newton's precision clockwork has been exposed as a myth: matter is inherently rebellious and nonconformist.

More recently, the theory of chaos and the study of physical systems capable of spontaneous self-organization have reinforced the new perspective of nature. Far from being imprisoned in a predestined pattern of change, the universe possesses a genuine openness, freedom to explore alternative pathways of evolution. In some ways the physical world more closely resembles a living organism than a machine. It is ironical that just as biologists are busy reducing life to a mechanism, so physicists are going the opposite way. Curiously the image of the universe as a living organism was common in many ancient cultures, but was cast aside by the ascendancy of physical science. Now that softer view of nature is in the process of being recaptured. History is turning full circle.

Physicists have come to recognize that inert, clodlike matter can, under the right circumstances, almost take on a life of its own. Certain physical and chemical systems have been discovered that display uncanny qualities of cooperation, or organize themselves spontaneously and unpredictably into complex forms. These systems are still subject to physical laws, but laws that permit a more flexible and innovative type of behaviour than the old mechanistic view of nature ever suggested.

Gone are the days when matter and energy were the hard currencies of physical theory. The new physics emphasizes instead the key role of concepts like information flow, complexity and organization in the behaviour of physical systems. Physicists no longer regard the world as merely a collection of particles being pushed and pulled by forces. They also perceive an elaborate network of creative activity. Reductionism has little place in this picture, for complex, chaotic or self-organizing systems are clearly more than the sum of their parts.

Cosmology—the study of the universe.

It is a perspective that has penetrated the new cosmology too. The evidence suggests that the universe was born in a state of almost total featurelessness, and has progressed, step by step, into the elaborate system we see today. The staggering richness and diversity of physical forms and structures that adorn the cosmos were not implanted at the outset but have emerged, spontaneously, in a long and complex sequence of creative, self-organizing processes.

This sweeping new view of nature will undoubtedly have profound implications for the way we view ourselves, and our relationship to the universe we inhabit. It is already being reflected in the manner that science impacts on the world's economy. The old material-based industries—mining, primary production, heavy engineering—are everywhere in decline. The wealth-creating industries of the future are systems-based and information-based. Today's so-called material scientists concern themselves with creating new structures on a molecular scale to produce "smart matter"—systems with novel qualities to perform tasks we never dreamt of. … The indicators are clear: in the twenty-first century real power will lie with those nations and institutions that control and manipulate information, not material resources.

The death of materialism will mean some painful adjustments in the decades ahead, but it also offers an exhilarating challenge. Mechanistic thought has undoubtedly had a stifling effect on the human spirit. Liberation from this centuries-old straitjacket will enable human beings to reintegrate themselves into the physical world of which they are a part.

It has been fashionable among scientists to suppose that mind is just an incidental and insignificant quirk of evolutionary fate, a meaningless accident in an ocean of blind and purposeless forces. As we move to embrace twenty-first century science, consciousness will come to be seen as a fundamental property of a generally creative cosmos. No longer will human beings feel marginalized—even trivialised—when set against the awesome outworking of cosmic forces. We live in a universe that has the emergence of conscious organisms written into its laws at the most basic level. There is no ghost in the machine, not because the ghost is dead, but because there is no machine.

ISSUE 2

The Illusion of Certainty

Organic life, we are told, has developed gradually from the protozoan to the philosopher, and this development, we are assured, is indubitably an advance. Unfortunately it is the philosopher, not the protozoan, who gives us this assurance.

Bertrand Russell

What men really want is not knowledge but certainty.

Bertrand Russell

Science cannot solve the ultimate mystery of Nature. And it is because in the last analysis we ourselves are part of the mystery we are trying to solve.

Max Plank

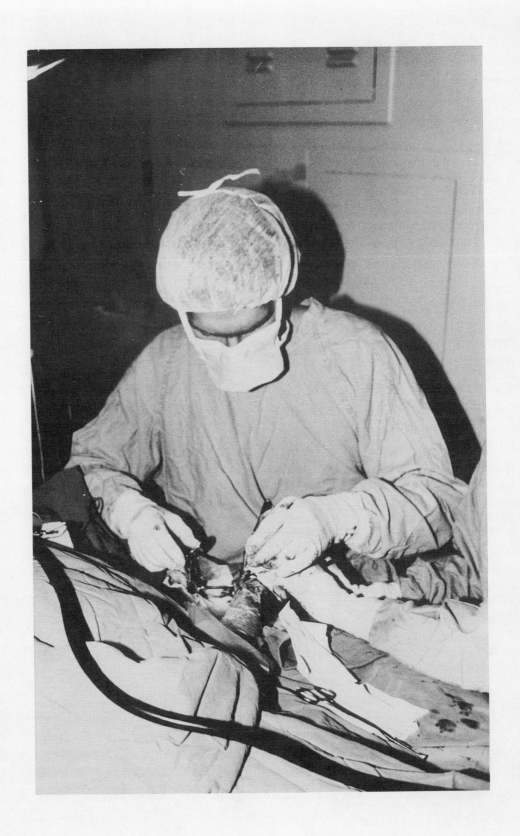

Limits of the Possible

Douglas Shenson

Cardiac intensive-care units are paradoxes. They are filled with the tools to delay dying but they keep the language of death at a distance. As an intern, I worked in such a place: a small, brightly lit area, partitioned into eight cubicles and filled with an overwhelming array of electronic equipment. Watching the nurses fit a patient into one of the cubicles was like watching an astronaut slip into a space capsule, engulfed and diminished by the machinery. But such thoughts did not immediately occur to me. My job was to work hard, attend to my patients, and leave the deeper problems of philosophy for later. Those were my priorities on the first day of my intensive-care rotation.

It was also the day we admitted a man I'll call Mr. Strap to the hospital. He came to us with an extraordinarily long and complicated history of heart ailments: three attacks, one bypass operation, and one heart-valve replacement. Now he had returned, complaining of chest pain— brought in by the paramedics when his wife suspected he was having another heart attack.

I met him in the emergency room. He was sitting up on a gurney, breathing slowly through an oxygen mask; he wore a patient's pajama top, but had on his trousers, shoes and socks. Like a minotaur, I would later kid him, neither man nor patient.

In his late seventies, Mr. Strap had the false robustness of a chronic smoker, and tired, apprehensive eyes. He spoke with the anxiousness and impatience of one who has met too many doctors, each seeking an understanding of his illness, which he himself had not yet found.

We talked about his previous hospitalization, his medications, his smoking. I examined him carefully, and told him I would be taking care of any day-to-day problems in consultation with more senior physicians. I communicated with that combination of signs doctors use when brought to a patient by crisis: the well-chosen word, the reassuring touch, the articulation of friendship, all mixed to support a sense of self, which, in parallel with his heart might also be collapsing.

It was not possible to assess how sick he was simply from his symptoms, I told him. It would be the laboratory that would indicate whether he had suffered another heart attack.

"I don't need a lab to tell me my chest hurts," he snapped, "I'm telling you, I'm having another bad one."

His family doctor soon arrived to evaluate his condition. After speaking at length to Mr. and Mrs. Strap, he moved away so we could discuss our initial therapeutic approach. I wrote the orders for Mr. Strap's medication and the family doctor rejoined the couple—only to be interrupted by the paging operator. Shortly, with a harried, fraternal look, he left for another patient.

I introduced myself to Mrs. Strap, who scrutinized me as we talked about the next steps in her husband's hospitalization. She spoke quietly, bracing herself for the unwanted intimacy inescapable in such encounters. We covered what must have been familiar material. I ordered medication and said he needs sleep now—that morning would be a better time to visit.

She turned to squeeze his hand and utter a few words before leaving; there was talk between them only of the magazines and family snapshots she would bring in—the soothing vocabulary of ordinary life, which she used instinctively to reduce their fright.

When she had left, he looked at me again.

"A kid like you really knows what he's doing?"

I smiled and assured him I had my medical school debt to prove it. Eventually he relaxed, and through the verbal jockeying I made myself a doctor in his eyes, as his disease had made him a patient in mine.

We came to know each other slowly. I was at first preoccupied with exploring his illness through the conventional prisms of medicine: evaluating the results of his blood tests and analyzing subtle changes in his X-rays and electrocardiograms. Every morning I checked his blood pressure, listened to his heart and lungs and watched for changes. I would in all likelihood be the first to detect it if he started to deteriorate.

Initially, the news was good: he had not had another heart attack. Yet the bouts of chest pain continued, only sometimes relieved by tablets of nitroglycerin. There were also episodes of difficulty in breathing. I was called repeatedly in the early hours to help him through these times. At one point, I found him struggling, sitting up in his darkened cubicle, neighboured by sleeping cardiac patients, a look of terrible fear in his eyes, nearly drowning as fluid seeped back in his lungs—the burden of a heart unable to pump blood through his arteries. An injection of medicine promised to bring back his breath to retrieve him from the disarray of his panic. As moments passed and the drug worked its way, I calmed him with explanations of how his heart was contracting more easily, of how his blood pressure was returning to normal, plying him softly with the reassurances of science, words in a kind of medical lullaby.

Soon it was over and we spoke again, like victorious confederates, conspiring now to exploit the coming day: there would be his wife's visit, family gossip, and reports of his young grandson's Little League accomplishments (there was greatness in this natural outfielder—he just knew it!). Before long, his energy dissipated and he fell asleep.

In time, we became chums. He seemed to depend on me more and more as his drug regimen was adjusted and readjusted. When a conference was called between his cardiologist and his family physician, he naively turned for my opinion first. With halting success, the team tried new approaches, investing him with our own sense of the possible. He clung fiercely to my medical powers, to my expert knowledge, to my white coat.

"You'll see me through, Doc. You're a magician," he would say.

•

Perhaps I could—my pride swelled and I told him that, with the right medicines, he'd soon be feeling much better. But by believing in the power I became a magician who had eaten his own rabbit; swallowing the illusion was simply the last possible trick, and nothing was left up my sleeve. The chest pain continued, exacerbated by his dread of each coming night and the fear of a body over which he had lost control.

Exacerbated—made worse.

More specialists met to consider therapies. Experimental drugs were proposed and other diagnostic tests were performed. As he was too old for a heart transplant and had already undergone extensive surgery, we searched for a successful pharmacologic approach. The cardiologist began his analysis by drawing graphs of a normal cardiac output: the contractility of muscles, the size and internal pressures of the heart chambers, the rates of cardiac contractions, all playing their parts. Then, superimposed upon these orderly studies, he drew in the distortions of Mr. Strap's cardiovascular machinery. Our goal was to find the ways to get it running properly again.

But as we concentrated on the mechanics, we became captives of our own metaphors. We had persuaded ourselves that his sick heart was simply a pump in disrepair, and had forgotten that his body, despite our exertions, would tell its own story. When his wife visited, she saw things we did not: his wilting posture, the altered resolution in his voice, a different look in his face.

"Just do what you can," she said.

Limits of the Possible

This article, which originally appeared in the *New York Times*, is about an interning doctor's first days in a cardiac intensive-care ward. In particular, it is about the nature of the relationship that develops between himself as "doctor" and the elderly, seriously ill "patient," named Mr. Strap.

At first, Mr. Strap responds well to various forms of treatment, and increasingly regards the novice medicine man as a kind of magician, seemingly able to correct any health problems with pills and machinery.

Over the next few days, the patient survives one medical crisis after another, and his faith in medical science grows. However, his wife seems to understand, even before the doctors, that her husband is dying and their reassurance that medicine can save him is their illusion.

Mr. Strap's condition deteriorates and the doctor-patient relationship is transformed; the doctor becomes "a young man watching an old man die" as he realizes the limitations of the discipline of medical science.

Evanescent—fading.

Her conversation had a premature sadness in it, coming—I thought then—from her lack of knowledge rather than her wisdom. She, better than we, understood the evanescent source of his deterioration.

As we turned more toward our pharmacopoeia, I watched his faith in the scientific arsenal ebb. And as the algorithms of the medical textbooks that guided our decisions failed him, so did the roles that went with them. Our relationship transformed itself again—I went subtly from doctor and saviour to friend and son. It was as if he had forgiven me for something he had known all along I could not do.

In this transformation our customary discourse dissolved with the inability of the machinery and the drugs to fulfill their promise. Each layer of formality faded away, and the two of us were left surrounded and unhindered by the equipment, simply as witnesses to a repeating, timeless process: a young man watching an old man die. And this teaching hospital, with its complex hierarchy and its ambitious science, became in that moment merely a place where young men and women, with titles of maturity and profession, oversee the dying of their elders.

Soon our conversations were punctuated by the empty dance of doctors confronting terminal illness. The pace of these activities quickened, and I worked to manipulate his failing blood pressure and improve his breathing. But Mr. Strap's death occurred while I was not in the hospital, and he seemed to leave me without transition. His last breath and heartbeat were caught immediately by the intensive-care nurse, and I was told that a long and energetic cardiac arrest code was performed on an unresponsive patient. I must have looked as though I was going to cry when they told me, because the resident on duty placed his hand on my shoulder and said it would be different next time. I wasn't sure.

QUESTIONS

1. Explain why Shenson calls his words "a kind of medical lullaby."

2. Explain what Shenson meant when he said that the doctors became "captives of our own metaphors" and why this resulted in the man's wife seeing, before the doctors did, that the man was dying.

Acid Rain

Michael Badyk

A cid rain is a term that is now in common use by us all, including most of the people involved in the study of this problem, such as biologists, ecologists and chemists. In reality, the problem includes not only acid rain but also acid snow, acid fog, acid dew, acid frost and dry fallout that occurs on perfectly sunny days. It is reaching the earth all day, all year and all over the planet.

The source of this problem is the technology that we have used over the last few hundred years. Acid rain is not new to the last 20 or so years. There is some evidence from illustrations made from carved wooden stamps and also from paintings originating in Germany in the late 1700s that suggests that acid has been damaging trees for some time. The main aspects of our technology that have contributed to these acids are: first, the refining and burning of fossil fuels (including the production of petrochemical-based materials such as plastics); and, second, the refining and manufacture of metals.

Our global economy is tied to these activities. Our technology often is measured by what we can produce from metal or plastic, and by using power contained in the carbon of the fossil fuels we can accomplish fantastic things. The burning of coal over the last few hundred years greatly improved life for all humanity, and the more recent use of oil and gasoline has changed our society forever. Automobiles and aircraft that we really can't do without any longer are perfect examples of the application of these technologies. The use of metal and the acquisition of the means to do things with it is woven through our past. It can be seen in such terms as the "Bronze Age" and the "Iron Age," used as labels for time periods based on the metallic achievements of the times. These two terms are used to denote our increasing sophistication in the application of technology over time.

Impurity as a Normal State

There is one aspect of the fossil fuels and metals that is not evident to most people—what we pull from the ground to use is seldom pure. Sulphur is commonly contained in coal, oil and natural gas. There are

ACID RAIN

Acid rain is a term that is now in common use. In reality, the problem includes not only acid rain but also acid snow, acid fog, acid dew, acid frost and dry fallout that occurs on perfectly sunny days.

Industrial societies are highly dependent upon sources of power that are harmful to the environment.

exceptions of course. In Pennsylvania, some of the oil is so pure that you could take it out of the ground and pour it right into your car. Normally, though, if you tried this with most crude oil, you would destroy the engine. The purer the oil or coal or natural gas is, the more its value increases. The less pure is known as dirty coal, or sour gas, and there are many different types of oil quality. Something like iron or nickel doesn't occur very often in purities that would allow us to use it directly out of the ground. Again, there are some exceptions. On the south shore of Lake Superior in what is now the State of Michigan there are deposits of copper that are almost pure. The aboriginal peoples who inhabited the area discovered it and were able to fashion useful items from it (which were traded all over the Great Lakes region). Again, normally what we get is the metal contained in something called an ore. Iron ore, for example, has lots of iron but also impurities, including other metals, silica, and most likely sulphur.

By-Products: The Result When Impurity Changes to Purity

These impurities are removed by refining. Most of the sulphur can be removed from the fossil fuels by chemical treatment. One of the common sights around a petrochemical refinery is a flame. This flame is fuelled by the sulphur waste being burned off. The same thing is true with natural gas. Further, more often than not, we don't even try to remove the impurities from coal—we just burn it as is. The product of this burning is a chemical compound known as sulphur dioxide.

An oxide is produced when a substance reacts with oxygen in the atmosphere to form a compound. Iron oxide, which we call rust, is a simple example. Sulphur dioxide denotes that there are two oxygen molecules linked with one sulphur molecule. When we turn on our automobiles we burn the gasoline and any sulphur that still may be in it, once again producing sulphur dioxide. We purify metals by heating them to liquefy the solid ore. We can then separate the part we want. The only thing wrong with this procedure is that the sulphur in the ore burns off rather than liquefying. And once again, this produces sulphur dioxides that enter the air. And, unfortunately it isn't just sulphur dioxides. There are oxides of nitrogen contained in there, too. There is also a range of other materials released into the atmosphere. They might not necessarily form acids, but their production goes hand in hand with acidic materials.

Basically, anywhere on earth where we refine fossil fuels or purify metals, we will be creating pollutants. You could look at the Tar Sands project in Alberta, the iron factories of Hamilton, the metal refining of Rouyn and Noranda in Quebec for Canadian examples. Everywhere that you can find an automobile you can find another source of pollutants.

From a chemical standpoint, the problem is that sulphur dioxide combines with water to form an acid. Nitrous oxides do the same thing. The water can be in a cloud (where the compounds of sulphur and nitrogen combine with the water) and then subsequently fall to earth. Or, the compounds can fall in a dry form (dry fallout), and when they encounter water they form an acid just as easily as the acids form in the clouds.

Acids and Bases

Acids carry the connotation of something harmful. However, we use acids quite often in our everyday lives. Lemon juice is an acid, and so is vinegar. Coffee and tea are acids. We also use acids to power batteries, thus creating the term "battery acid."

Almost everyone knows that acids are reactive—in other words they act upon whatever they come in contact with to form a new substance, which obviously alters the old substance permanently. That is, if an acid is poured on an object, then something is going to happen (e.g., if you pour acid on your hand and your hand dissolves). But there is a range of substances that are reactive that are not called acids; they

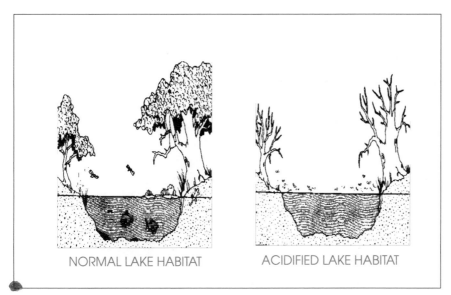

NORMAL LAKE HABITAT   ACIDIFIED LAKE HABITAT

THE LIFE AND DEATH OF A LAKE ECOSYSTEM

To support normal aquatic life, a lake habitat must have a balanced food chain and allow for normal reproductive cycles.

When acid is introduced to the ecosystem, either through acidic rainfall or runoff from acidic snowpack, the influx of acid may alter the lake's overall pH, creating a more acidic environment. Also, acidic runoff can release heavy metals—highly toxic for many aquatic species—from rocks and soil. Sensitive organisms may be wiped out and resistant life forms are weakened as their food supplies are affected.

are known as alkaloids or bases or antacids (the opposite of acids). This would include such things as hydrogen peroxide and ammonia.

There are two substances that make things reactive. For acids it is hydrogen ions (H), and for bases it is hydroxides (OH). If you combine the two of them in equal strengths and quantities you end up with something un-reactive that is very familiar: H_2O (water). Pure water is said to be neutral. If this is true, then we can use it as a means of comparing the other substances that may be acidic or basic.

In order to make comparisons between substances, chemists have devised a scale known as the *pH*, or *potential hydrogen scale*. It has values that run from 0 for the strongly acidic, to 7 for the pure water, and finally to 14 for those that are strongly alkaline. Vinegar would have a value of about 3.1 and ammonia would have a value around 11. Lemon juice comes in at around 2.2 and battery acid is about 1.8. You might ask how we can drink lemon juice with a *Ph* value not too far from battery acid when we know what would happen to us if we drank the battery acid. The way in which the *Ph* scale has been constructed is on a logarithmic basis. That implies that, for example, if the *Ph* value went from 5 to 4, then the actual acidity of the substance increases 10 times. So the difference of 0.4 *Ph* units between lemon juice and battery acid is very significant.

The Neutralizing Process

If acids can be so damaging, how can we get rid of them? To neutralize the acids a base of equal strength would have to be added.

NORMAL LAKE HABITAT

- Fish prey on insects and provide food for certain birds.
- Fish eggs hatch in the normal way.
- Insects provide food for fish and amphibians. Hunting birds, such as the osprey, live on fish.
- Frogs feed on insects.
- Trees are supported by local soil.

ACIDIFIED LAKE HABITAT

- Acid influx and heavy metal poisoning can kill sensitive fish, such as rainbow trout and salmon.
- Fish eggs can be destroyed or deformed by environmental changes. Certain insects, such as the whirligig beetle reproduce in an uncontrolled manner. They are resistant to acidification and their main predators are fewer.
- Birds must seek fish in other lakes. Frogs die in heavily acidic habitats.
- Acidic soil can damage or even kill certain trees.

If you have ever had a bitter cup of tea or coffee you would normally add milk or cream to it to reduce the bitterness. The bitterness comes from the acids that are contained in the beverage. The milk or cream contains a reasonable amount of calcium carbonate, which is the base. By combining the two of them, you approach the neutral value. If you have ever had an acidic stomach, then you have probably taken an antacid such as Rolaids or Tums, which contain calcium carbonate, just like the milk.

The Buffering Capacity of Rock

Lakes, rivers and the soil have a built-in neutralizer, similar to Rolaids. This usually comes from the type of rock that the body of water or the soil sits upon. This ability to neutralize an acid is referred to as the *buffering capacity*. This capacity is extremely variable on both a global and local basis. In southern Ontario the rock is mostly limestone, which is high in calcium carbonate. A lake that sits on this limestone will be able to neutralize a good deal of acid that falls into it because the soft and easily dissolved rock will enrich the water with minerals. The exact opposite is true of the area in central and northern Ontario, which is dominated by the type of rock known as the Canadian Shield. It is very different from the limestone. It is infinitely harder and is usually lacking in calcium carbonate. In fact, it is so hard that very few minerals ever dissolve into the water. This makes the buffering capacity very low. Unfortunately, both areas receive precipitation that has to be considered acidic.

Normal precipitation has a value between 5.5 and 7.0 on the *Ph* scale. Ontario quite regularly receives precipitation with values around 4. While the lakes in southern Ontario are still in good condition, and the soil and the vegetation seem to be reasonably good, on the Canadian Shield it is a very different story. Some of the trees seem to be dying and some of the lakes are dead.

What Makes a Lake Live

The death of the lakes is really what has attracted public attention. You have to understand how a lake lives before you can understand how it dies.

To make a lake you first of all need water. Then you need some sort of basin to put it in. That is a start, but it still doesn't make it suitable for life. You need certain dissolved minerals to feed the plants (mineral nutrients) and you also need sunlight and warm temperatures over a reasonable period of time. These variables mean that there can be many types of lakes and also a great variety in both the amount and type of life that a lake will have.

Just from this you could probably tell that a lake on the limestone of southern Ontario will potentially have more life in it than a lake on the Canadian Shield, based on the amount of dissolved minerals and the latitude. You might have noticed this on your own. The lakes of the tourism area of the Canadian Shield are noted for their clarity, while most lakes on the limestone turn into green soup by the end of the summer. The presence of all those mineral nutrients will feed a wide variety of aquatic plants. The plants in turn will feed a variety of plant-eaters (herbivores) and subsequently a variety of meat-eaters (carnivores). This interconnection is known as the food chain. The water and minerals of the lake make life possible for a wealth of plants and animals both in and around the lakes.

The Death of a Lake: How "Wet Deserts" Are Created

Acid affects the lakes in a number of ways. The first thing that happens is that the mineral nutrients that would normally feed the plants are used up in the neutralization of the acid. This, of course, implies that less is available for the plants, so the number of plants in the lakes decreases. This then lessens the herbivore and the carnivore population which affects the animal life directly. The acid in their systems forces dramatic chemical changes, the most insidious of which is that the animals' reproductive organs are slowly destroyed. This means that the existing animals are the last of their kind in the lake—they will not produce offspring. The overall effect on the lake is that life slowly winds down. It is a slow, gradual fade to oblivion over 20 years or even longer. The strangest thing is that the water looks to be in perfect health. It is absolutely crystal clear. That extreme clarity is achieved because there are no algae or bacteria or anything in there that would cloud the water—it has been called a "wet desert." Perhaps that is why we have not reacted to it until recently—the water is clear so it has to be healthy.

That is the scientific, objective, quantified assessment of this problem. We used chemistry, geology, geography and biology to assess the acidification of our lakes. You may not have understood all of the technical information, but you will understand the implication. Canada is dominated by the Canadian Shield geology. We have millions of lakes on this type of rock and they are all potentially threatened.

Human Losses: Where Science Ends

Science is able to illustrate the chemical and biological loss. However, it is unable to illustrate the losses to humanity. These losses are many and varied.

Psychological Losses

It is not possible to list these losses in any sort of hierarchy, or order of importance; that is up to the individual person to determine. But let us look at some of them. There is definitely a psychological loss. It is very common for people, even those in urban areas, to think that there are or should be areas on this planet where the hand of humanity has not reached. It is stressful to think that there are many remote lakes that are dead. Killarney Provincial Park, south-west of Sudbury, is officially designated as a wilderness park and is often called the "Crown Jewel" of the province's parks. It has magnificent high ridges of startling white quartzite rock, almost pure silica, and on a bright day it gives the illusion of snow on top of these high rounded ridges. These high ridges look down on brilliant blue lakes, but most of the lakes are dead. One can describe this but it is difficult to convey the profound feeling one gets when standing beside this clear lake knowing that it is dead. Or, what it feels like to cup your hand and drink some water from the lake and taste aluminum that has been pulled out of the rock by the acidic water. That impact is far greater than reading that there are so many parts per million of aluminum in the water or that the *Ph* is at a certain level. It is a profound sense that something is dreadfully and painfully wrong.

Social Losses

There is a social loss here as well. The native people of the area are now living with lakes that are not in the same condition as they were for thousands of years. We might not be able to appreciate this. The ridges of Killarney are holy places to these first peoples and are regarded as a source of great spiritual power. Natives today still seek the solitude and power emanating from nature in these ridges. To be on a ridge top and look down on a lake and know that it is now dead must be unbelievably sad to them. Or possibly it is maddening. Someone not from their culture can identify with their anguish and anger.

In non-Native society there is a loss as well. The people that would go to the north, the wilderness, and the solitude, are now faced with an altered world. We can't escape the hand of humanity even in the Canadian north. That hand is there in the lakes in which we fish, on which we canoe, in which we swim and by which we live. It may never be the same. Throughout this text, we have discussed the fact that societies do change, but are we prepared to see our world and that of Native peoples change so dramatically in this way?

Economic Losses

An economic loss is present here as well. Many of the communities of the north owe their existence to the recreation that occurs on the lakes around them. The small community of Killarney just outside of the park is a perfect example. Although it is not evident as yet, it is inevitable that people will stop coming to an area where all the lakes are poisoned and polluted. The loss of the tourism dollars will lead to the end of the community, a fact already appreciated by the people of the north. Their livelihood could disappear very soon. Their economic well-being will fall into our hands through unemployment insurance and welfare payments. We may even have to pay to have water brought into the community because the residents can no longer drink it. Acidic water can dissolve the copper in the plumbing of homes and businesses and poison people with copper sulphate, which can affect their liver and kidneys. Once again, the rest of society will have to pay for the health care costs to these victims of acid rain pollution. As our taxes will probably have to be increased to pay for all this, the standard of living of all Canadians will be directly affected.

Cultural Loss

In one sense, the greatest loss is a cultural one. The one thing that is deeply engrained in the Canadian mind is a sense that this great and untouched wilderness is just over the next hill. The sense of wilderness turns up in our art. Musicians such as Gordon Lightfoot, CANO, and Bruce Cockburn have composed lyrics and ideas based on these images. Writers such as Farley Mowat, Pierre Berton and Gabriel Roy craft pictures of wilderness which once read are never forgotten.

Probably the most distinctive appreciation of this wilderness is the paintings of the Group of Seven. The abstract landscapes of these artists are part of the Canadian identity. They are found in all of our museums and art galleries, and many of them are found as reproductions in our homes. They are part of our culture, and they are painted at Killarney. There is an A.Y. Jackson Lake in the park; there is also an O.S.A. Lake, standing for the Ontario Society of Artists which is the official working name for the Group of Seven. Most of us have seen paintings of the Killarney area in their art and not even known it. They depict rugged hills and lone gnarled pine trees. They are almost a stereotype of what

the north should be. And those lakes in those paintings are now dead. We, as Canadians, have lost something here.

The Role of the Subjective Self

We may now be at the limits of what science can do. It is not to say that we should abandon the science; it is just that science needs to be motivated by a profound sense of humanity and human emotion. To solve the problem of these dead lakes will take human emotion more than it will take a scientific solution. We will have to become concerned or angry enough to become involved with the solution. Science can supply us with the tools, but our emotions and our feelings will be a vital part of the solution. It might require a deep involvement in our economic or political system to say to the people in charge that the losses that have been detailed in this short essay are no longer acceptable, and those prepared to sacrifice our environment in the name of profit or science or both should be stopped.

Adding more science is not the answer. Science is sometimes seen as a way of automatically solving the problem that it has created. This is a false sense of security. It has been suggested that we could dump concentrated calcium carbonate, lime, in the lakes and then restock them with plants and fish, but this is only a band-aid solution that looks at the symptom but not the cure. We have to look at ourselves. We are the cause because of our demand for energy and consumer products. That point has to change before the problem is solved.

Ultimately our lives depend on the solution. If the food chains of our planet, both on land and in the water, fail, then the life-support system for us will also have failed. Are we, as a technically advanced society, prepared to die by our own hand? We can't ignore what we have done to this planet. We have to be aware of all this because "all this" is us—we are dependent on the whole variety of plants and animals that exist here. The tool we have in science is very powerful. With this power comes great responsibility. One can only hope we are responsible enough to make the right decision.

Our life depends on it.

Towards a Green Future

Petra Kelly

PETRA KELLY

Petra Kelly (1947-1992) was co-founder of the German Green Party and member of the German parliament, the Bundestag. She was a tireless organizer and speaker on behalf of environmental, women's and peace issues. What follows is a speech she made to an environmental conference in Mexico in 1991. Sadly, the world no longer benefits from her energy and vision. She was murdered at her home in Bonn in October 1992.

Dear friends! I am very happy to be able to be here in Mexico—my very first visit here—and to be able to share my thoughts with so many other friends in spirit and action. I am here first of all to learn from you—because we of the Western, industrialized, Eurocentric countries need to listen and to learn from others, more than most of us want to admit. In the past years of my political work I have learned especially from the indigenous peoples, the first peoples of the world. As environmental issues become increasingly urgent and Western models of development and economics become daily less sustainable, indigenous peoples, I believe, will come to occupy a position of considerable influence. Their views on a union of development and conservation could become a central factor on future decision-making.

Let me share with you what I have learned and experienced, not only while working on Green and social issues within the European Community in Brussels over ten years, but what I have learned from twenty-three years of grassroots work in the ecology and peace and women's movements in Eastern and Western Europe and in eight years of parliamentary work for the German Green Party in the national parliament.

First of all—though this view has made me rather lonely in the Green Party—I believe that if we want to transform society in an ecological way, we must transform ourselves profoundly first. I am more and more convinced that the kind of personal transformation I am talking about is, in itself, a very political act; it is politics or, as we would term it, "anti-politics!" One important ingredient, I believe, must be humility, and I have met very few politicians in the world who have that special quality of humility.

When we understand the interconnectedness of everything in Nature, we realize that countless beings walk within us, that Nature is our inexhaustible mirror, that humanness is a function of a wider system. To realize this is to begin to let go of the familiar individual self or ego, and to experience a sense of identification with wider circles of life.

Genuinely to experience "falling in love outward," as the poet Robinson Jeffers put it, is to experience a profound personal transformation.

There is one thought that I have come across that I would like to share with you in this regard:

To study the way, is to study the self:
To study the self, is to forget the self:
To forget the self, is to be enlightened by all things.
To be enlightened by all things, is to remove the barriers between one's self and others.

Petra Kelly (1947-1992).

What is needed in present-day politics is a change from both form and content, a vision of holism rather than separation and compartmentalism. To heal the planet Earth, we, especially in the West, must end the fragmentary problem-solving. And we must, of course, change our daily consciousness about our own lifestyles and our own attitudes. We must be acutely aware of our own habits and behaviour and the ways in which our personal action can contribute to the perpetuation of the present system.

I have, at the founding of the Green Party over eleven years ago, coined the term "anti-party party," trying to express with that word a new type of power, a new type of political party. When we speak about the power of non-violent change and non-violent transformation, we do not mean "power over," but we mean the power common to all, to be used by all and for all. "Power over" is to be replaced by shared power, by the "power to do things," by the discovery of our own strength as opposed to a passive receiving of power exercised by others, often in our name. The Green Party has tried to be a political lobby for those who have no voice, for those who are not represented, including the whales, the elephants, the dolphins, the plants and flowers on this planet.

Since those eleven years have gone by, I have also learned how quickly the old power from above and on top that "we" meant to transform has in fact changed us—or large parts of the Green Party who now see all salvation coming from joining regional governmental coalitions with the Social Democrats—at times almost at any price! But how can you, in fact, make non-violent politics, if there are only one or two Green ministers in a cabinet of ten others who oppose you? What happens when Green governmental partners in a coalition have to vote to increase the police forces and equip them with better water tanks that are used against non-violent protesters? And what happens when you have promised your grassroots movements not to build a test-road for Daimler Benz and then you go ahead and build it anyway?

Whatever we do to the Earth, we do to ourselves! Learning that we are not outside of Nature, but a part of it—that is the essence of ecological politics—but this is also a very spiritual statement.

Petra Kelly

Or when the Greens are forced to make compromises that touch life-and-death issues? For me, there is not a little bit of cancer or a little bit of deterrence or a little bit of dioxin or a little bit of plutonium—there are some ecological issues where you "do not" make any compromises, where you cannot repair irreparable damage. I have learned that foremost from my sister Grace who died at the age of ten-and-a-half from cancer, and from many other cancer-ill children that I have gotten to know. And I believe we should be very cautious about getting into power-sharing at governmental levels, unless we are very clear ourselves about when and where to compromise and when and where not to.

In fact, we must get away from the idea of "repairing" or of being able to repair all that we first destroy, because some things in nature cannot be repaired.

It was Mahatma Gandhi who spoke about not believing in the doctrine of the greatest good for the greatest number. Instead he believed the only real dignified human doctrine is the *greatest good for all!* The Brundtland Commission has put the dilemma in the following way:

> The Earth is one, but the world is not. We all depend on one biosphere for sustaining our lives. Yet each community, each country, strives for survival and prosperity with little regard for its impact on others.

As the German writer Siegfried Lenz put it, "A gravestone for our dying age could well bear the inscription: Everyone wanted the best—for themselves."

So this brings us right back to the interconnectedness of everything around us, in us, acting locally and thinking globally. Whatever we do to the Earth, we do to ourselves! Learning that we are not outside of Nature, but a part of it—that is the essence of ecological politics—but this is also a very spiritual statement.

The next point I would like to stress is the great misunderstandings that used to exist between those who come from Green movements in the West (movements that grew out of the seemingly unstoppable Western economic growth and movements that were and have been concerned about the wasteful destruction of Nature) and those in the so-called Third World countries who rightly so asked us *not* to ignore the questions of economic injustice and exploitation of the poor by the rich. Thinking on both sides has changed, and now it is understood that nurturing the environment is also central to tackling the grave problems of poverty. The transformation of forests into deserts or fertile earth into sunbaked concrete, of running rivers into silted flood-

"I only cut it down to put it out of its misery."

This cartoon, originally published in the former Soviet Union, touches upon what are now the region's enormous environmental problems.

The concern of the cartoon is universal.

waters—all proved that only through the care of the environment could the livelihoods of those most dependent on it be sustained.

Behind every environmental drama—and this can be seen right here in Mexico—there are in turn harsh realities of rural poverty, of landless villagers having to destroy nature to eat and drink and of governments pursuing economic growth at any cost to the environment (encouraged by Western companies and banks).

Of course, we must also speak about demilitarization—demilitarizing societies as radically as possible and of course beginning right at home in the North, for it is the North which is exporting those huge amounts of weapons and military materials to the South. If we are to have a chance at all, we must also tackle this problem of global militarization. We should not forget that superpower rivalry has brought even the most remote regions into the realm of military strategists. Whether in the Arctic homeland of the Inuit or the Dreaming Paths of the Aborigines of Central Australia, military installations are now in place that continue to be the key targets in the event of even a regional nuclear war (if there ever is such a thing as a regional nuclear war). In the industrialized

The seedbed of ecological destruction is the *global division* between *rich and poor!*

Petra Kelly

countries, traditional indigenous lands have been misused for bases and military test sites and the developing countries have often become the killing ground. Let me just quote one figure: although 80 percent of military expenditure is accounted for by NATO and the Warsaw Pact, spending on arms and weapons in the developing world doubled between 1978 and 1988. It doubled of course also, because we, the Western countries, have exported those weapons and have given the Third World countries the impression that you can only be an important member of this world community if you have enough weapons to deter others.

Within the Green Parties and movements, we believe that hope does not usually come from governments; hope, in fact, comes from the many grassroots efforts, from people working at grassroots levels and from their strength and their imagination eager to create a world without fear and without war. What we need more than ever before is a meeting of minds (like right here at this conference in Morelia) and a building of new alliances. The rape of the planet Earth cannot be halted simply by imposing environmental conservation or Green rules on all areas of the world. It must be remembered over and over again—the seedbed of ecological destruction is the *global division* between *rich and poor!*

As Ben Jackson wrote, "A series of Keep Out signs around the world's forest would not only be morally unacceptable, with the poor still hungry outside, it just would not work!"

If we finally have linked poverty, inequality and environmental degradation, then we must also form new alliances—groups concerned with ecology, human rights, peace, alternative production, world poverty, etc. In 1988, for example, over sixty thousand people from all walks of life came to Berlin to protest against the impact of the International Monetary Fund and the World Bank on poor countries and their environment, while the two institutions had met there. This is one important step in our strategy of building new alliances.

I believe that we can have ecologically based economies and socially useful, non-damaging investment, if only there is the political will. Of course, we must also reach the progressive people inside the trade union movement. To me, one of the most powerful movements in the trade union area has been the Australian Green Ban movement in the late sixties and early seventies, a movement that needs to be revived and extended in every country. In the Green Ban movement in Australia, trade unionists refused to work on environmentally damaging projects and, in fact, were imprisoned for their clear choice of conscience.

No official economic policy to date has taken the global damage resulting from human activity into consideration. The opposite, in fact,

is true. Considerable parts of our natural base have already been destroyed and other parts are seriously threatened by decisions made solely on the grounds of economic gain. In the end, the economic system will pull the rug out from underneath its own feet. We feel that what is ecologically necessary is also economically sound. Vandana Shiva puts it right to the point when she states that Amazonia is disappearing not because of the local inhabitants, but to supply cheap beef to Northern consumers and to supply charcoal for smelting iron for export. Southeast Asia's forests are disappearing to supply tropical hardwood to Japanese and European markets. And as commodity prices fall and the debt burdens spiral, the Third World is increasingly trapped in the vicious circle of exporting more to earn less. *It is as if the sick and dying are giving blood transfusions to the healthy and rich!*

The destruction of rain forest has repercussions throughout the entire world.

Let me add here that we must speak far louder than ever before about the connections between debt and environment. Indebted countries have not just borrowed money—they have mortgaged the future.

Nature, as Susan George writes, puts up the collateral! National economies, both state socialist and capitalist, proceeded as if there were no long-term costs for anything. They deny "limits of growth" or they do not even figure pollution and ecological destruction in their equation. We must expose the debt-environment connections: first, borrowing to finance ecologically destructive projects, and second, paying for them by cashing in natural resources! It is one vicious circle. Many of the mega-projects that helped put Third World countries on the debt-treadmill to begin with—large dams, hydro projects, nuclear power plants, etc.—are environmental disasters in their own right! The U.S. National Resources Defence Council stated, "Hydroelectric projects approved by the World Bank between 1979 and 1983 resulted in the voluntary resettlement (as they call it) of at least 450,000 people on four continents."

Massive deforestation, we all know, will change the whole world's weather for the worse—and it carries heavy economic penalties. Aside from harbouring untold numbers of animal and vegetable species, the forests are the habitat of native peoples. Deforestation is simply criminal—when we realize that rainforests are destroyed merely to extract the fifteen to twenty kinds of commercially valuable tree they contain and frequently 90 to 95 per cent of the trees are left unused when an area of rainforest is logged! And even now the World Bank admits that some 15 to 20 per cent of the world's estimated 3.5 to 10 million plant and animal species will become extinct by the year 2000! A tropical forest is a seamless web and all its components are necessary, or in time it will become as barren as a desert! And yet, forests are sold, then loans are given to reforest and repair the damages. And to pay for the loans more forest is cut, while the banks and lending countries acquire interest payments, export orders and political and economic power—and the environment is simply ruined.

And let us also consider the biological holocaust that is sweeping the Third World. Chemical transnational companies like Shell and Ciba Geigy are acquiring seed companies (merging pesticides and seed research). Of the five thousand food plants used centuries ago, our modern agriculture only uses 150! Most people rely on five cereals, three legumes and three root crops to meet their calorie needs. Even among these, variable strains are vanishing. As the *New Internationalist* reports in the issue of March 1991

> The destruction of rainforests in genetically rich areas of the world is the main cause of this biological holocaust. But the disappearing of native food plants can be blamed squarely on modern agricultural economics which demand uniformity. Developing countries, which have most of the world's genetic wealth, don't have the resources to

protect them. And Western transnational corporations, feed companies and privately funded research organizations have stepped up efforts to collect varieties in a form of "genetic imperialism."

It is thought that just ten transnational companies control nearly one-third of all cereal varieties. Their local firms gather seeds from remote regions of the Third World, breed them with other varieties or change them with biotechnology, and are beginning to patent the result and sell them back to the Third World.

I am at least now a little bit hopeful that the new alliances that are being forged between human rights activists, ecologists and members of the indigenous peoples movements will create a new political momentum! Greater pressure from Northern environmental movements on our own governments and on international finance institutions is very much needed.

The next point I would like to raise is that we ourselves must find new criteria for so-called "development models," because I believe that democratic, nonviolent and ecological development is possible. But this means of course that the North must "de-develop." The debt crisis is a symptom of a polarized world (the Iron Curtain is now between North and South), organized for the benefit of a minority that will stop at nothing to maintain and strengthen its control and privilege. Just look at the so-called New World Order, Pax Americana and the concepts of low-intensity warfare being discussed at the Pentagon. Even repression technology is being improved.

In the North there are many of us now working outside of the old development model. Many popular movements, for example, are working against the official developers. And in the South, we are learning from the courageous indigenous movements, from the courageous women of the Chipko movement, and from many others!

If we try to light a candle, let us look at the proposals of the South Commission, issued in Caracas in 1981, with its development strategy of self-reliance, its recognition that no country can be "developed" by outsiders, its determination to see people, their skills, creativity and wisdom as instruments as well as the ends of development. If we could light one small candle it could be the setting up of an alternative credit system to the International Monetary Fund and the World Bank. Perhaps a South Bank that a hundred or so countries of the South could devise as their own alternative! We can call this new idea "counter-development"—which means disengaging from the single, damaging present world-system.

Our own contribution in the North could be an ecological economy and lifestyle, as the German Green Party declared in 1983:

The release of atom power has changed everything except our way of thinking, and thus we are being driven unarmed towards a catastrophe... The solution of this problem lies in the heart of humankind.

Albert Einstein

A lifestyle and method of production which rely on an endless supply of raw materials and use those raw materials lavishly, also furnish the motive for the violent appropriation of raw materials from other countries. In contrast, a responsible use of raw materials, as part of an ecologically sound lifestyle and economy, reduces the risk that policies of violence will be pursued in our name. The pursuance of ecologically responsible policies within a society provides the pre-conditions for a reduction in tensions and increases our ability to achieve peace in the world. For the West, sustainable development requires a completely new paradigm. We cannot have both growth at any price and sustainable development. As long as we put economical considerations before ecological values, we are going to risk the latter.

Let me quickly turn to another development that is very worrying: Arrogant as we have been in the North, we are calling upon the struggling countries of the Third World to reduce their carbon-dioxide emissions, while the big polluters in the North refuse to do so. And yet it is we, the industrialized nations in the North, who are to blame for the threat to our Planet. We have caused 90 per cent of the greenhouse gas emissions to date. It is far too late to undo the damage that we have already done to our atmosphere, but every five years of delay in cutting pollution will lead to a 10 per cent increase in global warming. The United States, the Soviet Union, China, West Germany, Japan and the United Kingdom are the largest emitters of carbon dioxide. Between them they produce almost two-thirds of the world's CO_2.

One other issue that is very urgent today is how the changes in Eastern Europe affect the South. Vandana Shiva uses an African proverb:

When elephants make war, the grass gets trampled. When elephants make love, the grass gets trampled.

The Third World environment and the Third World communities are the ones who have paid the highest price for the superpower rivalry of the past. The Cold War in Europe had always been translated into real and burning wars in the Third World, for example, in Central America, Central Asia and in the Horn of Africa. Since 1945, two hundred wars have been fought in the Third World. And as the industrialized world now moves from an over-armed peace to a disarmed one, the military producers and traders merely find alternative markets in the Third World.

New ecological transformation and reconstruction in Eastern Europe is of course fundamental to social transformation towards a civil society. We must not forget, and this is one of the most important points, I believe, that it is again the Third World which will have to bear the ecological cost of the new industrialism and consumerism in the North,

including the cost of cleaning up Eastern Europe. Eastern and Western Europe will increasingly use the Third World as a dump for hazardous waste. This is, of course, "garbage imperialism." And eventually the West will use its own back yard, Eastern Europe, for its dumping ground. We call this the "Latin-Americanization of Eastern Europe."

Parts of Eastern Europe have been devastated by industrial strategies that disregarded many of the ecological safegards developed in the West.

The old repressive communistic system in Eastern Europe paralyzed many people and the soft and gentle revolutions that came overnight have given us much hope. But they have also left many of us in a state of shock. Communism institutionalized the surrender of the individual's decision-making and problem-solving capabilities to a state control. Now that the authoritarian powers have stepped down, how can individuals unravel their cultural conditioning and become free agents again? The West has never given Eastern European society, since the Revolution, a chance at all—no chance to think and rethink what kind of society they would now like to build.

Eastern Europe has to create almost a new economic, financial, social and ecological infrastructure—and we are asking them to do it in such a way that they can avoid our mistakes. But how will that be possible, if Western banks and financial institutions dictate what they are to produce, what they are to export and how they are to live in the coming months and years?

As the Iron Curtain dissolved in 1989, it revealed a land laid waste by industrial pollution. Under the assault of air pollution and acid deposition, Eastern Europe's medieval cities are blackened and crumbling, with entire hillsides deforested. Life expectancies in the dirtiest parts of these regions are as much as five years shorter and rates of childhood cancer, reproductive problems and other illnesses are far higher than in other areas. Restoring Eastern Europe's environment will be a most massive undertaking, but it cannot be done at the cost of exploiting the Third World once more. Eastern Europe, I believe, has a unique opportunity to implement only successful ecological strategies and sidestep those that did not work for us. Additionally, as obsolete factories in Eastern Europe are closed down, they could be replaced by ecological and safe and socially useful industries and production. But unfortunately, this is not happening. The shift to Western market-oriented economies in Eastern Europe has had little regard for clean industries, for we in Western Europe are sending our own old reactors and our own old dirty industries to Eastern European countries and to our own back yard, East Germany. There are two more points that will be perhaps a small candle of hope:

1. We must learn in the North that we must begin as critical consumers to reduce our consumption of goods to where we do not provide a market for big business. We can reduce our consumption to where we will use only our share of the world's resources and not take what belongs to someone else. This is for me just one very small aspect of non-violence and the ultimate dimension of non-cooperation with corrupt and inhuman practices. We are part of the problem, and thus we together are also part of the solution. The actual danger as well as the political solutions are not somewhere "out there"—both lie within us. And taking responsibility for our own personal behaviour every single day is the only thing in this world over which we have 100 per cent control.

2. *Feminization of power.* Feminism and the power of non-violence are to me essential concepts of Green politics. Male-led revolutions, so often and so tragically, have been mere power exchanges in a basically unaltered structure and have left behind dramatic accounts of their crisis and heroism (the siege of the Winter Palace or the taking of the Bastille). These revolutions were often based on the concept of dying for a cause; feminist-conceived transformation is all the more about daring to *live for a cause!*

Women represent half the global population and over one-third of the labour force and yet we women receive only one-tenth of the world's income and own less than one per cent of world prosperity. And yet we are also responsible for two-thirds of all working hours. Not only are females most of the poor, starving and the illiterate, but women and children constitute more than 90 per cent of all refugee populations.

Toxic pesticides, herbicides, chemical pollution, leakage from nuclear wastes, acid rain, etc., usually take their first toll as a rise in cancers of the female reproductive system, and in miscarriages, still births and congenital deformities. And furthermore, it is women's work which must compensate for the destruction of the ecological balance.

The overlooked factor in the power of women as a world political force is, I believe, the magnitude of suffering combined with the magnitude of women: women constitute not an oppressed minority, but a majority—of almost all national populations and of the entire human species. I truly believe that we can feminize power, and that we can, in fact, transcend patriarchal power. We can and must elect more ecological feminists to public offices and we must together dare to make new transnational, political and bold initiatives. I believe we must begin to do this with our Mexican sisters right here in Mexico! If there is a future, I believe, it will be Green and feminist!

UNIT 5

ARTS AND CULTURE

■ **ISSUE 1:**
The Role of the Arts

■ **ISSUE 2:**
Objective vs. Subjective Responses to Art

The Role of the Arts

Art is meant to disturb, science reassures.

Georges Braque

Art is the objectification of feeling, and the subjectification of nature.

Suzanne K. Langer

An artist is a dreamer consenting to dream of the actual world.

George Santayana

The purpose of art is the lifelong construction of
a state of wonder.

Glenn Gould

Portrait of the Arts

Morton Ritts

Propositional—tested using formal propositions.

In this unit we examine the role of the arts. Sometimes it's harder to say what art is than what it isn't. Art, for example, isn't science. As we saw in the previous unit, science is factual and propositional. It tries to provide knowledge that is objective and clear, with verifiable observations based on a rigorous method of enquiry.

Art, on the other hand, tends to be ambiguous and problematic. It is both factual and fictional. Indeed, on one level, narrative arts like literature and film proclaim themselves to be not "true" at all, to be "made-up." How can something that's made up be true? And yet, we know from our own experience that when we read certain novels or see certain films we're struck by just how "true to life" they are.

There is a profound paradox here. Characters in novels and films who are invented, who are fictions, often reveal more about human nature than real people. Fiction, in other words, has the capacity to provide us with greater insight to truth than truth. But fiction is just another kind of truth. All art is.

Of course, psychology and biology also provide us with truth. But their focus is always general, while art portrays the particular. In Unit 1, for example, we came across Freud's famous "oedipal complex." As a psychological theory, the oedipal complex is universal and abstract. But in his novel *Sons and Lovers*, D.H. Lawrence gives this theory specific, concrete form by creating a rich and complex character whose intense, troubled relationship with his mother dominates his life.

For another example compare the description of anxiety and fear in a psychology textbook with how these same emotions are depicted in a novel or film. The textbook account is analytical, factual. This is fine, but such an account doesn't convey to us what anxiety and fear "feel" like. A well-written novel or well-made film does, however, by locating these emotions in actions that compel our interest. This difference between fact and fiction is the difference between science and the arts. Science and the social sciences "tell" whereas the arts "show."

We've said that the arts "show" by giving us knowledge of the particular. As the *Sons and Lovers* example suggests, we come to know

Cave painting of a horse; about 15,000-10,000 BC. Lascaux, France.

The hunting-magic role of this painting is indicated by the trap emblem and the flying arrows.

an important universal relationship (mothers and sons) in the depiction of a specific relationship.

The arts "show" by way of creativity, discipline, expressiveness. They give form to our experience. Sometimes the result is indirect, as in expressionist painting. Sometimes it's brutally direct, as in *The Killing Fields*, a powerful film about the genocide that occurred in Cambodia in the 1970s. Different as the are, both examples represent some important aspect of truth.

Art and society

One thing we can say for certain is that artists work in a social context. On the walls of the vast cathedral-like caves at Lascaux in southwestern France, our paleolithic ancestors painted picture-stories of their communal hunts. These extraordinary images bind us to our own prehistoric beginnings some 20,000 years ago. At the same time, they're a good example of one of the underlying impulses behind art—the impulse to leave our mark, to say we were here.

In his essay in this book, "On the Meaning of Work", Mitchell Lerner makes much the same point. But is there a difference between work and art? Yes and no. No doubt, what a good painter or a writer produces is always the result of hard work. But if all art is work, the opposite—that all work is art—is not true. This is because most of us work to please someone else, while most artists work primarily to please themselves. In this sense, the more a job allows you to please yourself the closer you are to being an artist.

Sunday Afternoon on Island of La Grande Jatte, Georges Seurat (1859-91).

Most of us don't have this luxury. If we work in a factory, in an office or retail store, or in a school, our individual needs count for less than those of the company or our clients. Certainly we can find fulfilment in our work, but never at the expense of the group. While enlightened employers try to create the conditions for a balance between our individual interests and those of the company, this isn't often possible.

So in this way art is different from work. Unlike work, art, in western culture at least, stresses the primacy of the individual. In this tradition, even performing artists, like musicians, actors and dancers have a healthy regard for their own uniqueness. They may be part of a team, but some will always insist on shining more brightly than others—on being "stars."

Throughout history, societies have often objected to the idea of artists as individuals, arguing that their first loyalty is not to themselves but to the state. This was the case in the former Soviet Union, and is still the case in China. Even in democracies like Canada and the U.S., books, magazines, paintings, photographs and films are censored because they are deemed in some way a threat to society for reasons of obscenity, libel or blasphemy.

The Greek philosopher Plato would have heartily endorsed such censorship. For him, art was at best a distraction, at worst a danger. He believed it was difficult enough to know reality. Art only made it harder—instead of showing things as they were, it offered distorted representations of those things. Drama, poetry, painting gave us a kind of secret second-hand version of life, he argued. They served no constructive purpose.

According to Plato, only the study of science, philosophy or history enlightened us because these disciplines appealed to the mind, to our rational selves. Drama, poetry, music, the visual arts appealed to our senses, our irrational and emotional selves. In doing so, they not only distorted reality, they threatened the security and well-being of the state because they tended to mislead, confuse and excite people.

The need to imagine

Just as art differs from philosophy, science and history, writers, actors, dancers and other artists differ from philosophers, scientists and historians. Like them, artists attempt to impose their own sense of order on the random flow of life around them. But as we've already seen, their method is different—artists work with their senses, with feeling and intuition, with metaphor and imagination.

In his play, *A Midsummer Night's Dream*, William Shakespeare compared artists (poets) to lovers and lunatics. What connects them, he suggests, is precisely this power of the imagination:

And, as imagination bodies forth,
The form of things unknown, the poet's pen
Turns them to shapes, and gives to airy nothing
A local habitation and a name.

The artist, then, is someone whose imagination makes the unknown known, the invisible visible and the unconscious conscious—which is very close to the therapeutic process of Freudian psychoanalysis. Art itself is a way of exploring the mysteries of the human condition, not in the linear fashion of scientific enquiry but in the associative, circular manner of therapy. "We shed our sicknesses in books," D.H. Lawrence wrote. Art, he meant, heals.

That's perhaps one reason why people feel the need to write, paint, play an instrument or sing. Another reason, we've suggested, is the desire to leave some sign, some evidence of our existence. As children we seek even the most trivial kind of immortality, nothing more sometimes than carving our initials into the trunk of a tree or printing our name in the fresh concrete of a sidewalk.

The humanistic psychologist Abraham Maslow offers still another way of looking at the desire to create. We may recall that in his hierarchy of needs, Maslow speculates that physical survival is basic. Someone who lacks the requirements for physiological well being, including food and shelter, isn't much interested in writing novels or painting land-scapes.

But once these basic needs are satisfied, we often ask ourselves, "What more is there to life?" What's more, Maslow says, are the higher level needs for love, esteem and, above all, self-actualization. More than most people, artists are obsessed by the need to self-actualize, to be the best they can at whatever they are. A tale about two modern painters, Amadeo Modigliani and Chaim Soutine, illustrates this point.

Modigliani and Soutine were friends who shared a studio in a small garret in Paris at the turn of the century. They were almost stereotypes of the starving artist, deprived of material comforts but endowed with rich and productive imaginations.

One day, the story goes, they bought a chicken at the local butcher shop, as the subject for a "still life." They hung it from the rafters in their studio and set up their easels. In the midst of their preparation, however, it occurred to them that they hadn't had a decent meal in weeks. They'd spent their last francs on a chicken, but incredibly—foolishly, it seemed at that moment—they were intending to paint it, not eat it.

Maslow might explain their dilemma this way: If the two friends cooked the chicken, they'd satisfy their basic survival needs but not their need for art. On the other hand, if they painted the chicken, they'd satisfy their need for self-actualization, but might starve to death in the process. What to do? In fact, they arrived at one of those inspired compromises that are the mark of true genius—they painted very quickly (while the chicken was still fresh).

The story is a good example of the struggle between the demands of life and those of art. Someone once asked the great artist Picasso whether, if his house caught fire, he'd rescue his cat first or his paintings. He answered his cat. Picasso's point was that artists draw their inspiration from life. Without life there can be no art.

Art redraws the boundaries of our lives

As much as artists deal with the world of imagination and subjective perception, their messages of pain or celebration correspond in some way to life outside them, to the common experiences of humanity. When we see a film or hear a song that absorbs us, we feel this connection too. The artist redraws and enlarges the boundaries of our emotional and intellectual landscape.

At their best, the books and films and music that mean most to us tell us stories in provocative new ways. Since the beginning, the human species has always felt compelled to tell stories. There are the hunting

The Scream, 1895, Edvard Munch (1863-1944), Norway.

pictures in the caves at Lascaux. There was remarkable poetry, music and painting in the Nazi concentration camps. Plato was right to suggest that art is dangerous, but perhaps that's exactly what art should be—something that pricks the bubble of illusion, that exposes pain and injustice, that challenges us to think about old things in new ways.

Art is often most dangerous when it creates an experience for us that defies what is considered politically and morally "correct." That's why one of the first acts of dictatorial regimes is to imprison a country's writers. Or why police shut down exhibitions of "offensive" paintings and photographs. Or why some governments issue death threats against artists who have allegedly committed crimes against the state.

Yet those who want to create art, and not propaganda, will always affirm their right to see with their own eyes, to speak in their own voice. Their messages may indeed be subversive. But we soon forget books or paintings or music or films or plays that merely entertain us. We remember instead those that have astonished or disturbed, moved or changed us. They're part of who we are.

The Role of the Arts

Clive Cockerton

Think about the sports hero, after scoring a touchdown or a goal. Picture the athlete in uninhibited self-expression, the little dance that celebrates the moment, the moment when for once the event planned for and visualized actually takes place. Most of us share in the athlete's joy (unless we have a big stake on the other team) but a few people are embarrassed by this exuberance, and can be heard muttering words like "hot dog" or "grandstanding" that clearly indicate disapproval. For these people victory should be savoured quietly, with a certain decorum that might suggest that nothing unusual (goal/TD) has happened.

There's another moment, probably a great deal more important than the athlete's dance, and that's the moment of the Saturday night dance. Whether it takes place at a prom, a club or somebody's recreation room, the moment requires careful preparation. There's all the body prep, the showering and the hair, and the crucial choosing of clothes to achieve *the look*. There's the rehearsal in front of a mirror, not just the look, but the right *moves*. Some thought is given to the right music and where you can go to get it (do you have to bring it with you or can you request it?). And when you're finally dancing with someone important, and the right song comes on, you really *listen* as you move, because you want it to be perfect, no mis-steps, no awkwardness. Sometimes life then smiles, and says to both of you, "OK truehearts, you've prepared for this, you deserve it, you can have your moment." And then you can't believe it as you both surrender to the music and the mood, you can't put a foot wrong, you move in harmony, you pulse in rhythm AND you achieve insight, not really as a thought or an idea, something much more fleshy and salty, a strange union of perception and pleasure, that tells you that life is MAGICAL after all.

Of course, this is why many belief systems discourage dancing. It offers a competitive view of the world, one devoted to pleasure, the senses, the here and now. Parents, even liberal ones who want you to have a good time, want to be sure you've got your algebra homework done first. Their voice says, get the work done before you play.

Dancing, fooling around, the pursuit of pleasure are dangerous because they can distract us from our reality goals—getting our homework done, passing our courses, achieving a good education, getting a good job, getting ahead in life. Our reality goals demand that priorities be established, schedules be followed and discipline and order become a habit. In extreme form, this point of view is sceptical about pleasure itself, and seems to believe that anything pleasurable can't be serious. As anti-life as this view seems to be, the flip side, that anything serious can't be pleasurable appears thin and trivial to the same degree. This last notion reduces the idea of seriousness to a draggy sombreness, the domain of the long-faced and the stuffy. Perhaps both pleasure and seriousness need to be rescued from this debate.

At the very least, the reality instructors have convinced many of us that our success depends on the mind controlling the body and all its instincts for comfort, release and pleasure. Yet we are haunted by that moment on Saturday night, that perception that there's something else even more important than the progress we make in overcoming life's barriers.

These objections made to dancing are also voiced (in more muted tones, perhaps) about other arts (film, novels, music, etc.). In many people's eyes, the arts are the toy department of life, occasionally amusing perhaps but in the long run a waste of time for men and women of action and purpose. The Greek philosopher Plato (427–347 B.C.) argued that art was a distraction that someone looking for reality or truth would be better off without. According to Plato, art was a distraction because:

- art deals with images not truth; it doesn't advance knowledge, it doesn't discover anything, it only *seems* to understand.

- art imitates reality; to learn about reality it is much better to study reality itself rather than the pale imitation.

- art is sensual and distracts us from the more important quests (spiritual quests for instance). In its arousal of basic instincts, in its stimulation/simulation of violence and lust, it is anarchic, a force for disorder in the community.

Since Plato, many moralists have branched off of these arguments and have (less eloquently than Plato) argued, at various times, that bright colour and decoration is immoral because it calls attention to the self instead of singing the praises of God, or that "realistic" novels were too shocking for the delicate sensibilities of young women, or that rock'n roll would corrupt and deprave youth with its jungle rhythms. At a much less passionate level, business people, the folks of the bottom line, are sceptical of the arts, except where they can be trained to serve the purpose of promoting consumption of goods and services in advertising. Politicians of the small view frequently see the arts as frills, and in time of recession the artistic community is the first to feel the cuts of government spending and support. All of these views, whether held by philosophers, moralists, business people or politicians, have in common the conviction that art is not serious.

Television Fiction

Let's begin to look at the notion of seriousness by examining the art form most people spend the most time with (on average 24 hours per week)—television fiction. Television fiction, whether in the form of situation comedy, action adventure, or police drama *doesn't share* one very important ingredient with all other forms of fiction—suspense. The "what is going to happen next" question that accelerates into page-turning concentration in a novel or the laser-eyed excitement in the movie audience doesn't happen on TV. Only on rare occasions does suspense occur, such as the "who shot JR" question on *Dallas* or the "who killed Laura Palmer" question on *Twin Peaks*. So predictable are TV formulas, that having seen one it is usually possible to predict what will happen (in general terms at least) next week.

We keep watching for a number of reasons, one of them being the charm/presence/relationship of the main characters. TV is a small intimate medium and spends a lot of time focusing on the faces of main characters. If we find these characters attractive they become like family, invited into our homes every week, and the series becomes a success. It is interesting to note, however, that characters rarely change or develop. But if the plots are predictable and the characters don't develop, how does TV hold our attention? The main method is by multiple storylines, so that before we become bored with the plot, predicament, or character's reaction we are whisked off to another dimension (usually parallel) of the plot. Our interest is therefore spread over a larger field, reducing the chances of our becoming bored with any one aspect of the story. A look at a typical episode of the popular show *Magnum P.I.*, "Old Acquaintance," illustrates this process.

The program begins by showing the theft of a dolphin from an outdoor aquarium. Next we see Magnum at his home with T.C. and Rick. Magnum is preparing to meet an old acquaintance. Goldie Morris had been a friend of his in high school and had tutored him to help him pass English. T.C. and Rick tease Magnum about Goldie's unattractiveness in her high school photo. (At this point, the alert viewer is put on notice that this sexist fooling around will be rebuked by the now stunning presence of Goldie. This is as angry a rebuke as a TV series usually allow.) As Magnum is about to leave, Higgins enters, asking Magnum to drop off his credentials at the yacht of a visiting president of a mythical African nation. Higgins is planning to attend the meeting of the International Human Rights Advisory Council on this yacht as an unofficial representative of the British government which wants to keep its distance from President Kole and his record of atrocities towards his people. So, in the first three minutes, three storylines are set in motion:

1. The theft of the dolphin. Who took it and why? Will it be recovered?

2. Magnum and Goldie's relationship. When it turns out that she's become quite pretty, will their friendship change to romance?
    and

3. Higgins meeting with President Kole. Should he go? What is to be done about Kole's crimes?

It turns out, however, that these three storylines are intimately interconnected: Goldie was involved in the theft of the dolphin (out of over-zealous concern for animal rights), but her politically extreme cohorts have actually kidnapped the dolphin to use it to carry a bomb to blow up Kole and all those aboard his yacht. Magnum recovers the dolphin, saves everyone's lives (assassination is not the answer to dealing with dictators) and affectionately, but paternally, extricates Goldie from her difficulties (thereby paying her back for past kindnesses and reasserting his superiority). (From Sarah Ruth Kozloff, *Channels of Discourse*.)

Perhaps the hard-nosed critics of the arts can be forgiven for thinking of the arts as the toy department. The storylines interconnect in ways that are incredible and Magnum navigates his way through the maze without ever really being in great danger.

Episodes conclude at the same place they begin—with the unchanging hero ready to resolve new predicaments next week. Think of *Miami Vice*. Over four seasons of being spectacularly under-cover, the audience was expected to wonder if Crockett and Tubbs would be (a) exposed or (b) corrupted. Miraculously, the Miami drug barons never figured out that the chicly-dressed pair in the Ferrari were always involved when one of their number went down. Towards the end of the run, the producers began to flirt with the notion of (b), Sonny being corrupted and going over to the other side. As soon as that happened, the air went out of the Mi-Vi balloon. These ultimate questions that lurk behind the action should only be implicitly present, like an ominous shadow, and never explicitly dealt with. Much better to return the

Since television interprets the world for so many people, it is crucial that they are not innocent of the warp that television brings to the world.

———

Illustration by
Thomas Dannenberg

heroes to the police station, safe and secure, ready for next week's villains.

OK. The world of TV fiction is a fantasyland. But what happens when fantasyland tries to deal with serious issues from the real world? Issues of gender are usually presented as a "fun battle of the sexes," as in *Designing Women*. Single-parent families also share in a life that can be described as a *Kate and Alie* laugh riot. Being black in America becomes the cozy, comfortable *Cosby Show* or the loony *Fresh Prince of Bel-Air*. Homosexuality is the latest "issue" to surface on TV. *Hooperman* had a gay cop. *L.A. Law* has a lesbian lawyer; *thirtysomething* featured a homosexual relationship in which two men were seen in bed together, enjoying the afterglow but not actually touching. Despite the noble attempts of *thirtysomething* to present a real situation involving gay men, most TV dramas play up the "gayness" as a gag, focusing on the alarmed and frustrated reactions of parents and peers.

As irritating as this downsizing of their dilemmas may be to women, single parents, blacks and homosexuals, TV does take away the threat to the status quo implicit in any political cause or vocal minority. It's a trade-off; something is lost and something won. When a group or cause makes it to TV, television domesticates the dilemma, reducing it to manageable proportions suitable for the living room. Still, something has been gained from this understandably annoying process. Television reduces fear, encourages tolerance if not acceptance, and most importantly confers normalcy on what had previously been regarded as aberrant and threatening.

Television Fact

Many people rely on television news/documentary as their chief source of information. By and large, Canadian news teams do a creditable job of providing and interpreting information. However, an awareness of the limitations of the medium is essential if the audience is not to be deceived.

The first and most obvious limitation is that television must photograph something. When a story is relatively difficult to film, such as inflation, the producers may try to illustrate the falling purchasing power of the dollar graphically by showing $100 worth of groceries in two shopping carts. Shopping cart no. 1 contains $100 worth of groceries in 1975; shopping cart no. 2 contains $100 worth of groceries in 1991. See the difference. Yes, it's a neat visual summary of inflation, but once you've done this once, it's hard to keep repeating it. What in fact happens is that the non-visual story gets less air-time; it is devalued as a news item because of the presentation difficulties, however important it may remain to the economy and the viewer.

The second major limitation comes from the news/documentary team's goal to entertain as well as inform. What's the matter with entertainment? Who wants a stuffy, dry presentation of events that may seem very distant to the average viewer? As much as I agree with the spirit of those questions, it is also true that in practice the efforts of producers/directors and writers are bent towards telling a compelling story. The real world is chaotic, with events sometimes happening at random, without satisfactory explanation. However, a news story that can't make up its mind, that tells us that country X could go to war with country Y, or maybe country Y would align itself with Z, making war unlikely, or that internal dissension in country X could prevent any action—well, that is a news story fast on the way to losing our attention. We don't look for nuances on TV. We want to know—war or peace? Which is it? The producers are well aware of this need for a clear and dramatic answer and they're prepared to find it. And if finding it at times seems a little difficult, perhaps they can invent a thesis and hope their educated judgment stands them in good stead. All too frequently a camera crew is let loose on a situation, not to make discoveries, but to search for preconceived moments that support a satisfying interpretation.

The temptation to use television techniques (such as skilful editing of opposing views, or excessively tight close-ups of the "villain" in the piece) to colour the story, is enormous. In a now famous dispute between the head of the American Army in Viet Nam, General Westmoreland, and the CBS network, the program *60 Minutes* implied that General Westmoreland set out to conceal estimates of enemy strength from the President of the United States, Lyndon Johnson. Although there were plenty of knowledgeable people prepared to support the General, many were not approached for interview. Of those interviewed, those in favour of the *60 Minutes* thesis outnumbered those against by 9–2. Of course, they had to include *some* contrary views, to avoid charges of bias, but by following the statements of support for the General with, for instance, shots of the interviewer in mouth-opened disbelief, it can be very easy to undermine what has just been said. As much as many people are inclined to believe ill of the U.S. military in Viet Nam, when they ran up against the might and technique of CBS, they became the victims of reporting. The American military has learned much about dealing with the media, and during the recent Gulf War, managed to control the news of the war and to shape the debate over the war. What was permitted to be shown were neat images of high-tech weapons searching out the door of a bunker. We marvelled at the stunt, the techno-wizardry of it all, and didn't much think about the human misery that is attendant to all wars.

Because television shows us real people in real situations we tend to believe it too much. Since television interprets the world for so many people, it is crucial that they are not innocent of the warp that television brings to the world.

Television Propaganda (Commercials, Advertising)

Now, who takes commercials seriously? Well, the average Canadian spends 32 working days per year watching them (according to the Bureau of Broadcast Measurement, 1989 figures). Commercials underwrite everything you see on TV—fiction and news/documentary programming. Without commercials our present system of programming would collapse. Business people take commercials very seriously indeed, spending large portions of their budgets to advertise and promote their products. And, of course, the commercials are the best made element in TV. The budget for a 30-second commercial can exceed the budget for the half-hour or even hour-long program. Commercials present their messages with a dazzling display of technique.

Of course they have to be dazzling for they are meant to be viewed over and over again, sometimes within the same hour. If suspense is absent to a surprising degree from most of television fiction, it is totally absent from commercials after the first viewing. The rapid succession of images (sometimes faster than 1 image per second) sets up a visual

Disturbing images are sometimes used in advertising.

UNITED COLORS OF BENETTON.

rhythm, the soundtrack an aural rhythm, and the narration punches us silly with the slogan.

Commercials adopt one of three basic approaches. They can present their case in a visual essay, a mini-documentary, arguing that Brand X really is preferred by most doctors over Brand Y. (Pain relief ads seem particularly fond of this approach.) The lyrical, image-laden car/beer commercial presents another approach, full of vitality, sex and adventure. The third and perhaps most often used approach is the mini-story. Part 1: Your laundry powder doesn't seem to get things clean any more, your drains are plugged, your hands are chapped, your muffler falls off. Part 2: Someone suggests you try new Sunlight, Liquid Plumber, Vaseline Intensive Care, or Speedy. Part 3: Your whites are whiter now, your drain sucks water, your hands are touchable again, and not only is your car fixed, you're a Somebody, too. It is the pattern of the faery-tale. The problem is stated, the magic wand appears, the problem not only vanishes but also the very quality of one's life has been enhanced.

But it doesn't stop at just the small vexatious problems of everyday life. The world of the commercial is a world where most women have now become airline pilots, bank managers and entrepreneurs. It is a world where racial tension is replaced by harmony and mutual understanding (think of the Bennetton ads). It is a world where everybody behaves with great respect for Nature, and sees in the communication of wolves or whales an organic system worthy of being copied. It is a world of our fondest wish and the message is that it can be ours, here and now. It is a vision of great innocence and attractiveness, despite its lack of any clues as to how to achieve this world. You have to remind yourself that it is a vision bent to the task of selling—soap, mufflers and hand cream. Those thirty-second visions are important because they create urgency around a purchase and complacency around a world.

Film

Television is like someone you know who's "nice enough" but who you have no desire to know further; film is like someone who breaks through your social reserve, someone who has a hold on you, someone to be passionate about. They are very different media as anyone who has studied them will tell you. As television domesticates issues and renders people predictable and safe, film casts a magic light, transforming events into crises and people into heroes. Partly it has something to do with scale; the size of the image in film is heroic. Partly it has to do with the intensity of the image; it's so much brighter, sharper, you can see much more than you can see with current TV technology. Partly it has to do with technique; in film the camera explores its subject with imagination, from a variety of angles, with dramatic lighting falling on the subject. As well, the camera *moves through* a situation, a crowd, a landscape, which psychologically creates the illusion that you, the viewer, are in the scene, surrounded by action. This seductive camera movement is in stark contrast to the more static point of view of television, which imitates the point of view of the tennis spectator, "thwack"—look left, "thwack"—look right. The images change (on average every 3.5 seconds) but they are seen from a relatively unchanging perspective. On film it is possible to leap onto the court, to visually both serve the ball and return it. It is a more complex, more varied and more intense experience.

Film is also a bigger adventure. There are bigger risks, the heroes sometimes die, the lovers sometimes end tragically. The predictability that we find on TV is available only on certain types of film (those starring Sylvester Stallone, for instance) and even in these films there lies the compensation of truly spectacular effects. But generally in film the question "What is going to happen next?" carries some force; far more options, both happy and sad await. We watch the story unfold, acted by recognizable if heroic people, told by a dynamic and fluid

People hardly ever quote movie lines exactly or remember accurately what happens in a single scene. The most powerful art form of our day depends on passionate incoherence for its effects. The eye is glazed, the mouth hangs in a flat, slack face.

Leonard Michaels

camera, and for the two hours of watching, the film reality can be almost as strongly experienced as any other reality. As we face the dilemmas with the characters in the film, our sense of what drives, disturbs and delights other people is deepened.

The Novel

Deepened by film, but if we want to get to the source of all human understanding, that quivering voice within us all, we have to go to novels. For in novels we can not only see behaviour as we do in film, but we can follow the contents of the mind as it responds and reacts to the world around it. We are not just limited to experience another's external behaviour, but, by crawling into the fictional character's mind, we can experience another's experience as well. It is this ability that makes literature the most intimate of the arts, able to explore the faintest shadows of thought and the most powerful of emotions.

We experience novels as we do the world—from a perspective, a point of view that is both emotional and rational. Despite the major role that the scientific process has played in expanding our understanding, we generally don't experience life as detached observers. Instead we grope about through our lives, using bits of knowledge and lots of emotion in a constantly shifting understanding—as we do in novels. When we persevere through a novel, we may come to know a situation or a character very intimately; indeed, we may know all the significant details about a person's life (thoughts as well as actions). It's possible to know fictional characters better than our close friends. By providing us with all the information we need and by coming to a conclusion, novels present a complete vision. This completeness necessarily lacks some of life's random quality. Novels conclude, life goes on. By concluding, novels ask us to stop and think. By focusing on some of the most fundamental issues (growth, independence, love, pain, death) that we encounter in the real world, novels ask us to reflect on our own lives. But they don't just ask, they seduce us with pleasure, with worlds spun from word-magic; they seduce us with intimacy, they leave us with insight.

If you've ever seen a film adapted from a favourite book, you know the two media have very different insights, very different strengths. To put it in simple terms, the film paints a physical landscape, shows us physical action. The novel gives us an interior landscape, lets us hear the deepest voice. Of course, films are not satisfied with telling just physical tales; actors speak and gesture and through these techniques suggest interior emotion. Lighting and camera work can create an emotional atmosphere. Voice-over narration can tell us (usually in an awkward fashion) what a character is thinking. Still, despite film-makers' efforts to stretch the structure of their medium it is generally true that they do not succeed in going as clearly, completely inside the individual as do novelists. However, this fact doesn't mean that novels are always more serious than the films that get made from them. Some novels (*The Godfather*, for instance) don't exploit the structural advantages available to a novel, while the film version does stretch the structural limitations of film resulting in a great and serious film based on an inconsequential and superficial book.

Literature is the most intellectual art form. Ideas are produced by scientists, philosophers, academics, teachers, journalists but it is in literature that the ideas are given flesh, tested not in debate, but in a re-creation of life. Through this process we find what ideas are useful, not just as ideas but as guiding principles. We learn what works, what is credible, what plays. The pages of literature contain a great sifting and a great pleasure.

It is unfortunate that seemingly fewer and fewer people partake of this great pleasure. A few years ago, parents were concerned that if their children weren't computer literate, that somehow they would be condemned to a powerless position in society. Computers were brought into the home, computer courses introduced into the curriculum. Now everyone computes, but only the powerful still read. It is a pity, for its pleasure and insight should be shared by all.

Conclusion

Whenever it occurs, the combination of pleasure and insight is compelling. The pleasure can take the form of delight in a line of melody, the turn of a phrase or the intensity of vision. While pleasure is frequently found on the shimmering surface of the art, the insight cuts to the heart of issues, towards a deeper understanding of people and human experience. The answer to Plato's desire to rid his world of art lies in the value of pleasure and insight to the individual reader, viewer and listener. But it doesn't stop with value to the individual, but extends to a community. Indeed, the shared experience of art helps to create a sense of community. Many cold winds blow through an individual's life, but the arts tell you that you're not alone, that others have cried as hard, laughed as loud, and loved as deeply. There's pleasure in that—in the community with others that the arts magically bring to us. Serious pleasure.

On Photography

Susan Sontag

Photographs furnish evidence. Something we hear about, but doubt, seems proven when we're shown a photograph of it. In one version of its utility, the camera record incriminates. Starting with their use by the Paris police in the murderous roundup of communards in June 1871, photographs became a useful tool of modern states in the surveillance and control of their increasingly mobile populations. In another version of its utility, the camera record justifies. A photograph passes for incontrovertible proof that a given thing happened. The picture may distort; but there is always a presumption that something exists, or did exist, which is like what's in the picture. Whatever the limitations (through amateurism) or pretensions (through artistry) of the individual photographer, a photograph—any photograph—seems to have a more innocent, and therefore more accurate, relation to visible reality than do other mimetic objects. Virtuosi of the noble image like Alfred Stieglitz and Paul Strand, composing mighty, unforgettable photographs decade after decade, still want, first of all, to show something "out there," just like the Polaroid owner for whom photographs are a handy, fast form of note-taking, or the shutterbug with a Brownie who takes snapshots as souvenirs of daily life.

•

Recently, photography has become almost as widely practised an amusement as sex and dancing—which means that, like every mass art form, photography is not practised by most people as an art. It is mainly a social rite, a defense against anxiety, and a tool of power.

Memorializing the achievements of individuals considered as members of families (as well as of other groups) is the earliest popular use of photography. For at least a century, the wedding photograph has been as much a part of the ceremony as the prescribed verbal formulas. Cameras go with family life. According to a sociological study done in France, most households have a camera, but a household with children is twice as likely to have at least one camera as a household in which there are no children. Not to take pictures of one's children, particularly

Young Boy,
Paul Strand (1890-1976).

when they are small, is a sign of parental indifference, just as not turning up for one's graduation picture is a gesture of adolescent rebellion.

Through photographs, each family constructs a portrait-chronicle of itself—a portable kit of images that bears witness to its connectedness. It hardly matters what activities are photographed so long as photographs get taken and are cherished. Photography becomes a rite of family life just when, in the industrializing countries of Europe and America, the very institution of the family starts undergoing radical surgery. As that claustrophobic unit, the nuclear family, was being carved out of a much larger family aggregate, photography came along to memorialize, to restate symbolically, the imperiled continuity and vanishing extendedness of family life. Those ghostly traces, photographs, supply the token presence of the dispersed relatives. A family's photograph album is generally about the extended family—and, often, is all that remains of it.

As photographs give people an imaginary possession of a past that is unreal, they also help people to take possession of space in which they are insecure. Thus, photography develops in tandem with one of the most characteristic of modern activities: tourism. For the first time in history, large numbers of people regularly travel out of their habitual environments for short periods of time. It seems positively unnatural to travel for pleasure without taking a camera along. Photographs will offer indisputable evidence that the trip was made, that the program was carried out, that fun was had. Photographs document sequences of consumption carried on outside the view of family, friends, neighbours. But dependence on the camera, as the device that makes real what one is experiencing, doesn't fade when people travel more. Taking photographs fills the same need for the cosmopolitans accumulating photograph-trophies of their boat trip up the Albert Nile or their fourteen days in China as it does for lower-middle-class vacationers taking snapshots of the Eiffel Tower or Niagara Falls.

A way of certifying experience, taking photographs is also a way of refusing it—by limiting experience to a search for the photogenic, by converting experience into an image, a souvenir. Travel becomes a strategy for accumulating photographs. The very activity of taking pictures is soothing, and assuages general feelings of disorientation that are likely to be exacerbated by travel. Most tourists feel compelled to put the camera between themselves and whatever is remarkable that they encounter. Unsure of other responses, they take a picture. This gives shape to experience: stop, take a photograph, and move on. The method especially appeals to people handicapped by a ruthless work ethic—Germans, Japanese, and Americans. Using a camera appeases the anxiety which the work-driven feel about not working when they are on vacation and supposed to be having fun. They have something to do that is like a friendly imitation of work: they can take pictures.

People robbed of their past seem to make the most fervent picture takers, at home and abroad. Everyone who lives in an industrialized society is obliged gradually to give up the past, but in certain countries, such as the United States and Japan, the break with the past has been particularly traumatic. In the early 1970s, the fable of the brash American tourist of the 1950s and 1960s, rich with dollars and Babbittry, was replaced by the mystery of the group-minded Japanese tourist, newly released from his island prison by the miracle of overvalued yen, who is generally armed with two cameras, one on each hip.

●

A photograph is not just the result of an encounter between an event and a photographer; picture-taking is an event in itself, and one with ever more peremptory rights—to interfere with, to invade, or to ignore whatever is going on. Our very sense of situation is now articulated by the camera's interventions. The omnipresence of cameras persuasively suggests that time consists of interesting events, events worth photographing. This, in turn, makes it easy to feel that any event, once underway, and whatever its moral character, should be allowed to complete itself—so that something else can be brought into the world, the photograph. After the event has ended, the picture will still exist, conferring on the event a kind of immortality (and importance) it would never otherwise have enjoyed. While real people are out there killing

On Photography

In this thoughtful essay, the author studies the camera and the role the related practice of photography plays in our lives.

As Sontag suggests, photographs are regarded as such an accurate representation of what lies "out there" that they are commonly admissible as evidence in a court of law. We "take" wedding, baby and other pictures to chronicle important events.

And we use the camera, Sontag argues, as a defense against our anxieties and fears to make us feel comfortable in foreign spaces. "Most tourists feel compelled to put the camera between themselves and whatever is remarkable that they encounter," she observes. "Unsure of other responses, they take a picture."

So, when encountering amazing works of nature or humans, like Niagara Falls or the Great Wall of China, the Grand Canyon or the Parthenon, the tourist aims, frames and clicks the shutter. The camera shapes the experience and by default establishes a passive role for the tourist, who by seeing the world through a viewfinder becomes a chronic voyeur, a spectator, an observer instead of a participant. The tourist denies his own awe and sense of wonder, capturing though diluting the power of the moment.

According to Sontag, the camera, and thereby the person using it, takes a morally neutral position towards the photographic subject. Taking a photograph, she writes, is "an act of non-intervention." The media show astonishing, even shocking photographs related to natural and human-made disasters and tragedies, floods, famines, assassinations and other events focusing on human suffering that are repetitiously the central component. By snapping the picture, the photographer preserves the unfortunate situation on film before attempting to improve it. And so, says Sontag, the picture taker may end up prolonging the suffering for as long as it takes to get a "good" picture.

themselves or other real people, the photographer stays behind his or her camera, creating a tiny element of another world: the image-world that bids to outlast us all.

Photographing is essentially an act of non-intervention ... how plausible it has become, in situations where the photographer has the choice between a photograph and a life, to choose the photograph. The person who intervenes cannot record; the person who is recording cannot intervene. ... Even if incompatible with intervention in a physical sense, using a camera is still a form of participation. Although the camera is an observation station, the act of photographing is more than passive observing. Like sexual voyeurism, it is a way of at least tacitly, often explicitly, encouraging whatever is going on to keep on happening. To take a picture is to have an interest in things as they are, in the status quo remaining unchanged (at least for as long as it takes to get a "good" picture), to be in complicity with whatever makes a subject interesting, worth photographing—including, when that is the interest, another person's pain or misfortune.

The Story of Stories

Sarah Sheard

Narrating, according to the *Oxford English Dictionary*, is the act of telling a story, of giving a full and detailed account of the facts of the matter. Or is it a *fiction* of the matter? An Ashanti African storyteller traditionally begins a tale with the warning: "I do not mean, I do not really mean, that what I am going to say is true." Similarly a Sudanese storyteller traditionally opens his or her sessions with an exchange that goes something like this:

"I'm going to tell a story."
"Right!" the audience shouts back.
"It's a lie."
"Right!"
"But not everything in it is false."
"Right!"

The storyteller concludes the narration with the words: "I put the tale back where I found it."

So narration needs not only a storyteller but also an attentive listener who agrees to accept the conventions of the tale and its telling. Compare the African storytellers' approach to the disclaimer we usually find printed in the front matter of novels or after the credits have rolled in movies: "Any similarity between actual persons, places or events and those depicted here are purely coincidental." (Right!)

The telling of stories is crucial to our daily lives and has been so since birth. Whether awake or asleep, we are continuously swimming down an ancient river of narrative that began flowing the moment humans first mastered speech itself. The categories of narrative genres today include allegory, poetry, satire, novel, short story, epic, drama, legend, fable, history, biography, pamphlet and essay, but we could stretch our definition of narrative a little to include, say, dreams, daydreams, nightmares, chronicles, diaries, records, reports, lies, gossip, local news, confessions, plans, predictions, announcements, pronouncements, prophesies, fantasies, intentions, as well as dances, popular music, pantomimes, paintings, stained glass windows, movies, cartoons and combinations of any of the above.

Our well-being and sometimes our very survival can depend on the story we hear. A revised scrap of memory, a secret location disclosed, the winning number leaked, a name overheard, or a crucial detail omitted from someone's testimony in court can actually change the course of history.

Even if almost anything with words can be considered a kind of narrative, we still need to know more about what defines it. We already accept that a story requires both a teller and a listener, but what about length? A narrative can nestle inside a single sentence like, "People in glass houses shouldn't throw stones"—or can take a thousand and one nights in the telling, like *The Arabian Nights*.

According to Aristotle, a narrative should have a beginning, a middle and an ending. "The middles should develop in a linear way to connect beginnings with ends sequentially in order to produce unified and harmonious effects upon readers … ." He also thought that middles, unlike highways and Canada Post, oughtn't to take the shortest track between two points. Pleasure was to be taken in the scenery along the way.

Everything in a narrative also has to take place through *time*. The separate elements of theme, characters, plots, events, relationships, imagery and symbols all need time in which to be developed. If the story has been clearly told, with sufficient details, ordered in an coherent and memorable fashion, then the reader will accumulate a sense of the story's past.

Narrative also needs to convey a clear sense of *sequence*, or order of occurrence. The organisation of experience created by the writer is recreated in the reader's mind, although the events themselves need not be presented chronologically. Readers today are all comfortable with the flashback or the story that opens in the middle of the character's life in which we may discover a tremendous amount about the person's life (or death) before we are told the first things about his or her childhood. A well-crafted narrative conveys a feeling of rightness in its order of unfolding of the events. Aristotle felt that the order must be such "that repositioning or removal (of a section of narrative) would cause confusion or misshapenness."

With sequence comes *consequence*. Part of a reader's pleasure (and proof of a writer's skill) is in being able to anticipate a probable outcome to the story based on an understanding and recollection of the characters and events of that particular story-world. How many of us emerge blinking from the movie theatre lost in the predictions of possible futures for the characters with which we've come to identify?

Yet writers are the first to admit the chaotic impulses that go into creating narratives. Richard Ford, a contemporary American novelist, describes the process this way: "Stories and novels too—are makeshift things. They originate in strong disorderly impulses that are supplied by random accumulations of life-in-words and proceed in their creation by mischance, faulty memory, distorted understanding, weariness, deceit of almost every imaginable kind, by luck and by the stresses of increasingly inadequate vocabulary and waning imagination—with the result being a straining, barely containable object held in fierce and sometimes insufficient control."

These would seem unlikely conditions by which well-ordered, elegantly styled, realistic narratives such as Ford's are spun; yet, if he and other writers are to be believed, they are precisely the ones which seem to work best.

So what were the first narratives? Perhaps they were tales of exploits brought back from the hunt and told to the others around a flickering fire, accompanied by broad gestures and pantomime, some collaboration from other witnesses in recalling the details and inevitably a little embroidery. Mothers and elders captured the interest of children with cautionary tales and parables about human nature and the natural kingdom that both instructed and amused them passing on wisdom in a form that was both pleasant and memorable. Eventually, inside any community, artists of narrative naturally would have emerged to become the shamans, sages and entertainers. Stories eventually expanded as people became spiritually sophisticated to include those about the world of gods and superhuman creatures living above earth as well as those of subhumans dwelling below—myths that explained and illustrated the origins of a people and their beliefs. Stories told in songs and rhyming verse gave rise to epic poems of warriors or sailors on brave quests, of knights and the women they loved, the dragons they fought.

With the revolution of printing techniques and the rise of literacy, narrative could be written and bound into books. The reader no longer needed to depend on a storyteller, priest or shaman for stories and information and thus, the pursuit of reading as a private pleasure was born. Stories in book form could easily travel around the world, be translated, and exchanged with those of other cultures. Stories could also exist, independent of their storytellers. In oral cultures, both singer or orator and listener shared a common reality simply because they were both present at the same place and time and shared an understanding of the world around them. Now with literacy, narratives could enjoy a kind of word-perfect immortality. Fixed on the printed page and passed down from generation to generation, they became permanent—and increasingly more detailed—records of realities that other-

Salman Rushdie has been condemned to death by Islamic fundamentalist leaders in Iran for his book *Satanic Verses*. He is seen here (centre) in Toronto with members of the Board of Directors of PEN Canada. Rushdie was the surprise guest at a PEN benefit on December 7, 1992.

wise tended to pass into oblivion or suffered alteration by the imperfect recollections and biases of those who repeated them.

The revolution of print brought the first pamphlets, forerunners of the newspaper, to the common reader, featuring short essays of fact and opinion which gave rise to longer accounts of factual experience— or experience that declared itself to be very similar to fact—like Daniel Defoe's *Robinson Crusoe*, published in serial form in 1719. There have always been people curious to know the thoughts and feelings of others and written narrative was the only art that could reveal that interior. Writing expanded into the larger picture of life called the novel and became the dominant form of literature for the next two hundred or so years—"a key that lets us into the hearts of men we have never seen and not infrequently opens our own to us," as Oscar Wilde put it.

The hearts, minds and experiences of women also found their way into printed record for the first time as women picked up pens and wrote their own stories (sometimes under a male pseudonym like Mary Ann Cross who used the name George Eliot). To think of the development of the novel is to think of the works of Jane Austen, the Bronte sisters, Virginia Woolf, Harriet Beecher Stowe, and others. Novels began, more and more, to depict the real lives of men and women.

Books are powerful symbols of freedom and truth, records of the knowledge and wisdom of people accumulated throughout time, available to anyone possessed of the skill to decipher words. Smashing the vessel that holds ideas does not, of course, destroy the ideas themselves, but throughout history the burning of books has occasionally been resorted to in times of purge and oppression and is almost universally viewed as an act of sacrilege against humanity, demoralizing to those forced to stand by and watch—from Savonarola's bonfire of the *Vanities* during the Renaissance to Krystalnacht, the infamous night of Nazi book-pyres to the *Fatwah*-incited burnings in Manhattan of Salman Rushdie's *Satanic Verses*.

Yet, the story of ourselves will survive! Narratives have been written on tiny scraps of paper and smuggled out of prisons, stuffed inside the tires of cars and driven across borders, packed into rockets and shot into space, interred with mummies in pyramids, chiselled into cliff faces and scratched into biscuit lids at the North Pole. The technology of recording and displaying narrative inevitably grows ever more sophisticated but the basic recipe—and hunger—for stories has not changed since the first account given by the first teller to the first listener.

Appetizer

Robert H. Abel

I'm fishing this beautiful stream in Alaska, catching salmon, char and steelhead, when this bear lumbers out of the woods and down to the stream bank. He fixes me with this half-amused, half-curious look which says: You are meat.

The bear's eyes are brown and his shiny golden fur is standing up in spikes, which shows me he has been fishing, too, perhaps where the stream curves behind the peninsula of woods he has just trudged through. He's not making any sound I can hear over the rumble of the water in the softball-sized rocks, but his presence is very loud.

I say "his" presence because temporarily I am not interested in or able to assess the creature's sex. I am looking at a head that is bigger around than my steering wheel, a pair of paws awash in river bubbles that could cover half my windshield. I am glad that I am wearing polarized fishing glasses so the bear cannot see the little teardrops of fear that have crept into the corner of my eyes. To assure him/her I am not the least bit intimidated, I make another cast.

Immediately I tie into a fat Chinook. The splashing of the fish in the stream engages the bear's attention, but he/she registers this for the moment only by shifting his/her glance. I play the fish smartly and when it comes gliding in, tired, pinksided, glittering and astonished, I pluck it out of the water by inserting a finger in its gill—something I normally wouldn't do in order not to injure the fish before I set it free, and I do exactly what you would do in the same situation—throw it to the bear.

The bear's eyes widen and she—for I can see now past her huge shoulder and powerful haunches that she is a she—turns and pounces on the fish with such speed and nimbleness that I am numbed. There is no chance in hell that I, in my insulated waders, am going to outrun her, dodge her blows, escape her jaws. While she is occupied devouring the fish—I can hear her teeth clacking together—I do what you or anyone else would do and cast again.

God answers my muttered prayer and I am blessed with the strike of another fat salmon, like the others on its way to spawning grounds upstream. I would like this fish to survive and release its eggs or sperm to perpetuate the salmon kingdom, but Ms. Bear has just licked her whiskers clean and has now moved knee-deep into the water and, to my consternation, leans against me rather like a large and friendly dog, although her ears are at the level of my shoulder and her back is broader than that of any horse I have ever seen. Ms. Bear is intensely interested in the progress of the salmon toward us, and her head twists and twitches as the fish circles, darts, takes line away, shakes head, rolls over, leaps.

With a bear at your side, it is not the simplest thing to play a fish properly, but the presence of this huge animal, and especially her long snout, thick as my thigh, wonderfully concentrates the mind. She smells like the forest floor, like crushed moss and damp leaves, and she is as warm as a radiator back in my Massachusetts home, the thought of which floods me with a terrible nostalgia. Now I debate whether I should just drift the salmon in under the bear's nose and let her take it that way, but I'm afraid she will break off my fly and leader and right now that fly—a Doctor Wilson number eight—is saving my life. So, with much anxiety, I pretend to take charge and bring the fish in on the side away from the bear, gill and quickly unhook it, turn away from the bear and toss the fish behind me to the bank.

The bear wheels and clambers upon it at once, leaving a vortex of water pouring into the vacuum of the space she has left, which almost topples me. As her teeth snack away, I quickly and furtively regard my poor Doctor Wilson, which is fish-mauled now, bedraggled, almost unrecognizable. But the present emergency compels me to zing it out once again. I walk a few paces downstream, hoping the bear will remember an appointment or become distracted and I can sneak away.

But a few seconds later she is leaning against me again, raptly watching the stream for any sign of a salmon splash. My luck holds, another fish smacks the withered Wilson, flings sunlight and water in silver jets as it dances its last dance. I implore the salmon's forgiveness: something I had once read revealed that this is the way of all primitive hunters, to take the life reluctantly and to pray for the victim's return. I think my prayer is as urgent as that of any Mashpee or Yoruban, or Tlingit or early Celt, for I not only want the salmon to thrive forever, I want a superabundance of them now, right now, to save my neck. I have an idea this hungry bear, bereft of fish, would waste little time in conducting any prayer ceremonies before she turned me into the main course my salmon were just the appetizer for. When I take up this fish, the bear practically rips it from my hand, and the sight of those teeth so close, and the truly persuasive power of those muscled, pink-rimmed jaws, cause a wave of fear in me so great that I nearly faint.

My vertigo subsides as Ms. Bear munches and destroys the salmon with hearty shakes of her head and I sneak a few more paces downstream, rapidly also with trembling fingers tie on a new Doctor Wilson, observing the utmost care (as you would, too) in making my knots. I cast and stride downstream, wishing I could just plunge into the crystalline water and bowl away like a log. My hope and plan is to wade my way back to the narrow trail a few hundred yards ahead and, when Ms. Bear loses interest or is somehow distracted, make a heroic dash for my camper. I think of the thermos of hot coffee on the front seat, the six-pack of beer in the cooler, the thin rubber mattress with the blue sleeping bag adorning it, warm wool socks in a bag hanging from a window crank, and almost burst into tears, these simple things, given the presence of Ms. Hungry Bear, seem so miraculous, so emblematic of the life I love to live. I promise the gods—American, Indian, African, Oriental—that if I survive I will never complain again, not even if my teenage children leave the caps off the toothpaste tubes or their bicycles in the driveway at home.

"Oh, home," I think, and cast again.

Ms. Bear rejoins me. You may or may not believe me, and perhaps after all it was only my imagination worked up by terror, but two things happened which gave me a particle of hope. The first was that Ms. Bear actually belched—quite noisily and unapologetically, too, like a rude uncle at a Christmas dinner. She showed no signs of having committed any impropriety, and yet it was clear to me that a belching bear is probably also a bear with a pretty full belly. A few more salmon and perhaps Ms. Bear would wander off in search of a berry dessert.

Now the second thing she did, or that I imagined she did, was to begin—well, not *speaking* to me exactly, but communicating somehow. I know it sounds foolish, but if you were in my shoes—my waders, to be more precise—you might have learned bear talk pretty quickly, too. It's not as if the bear were speaking to me in complete sentences and English words such as "Get me another fish, pal, or you're on the menu," but in a much more indirect and subtle way, almost in the way a stream talks through its bubbling and burbling and rattling of rocks and gurgling along.

Believe me, I listened intently, more with my mind than with my ears, as if the bear were telepathizing—I know you're not going to believe this, but it's true, I am normally not what you would call an egomaniac with an inflated self-esteem such that I imagine that every bear which walks out of the woods falls in love with me—but I really did truly believe now that this Ms. Bear was expressing feelings of, well, *affection*. Really, I think she kinda liked me. True or not, the feeling made me less afraid. In fact, and I don't mean this in any erotic or perverse kind of way but, I had to admit, once my fear had passed, my feelings were kinda mutual. Like you might feel for an old pal of a dog. Or a favourite horse. I only wish she weren't such a big eater. I only wish she were not a carnivore, and I, carne.

Now she nudges me with her nose.

"All right, all right," I say. *"I'm doing the best I can."*

Cast in the glide behind that big boulder, the bear telepathizes me. *There is a couple of whoppers in there.*

I do as I'm told and wham! the bear is right! Instantly I'm tied into a granddaddy Chinook, a really burly fellow who has no intention of lying down on anybody's platter beneath a blanket of lemon slices and scallion shoots, let alone make his last wiggle down a bear's gullet. Even the bear is excited and begins shifting weight from paw to paw, a little motion for her that nevertheless has big consequences for me as her body slams against my hip, then slams again.

Partly because I don't want to lose the fish, but partly also because I want to use the fish as an excuse to move closer to my getaway trail, I stumble downstream. This fish has my rod bent into an upside-down *U* and I'm hoping my quick-tied knots are also strong enough to take this salmon's lurching and his intelligent, broadside swinging into the river current—a very smart fish! Ordinarily I might take a long time with a fish like this, baby it in, but now I'm putting on as much pressure as I dare. When the salmon flips into a little side pool, the bear takes matters into her own hands, clambers over the rocks, pounces, nabs the salmon smartly behind the head and lumbers immediately to the bank. My leader snaps at once and while Ms. Bear attends to the destruction of the fish, I tie on another fly and make some shambling headway downstream. Yes, I worry about the hook still in the fish, but only because I do not want this bear to be irritated by anything. I want her to be replete and smug and doze off in the sun. I try to telepathize as much. Please, Bear, sleep.

Inevitably, the fishing slows down, but Ms. Bear does not seem to mind. Again she belches. Myself, I am getting quite a headache and know that I am fighting exhaustion. On a normal morning of humping along in waders over these slippery softball-sized rocks, I would be tired in any case. The added emergency is foreclosing all my energy reserves. I even find myself getting a little angry, frustrated at least, and I marvel at the bear's persistence, her inexhaustible doggedness. And appetite: I catch fish, I toss them to her. At supermarket prices, I calculate she has eaten about six hundred dollars worth of fish. The calculating gives me something to think about besides my fear.

At last I am immediately across from the opening to the trail which twines back through the woods to where my camper rests in the dapple shade of mighty pines. Still, five hundred yards separate me from this imagined haven. I entertain the notion perhaps someone else will come along and frighten the bear away, maybe someone with a dog or a gun, but I have already spent many days here without seeing another soul, and in fact have chosen to return here for that very reason. I have told myself for many years that I really do love nature, love being among the animals, am restored by wilderness adventure. Considering that right now I would like nothing better than to be nestled beside my wife in front of a blazing fire, this seems to be a sentiment in need of some revision.

Now, as if in answer to my speculations, the bear turns beside me, her rump pushing me into water deeper than I want to be in, where my footing is shaky, and she stares into the woods, ears forward. She has heard something I cannot hear, or smelled something I cannot smell, and while I labour back to shallower water and surer footing, I hope some backpackers or some bear-poaching Indians are about to appear and send Ms. Bear a-galloping away. Automatically, I continue casting, but I also cannot help glancing over my shoulder in hopes of seeing what Ms. Bear sees. And in a moment I do.

It is another bear.

Unconsciously, I release a low moan, but my voice is lost in the guttural warning of Ms. Bear to the trespasser. The new arrival answers with a defiant cough. He—I believe it is a he—can afford to be defiant because he is half again as large as my companion. His fur seems longer and coarser, and though its substance is as golden as that of the bear beside me, the tips are black and this dark surface ripples and undulates over his massive frame. His nostrils are flared and he is staring with profound concentration at me.

Now I am truly confused and afraid. Would it be better to catch another salmon or not? I surely cannot provide for two of these beasts and in any case Mister Bear does not seem the type to be distracted by or made friendly by any measly salmon tribute. His whole bearing— pardon the expression—tells me my intrusion into this bear world is a personal affront to his bear honour. Only Ms. Bear stands between us and, after all, whose side is she really on? By bear standards, I am sure a rather regal and handsome fellow has made his appearance. Why should the fur-covered heart of furry Ms. Bear go out to me? How much love can a few hundred dollars worth of salmon buy? Most likely, this couple even have a history, know and have known each other from other seasons even though for the moment they prefer to pretend to regard each other as total strangers.

How disturbed I am is well illustrated by my next course of action. It is completely irrational, and I cannot account for it, or why it saved me—if indeed it did. I cranked in my line and lay my rod across some rocks, then began the arduous process of pulling myself out of my waders while trying to balance myself on those awkward rocks in that fast water. I tipped and swayed as I tugged at my boots, pushed my waders down, my arms in the foaming, frigid water, then the waders also filling, making it even more difficult to pull my feet free.

I emerged like a nymph from a cocoon, wet and trembling. The bears regarded me with clear stupefaction, as if one of them had casually stepped out of his or her fur. I drained what water I could from the waders, then dropped my fly rod into them, and held them before me. The damned rocks were brutal on my feet, but I marched toward the trail opening, lifting and dropping first one, then the other leg of my waders as if I were operating a giant puppet. The water still in the waders gave each footfall an impressive authority, and I was half thinking that, well, if the big one attacks, maybe he'll be fooled into chomping the waders first and I'll at least now be able to run. I did not relish the idea of pounding down the trail in my nearly bare feet, but it was a damn sight better way to argue with the bear than being sucked from my waders like a snail from its shell. Would you have done differently?

Who knows what the bears thought, but I tried to make myself look as much as possible like a camel or some other extreme and inedible form of four-footedness as I plodded along the trail. The bears looked at each other, then at me as I clomped by, the water in the waders making an odd gurgling sound, and me making an odd sound, too, on remembering just then how the Indians would, staring death in the eye, sing their death song. Having no such melody prepared, and never having been anything but a bathtub singer, I chanted forth the only song I ever committed to memory: "Jingle Bells."

Yes, "Jingle Bells," I sang, "jingle all the way," and I lifted first one, then the other wader leg and dropped it stomping down. "Oh what fun it is to ride in a one-horse open sleigh-ay!"

The exercise was to prove to me just how complicated and various is the nature of the bear. The male reared up, blotting out the sun, bellowed, then twisted on his haunches and crashed off into the woods. The female, head cocked in curiosity, followed at a slight distance, within what still might be called striking distance whether I was out of my waders or not. Truly, I did not appreciate her persistence. Hauling the waders half full of water before me was trying work and the superfluous thought struck me: suppose someone sees me now, plumping along like this, singing "Jingle Bells," a bear in attendance? Vanity, obviously, never sleeps. But as long as the bear kept her distance I saw no reason to change my *modus operandi*.

When I came within about one hundred feet of my camper, its white cap gleaming like a remnant of spring snow and beckoning me, I risked everything, dropped the waders and sped for the cab. The bear broke into a trot, too, I was sure, because although I couldn't see her, had my sights locked on the gleaming handle to the pickup door, I sure enough could hear those big feet slapping the ground behind me in a heavy rhythm, a terrible and elemental beat that sang to me of my own frailty, fragile bones and tender flesh. I plunged on like a madman, grabbed the camper door and hurled myself in.

I lay on the seat panting, curled like a child, shuddered when the bear slammed against the pickup's side. The bear pressed her nose to the window, then curiously, unceremoniously licked the glass with her tongue. I know (and you know) she could have shattered the glass with a single blow, and I tried to imagine what I should do if indeed she resorted to this simple expedient. Fisherman that I am, I had nothing in the cab of the truck to defend myself with except a tire iron, and that not readily accessible behind the seat I was cowering on. My best defense, obviously, was to start the pickup and drive away.

Just as I sat up to the steering wheel and inserted the key, however, Ms. Bear slammed her big paws on to the hood and hoisted herself aboard. The pickup shuddered with the weight of her, and suddenly the windshield was full of her golden fur. I beeped the horn loud and long numerous times, but this had about the same effect as my singing, only causing her to shake her huge head, which vibrated the truck terribly. She stomped around on the hood and then lay down, back against the windshield, which now appeared to have been covered by a huge shag rug.

Could I believe my eyes?

No, I could not believe my eyes. My truck was being smothered in bear. In a moment I also could not believe my ears—Ms. Bear had decided the camper hood was the perfect place for a nap, and she was snoring, snoring profoundly, her body twitching like a cat's. Finally, she had responded to my advice and desires, but at the most inappropriate time. I was trapped. Blinded by bear body!

My exhaustion had been doubled by my sprint for the camper, and now that I was not in such a desperate panic, I felt the cold of the water that had soaked my clothes and I began to tremble. It also crossed my mind that perhaps Mister Bear was still in the vicinity, and if Ms. Bear was not smart enough, or cruel enough, to smash my window to get at me, he just might be.

Therefore, I started the engine—which disturbed Ms. Bear not a whit—and rolled down the window enough to stick my head out and see down the rocky, limb-strewn trail. I figured a few jolts in those ruts and Ms. Bear would be off like a shot.

This proved a smug assumption. Ms. Bear did indeed awaken and bestir herself to a sitting position, a bit like an overgrown hood ornament, but quickly grew quite adept at balancing herself against the lurching and jolting of my truck, which, in fact, she seemed to enjoy. Just my luck, I growled, to find the first bear in Alaska who wanted a ride into town. I tried some quick braking and sharp turn maneuvers I thought might send her tumbling off, but her bulk was so massive, her paws so artfully spread, that she was just too stable an entity. She wanted a ride and there was nothing I could do about it.

When I came out of the woods to the gravel road known locally as the Dawson Artery, I had an inspiration. I didn't drive so fast that if Ms. Bear decided to clamber down she would be hurt, but I did head for the main road which led to Buckville and the Buckville Cannery. Ms. Bear swayed happily along the whole ten miles to that intersection and seemed not to bat an eye when first one big logging truck, then another plummeted by. I pulled out onto the highway, and for the safety of both of us—those logging trucks have dubious brakes and their drivers get paid by the trip—I had to accelerate considerably.

I couldn't see much of Ms. Bear except her back and rump as I had to concentrate on the road, some of which is pretty curvy in that coastal area, shadowed also by the giant pines. But from the attitude expressed by her posture, I'd say she was having a whale, or should I say a salmon, of a time. I saw a few cars and pickups veering out of the oncoming lane onto the shoulder as we swept by, but I didn't have time, really, to appreciate the astonishment of their drivers. In this way, my head out the window, Ms. Bear perched on the hood, I drove to the Buckville Cannery and turned into the long driveway.

Ms. Bear knew right away something good was ahead for she rose on all fours now and stuck her nose straight out like a bird dog on a pheasant. Her legs quivered with nervous anticipation as we approached, and as soon as I came out of the trees into the parking area, she went over the front of the camper like someone plunging into a pool.

Don't tell me you would have done any differently. I stopped right there and watched Ms. Bear march down between the rows of cars and right up the truck ramp into the cannery itself. She was not the least bit intimidated by all the noise of the machines and the grinders and stampers in there, or the shouting of the workers.

Now the Buckville Cannery isn't that big—I imagine about two dozen people work there on any given day—and since it is so remote, has no hurricane fence around it, and no security guard. After all, what's anybody going to steal out of there besides a few cases of canned salmon or some bags of frozen fish parts that will soon become some company's cat food? The main building is up on a little hill and conveyors run down from there to the docks where the salmon boats pull in—the sea is another half mile away—and unload their catch.

I would say that in about three minutes after Ms. Bear walked into the cannery, twenty of the twenty-four workers were climbing out down the conveyors, dropping from open windows, or charging out the doors. The other four just hadn't got wind of the event yet, but in a little while they came bounding out, too, one fellow pulling up his trousers as he ran. They all assembled on the semicircular drive before the main office and had a union meeting of some vigor.

Myself, I was too tired to participate, and in any case did not want to be held liable for the disturbance at the Buckville Cannery, and so I made a U-turn and drove on into Buckville itself where I took a room above the Buckville Tavern and had a hot shower and a really nice nap. That night in the Tap and Lounge I got to hear many an excited story about the she-bear who freeloaded at the cannery for a couple of hours before she was driven off by blowing, ironically enough, the lunch whistle loud and long. I didn't think it was the right time or place to testify to my part in that historical event, and for once kept my mouth shut. You don't like trouble any more than I do, and I'm sure you would have done about the same.

Self-Portrait, Van Gogh (1853-90)

Objective vs. Subjective Responses to Art

The whole of art is an appeal to a reality which is not without us but in our minds.

Desmond MacCarthy

Art is ruled uniquely by the imagination. Images are its only wealth. It does not classify objects, it does not pronounce them real or imaginary, does not qualify them, does not define them; it feels and presents them—nothing more.

Benedetto Croce

A work of art has no importance whatever to society. It is only important to the individual, and only the individual reader is important to me.

Vladimir Nabokov

Art is the imposing of a pattern on experience, and our aesthetic enjoyment is recognition of the pattern.

Alfred North Whitehead

Objectivity and Subjectivity

Clive Cockerton

When we attempt to choose a movie for Saturday night, we might begin by poring over the newspaper, scanning the listings, reading the reviews. We might weigh and balance the fact that Costner is "one prince of a thief" in *Robin Hood*, whereas Anthony Hopkins' performance is "chilling and brilliant" in *Silence of the Lambs. Jungle Fever* is mercilessly funny while *Thelma and Louise* is one of the best films of the year. This film is an "absolute delight," that film is "irresistible," this one "touching and sensitive." Choices, choices. How does one sort the good from the bad from such a list? Add to the questions of the intrinsic worth of the film the problem of the individual's mood. Sometimes "touching and sensitive" just doesn't stand a chance against "frivolous and fun."

In fact, most of the decisions regarding choosing a film are subjective. After all, how can one effectively compare a musical to a thriller except on the basis of how one feels at the moment? In choosing a film we make decisions based on content that is suitable to our mood and a faith that the form of the film will measure up to its content. Once we have seen the film, however, we usually wish to weigh the success of our choice. Our conclusions usually fall into two categories:

1. "I really like the film because … "
2. "That is a good film because … "

These statements are really very different from each other, with the first statement recording a subjective preference while the second attempts an objective evaluation. Preference tends to be more content-oriented as in "I really liked the ending," or "It was a great love story," while attempts to prove the worth of the film tend to be more form-oriented as in, "The photography was beautiful" or "The pace was exciting."

For most of us, whether or not we like a film is much more important than whether the film is any good. As well, it is clearly possible to like a film we know we cannot defend as a good film. Our preference may be formed because of the presence of a favourite actor, a locale such as Africa or New York that fascinates us, or moments such as steamy love scenes or violent car chases that we find irresistible. The presence of these elements in no way forms a criterion for excellence, and the absence of these elements does not indicate a bad film. Indeed, our preference for these elements declares a lot about ourselves and our own feelings but says virtually nothing about the film. As well, it is quite possible to dislike a film that we know to fulfill all the requirements of a good film, again for strictly personal reasons such as the fact that the film reminds us of unpleasant or painful moments in our own lives.

Although there is clearly no possibility of argument or contradiction about personal feelings on an art object (they just simply are what they are), it is also clear that we can change our minds about works of art. A painting can look shapeless and disorganized to us until someone more expert reveals a previously overlooked organizing principle. A novel can sometimes seem obscure and difficult until we become familiar with its language and world view. We might condemn a film as confusing and subsequently read an interview with the director where he states that he wants his audience to feel confused. If the film achieves its aim, how can we condemn it? These examples happen frequently and point to the fact that proper artistic evaluation is more than just a subjective statement about our perspective at the moment. It is not simply a case of thinking one thing on Monday and another on Friday. We replace the first view with the second because we think that the second view more accurately and objectively describes the art. It is as if at first glance we perceive a frog, but after consultation with experts we begin to discern the prince hiding within. Of course, there are many more frogs than princes, and we are more frequently deceived by art works that initially seem good but over time don't stand up to close examination.

Experts attempt to engage our minds in the task of analyzing the aesthetic emotion. They teach us to analyze the art work, to look separately at its elements, and to establish standards or criteria to evaluate the elements. The use of this largely mental process can help us to understand more about the art work independent from our own subjective bias. Aristotle identified three criteria based on his study of Greek poetry and drama: unity, clarity, and integrity. Unity (of mood, of time and place among others) as a criterion didn't have the longevity of the other two: Aristotle couldn't anticipate the successful mixing of comic and tragic mood that would take place in Shakespeare's plays and other later works. However, clarity of expression seems as useful a standard by which to judge as any. Integrity, in the relationship of the parts of the play/poem to the whole and in the relationship of the whole to reality, forms the basis of much critical judgment. If we substitute simplicity of design, or perhaps more appropriately, focus for the concept of unity, we have a starting point in our discussions of criteria.

However, in our search for objective criteria by which to judge art objects, it must be admitted that no criteria work universally for all art objects. We praise the playful fantasy in the paintings of Henri Rousseau yet we do not condemn the paintings of Eduoard Munch for lacking that quality; indeed we praise Munch for his graphic rendering of inner torment. We appreciate one novel's realistic depiction of character and delight in another's cartoon-like parodies. We appreciate the grim honesty of films like *Full Metal Jacket* and at the same time are charmed by the simple beauty of films like *The Black Stallion*. Yet on occasion films displaying "simple beauty" or "grim honesty" lack other qualities and we find them unsatisfactory. The fact that no one criterion or element guarantees a work's value makes the job of appraisal that much more difficult. One thing is clear: on different occasions we judge by different criteria. Moreover, the skilled and open-minded consumer of art lets the individual work of art dictate by which criteria it is to be judged.

Some contemporary critics suggest that in a modern consumer society we are so overwhelmed with artistic experiences and images that the task of sorting them into piles of good and bad is a hopeless one. These critics see a rough equality of banality in all objects, and find that wit and beauty come from the perspective of the audience, and are not necessarily contained in the art. It is how you see a TV program, for instance, not the TV program itself that makes the experience lively and intelligent or dull and stupid. Some of these critics would go so far as to say that a book has no meaning by itself, that an unread book is a vacuum, and that the reader is the one who provides the meaning. Since every reader's experience is shaped by their gender, their class and cultural background, there can be no universal objective meaning, only a collection of diverse and subjective impressions. As one recent critic, Frank Lentricchia, has written of his relationship to literature:

> I come to the text with specific hangups, obsessions, worries, and I remake the text, in a sense, for me, for my times. ... The moment you start talking about it, you have injected interpretation. The text is not speaking; you are speaking for the text. You activate the text.

Still other critics focus on the possibility of consensus (among informed observers) operating as a kind of objectivity. This agreement by experts operates as a kind of "rough guide" to truth. However, these "agreements

Nighthawks, 1942,
Edward Hopper
(1882-1967).

by experts" do not always have the shelf life that one would expect. It is clear that some art work does not seem to travel well from one historical period to the next. The novels of Sir Walter Scott (*Ivanhoe, The Heart of Midlothian*) were extremely popular in the nineteenth century, and are hardly read today. In our own twentieth century, the literary reputation of Ernest Hemingway was extraordinarily high in the '20s and '30s but today Hemingway is more often seen as an interesting but minor writer.

One historical period may form an aesthetic preference for certain artistic qualities, preferring, for instance, clean and simple elegance to the previous generation's taste for exuberant and stylized decoration. When watching old films on television, we can be initially struck by what now seems bizarre fashion and style. Our experience of these films can be even more seriously undermined by outmoded attitudes, particularly sexist and racist ones. Everything that has happened to form our present consciousness stands as an obstacle to the appreciation of these films.

Even within an historical period critics sometimes disagree about the value of an individual work. Recently, films such as *The Prince of Tides, Pretty Woman,* and *Gandhi* have received very diverse reviews. All the critics may agree for instance, that pace in editing and structure is a very important element in a film's success. They may all agree that pace is a problem in a film such as *Gandhi.* But some critics will find that the other elements of the film compensate for the weakness in pace and will give the film an overall high evaluation. Some of the disagreement can be explained by the fact that, despite agreement *in theory* on the importance of pace, *in practice* many critics habitually weigh some criteria more than others. Therefore those critics who regard editing as the most essential creative act in film will habitually favour films that possess skilful editing in spite of other problems that may exist in the film. Other critics may habitually value elements of script, acting or cinematography more highly than editing and refuse to accept that the obvious virtues in editing make up for the perceived weakness in acting. When a preference is habitual, we can be pretty sure that its origin is rooted deeply in our own personality and experience.

In spite of the effort of art critics to focus on the art rather than themselves, to analyze and evaluate the elements of art rather than narrate and describe their own experiences, it remains obvious that elements of personality can't always be overcome or transcended. Perhaps the relationship between art and our experience of art is circular. The more we possess the inner experience, the more we grow curious about that external art object. The more we learn about art, the more we learn about what makes us who we are. That moment on Saturday night when the theatre goes dark, we watch the slowly brightening screen and wonder what this film world will be like. At the end of the film, if we have been moved by the film, the natural instinct is to be quiet, to digest our own experience before surfacing to the workaday world. But watching movies is a social activity, and it's irresistible to turn to our friends and ask "What do you think? Wasn't it good? I really liked the part where …" We share our delight, and we compare experiences. Our view becomes larger.

* * *

Ultimately, the question is much larger than whether our statements about art are objective or not. The question applies not only to art. It's about the world. It's just that art is a convenient place to begin the argument. If we cannot agree on the meaning of a single art object, with its known borders, its beginning, middle and end, with its human author, how can we make statements about a limitless universe—a universe not divided into neat stages of development, ending in closure, but a universe (caused/uncaused) constantly evolving, stretching out to infinity and a universe whose author is either unknown or not available to interview.

Is the external world totally independent of us or as the Greek philosopher Protagoras held, is it us, and our perceptions that are the measure of all things? Even if we grant the existence of the external world, it doesn't seem possible to get beyond our perceptions of it. Scientists have their protocol, the scientific method, that is meant to banish subjective interpretation. In the search for the underlying principles of things as they are (remember Tom Olien's article), science took over from religion the chief role of establishing truth. And what a magnificent job science has done. In revealing the structure of sub-atomic particles, in predicting the location and timing of an earthquake or volcano, in isolating a deadly virus and developing vaccines and in improving the quality of life for millions, science can lay claim to being humanity's most successful enterprise.

Think of the surgeon holding a human heart in his or her hands, repairing a faulty valve and placing it back into the person's chest, giving them twenty years more of life. All of the knowledge, the complex theory and practical skill that go into a successful operation rest on a physician's informed judgment that an operation is called for. That judgment is fallible, as are all human judgments. For the history of science is full of examples of misreadings, of scientists finding only what they were looking for, and not finding what they weren't, of finding solutions to problems that not only fit the hypothesis but also the prevailing ideology. Ultimately, scientists too must depend on their very fallible senses (or their high tech extensions) to draw conclusions. As well the role of the scientist confers no immunity to normal human pressures, the ego needs, the economic necessity to succeed, the political compulsion to research in certain directions. Scientists may be the most objective amongst us, but even in this highly trained class of people, subjective considerations colour many perceptions.

The truth about the world, the final objective Truth, is getting harder to find, yet meaning, subjective meaning is everywhere. A single rational explanation for the universe and all it contains may no longer be possible. Our knowledge (scientific and otherwise) has grown and grown until it has reached a point beyond where any one individual can comprehend the whole. To see the whole domain of our knowledge we need to climb a very high mountain; we haven't found the mountain yet (although on several occasions we thought we had) and are beginning to doubt if it exists.

Instead of the overview from the mountain, what we have is the micro-view of the specialist. What we have are fragments of the whole, knowledge and insight from the physicist, the philosopher, the biologist, the historian, the psychologist, the literary critic, the political economist. The fragments don't cohere into one magnificent interpretation of the universe. They exist as beams of light that illuminate the darkness for a certain time, as probes that reveal something about the world, and as a point of view.

We both rely on and are suspicious of experts. We rely on them, for their fragmentary understanding of the world is the best insight that we've got. But in a deeper sense we know them to be fallible. No political thinker predicted the collapse of communism in Eastern Europe, yet we continue to tune into the TV to hear what they have to say. Young parents read everything they can get their hands on about child rearing, yet are highly selective in what ideas they apply to their own children. We may listen with interest to the reasoned arguments of the nuclear power experts, but when they tell us that we have nothing to fear the shadow of Chernobyl falls over the discussion.

Every discipline of study is currently racked with conflict, with dissenting voices. If even the experts can't agree, are the rest of us just gambling on what and who we choose to believe? It becomes so difficult to judge the worth of arguments that quickly threaten to go beyond our expertise. The difficulty causes many of us to give up the task of sifting through the ideas, adopting instead a weary and cynical assumption that all views are equal. Many of us come from school systems that value self-expression as the highest good. It doesn't so much matter what gets expressed (all views are roughly equal anyway); just so long as a view gets expressed, the system will applaud. This emphasis involves a radical turning away from the searching after truth that has so long inspired our education. If there's no truth to search for, why struggle so hard?

If there's no truth, then what we have left is competing views, subjective perceptions. My view becomes as valuable as yours because there's no way to successfully weigh and measure them against each other. On the surface, there's an increase in tolerance as we all recognize that what may be true for me may not be true for you. But beneath the surface lurks the urge for dominance, the recognition that the prevailing view belongs to the loudest, most powerful voice.

And so we have the competition of interests and perspectives: Quebec, the West, free trade, feminists, unionists, native peoples, blacks, environmentalists. The competition is healthy, the diversity of views enriching. But without truth as a goal, the contest of ideas has no referee; it's too easy for reason to become a weapon to beat your opponent, not a tool to dig for understanding. Still, we're in the middle of a huge process in our relationship to the world and each other. If fragmentation into competing perspectives and specialized bits of knowledge is the current mode, perhaps all we need to do is wait for the emergence of new and better ideas that might reconcile some of the conflicts and satisfy our yearning for something to believe in. The competition of ideas has been evident throughout this text: are we free or determined in Unit One; what changes and what remains the same in Unit Two; do we have the sense to co-operate with each other or are we doomed to conflict in Unit Three; can science provide the solutions to the problems it creates in Unit Four? Do we have to make a choice? Do we have to run to the comfort of certainty? Or do we have to learn to love the paradox—to see in contradiction the breathing in, the breathing out of ideas?

The arts, particularly narrative arts such as film and the novel, may have a role to play in helping us to reconcile apparent contradiction. By successfully creating a fictional world that re-creates the real world, the author/artist sets artificial boundaries to what is included in the story, how many characters, subplots and themes. Fictionalizing the world tells us everything we need to know; the author/artist creates a vision of life that is remarkable in its completeness. The sharing of this vision creates a sense of community between artist and audience and holds out the possibility of consensus. We are not alone; others see the same world, sometimes with great clarity and undeniable insight. It's as if the film or novel creates a fictional mountain, from which we can finally see the human truth stretched out below, in all its complexity and contradiction. It is just a glimpse, but reassuring. In the midst of the darkest night-time thunderstorm, the lightning can suddenly illuminate our world in a flash of brilliant light, letting us know that the world is still there, under the cover of darkness.

The Search for Form

Clive Cockerton

It is clear that the Canadian government, through its body of experts, believes that objective evaluations can be made about works of art and about what they can contribute to a culture. The experts reward the good art with government money and discourage the bad by withholding funding. Each of the experts from the different artistic areas brings criteria drawn from years of experience to judging art. As well as the criteria for good art, they also bring some sense of what might contribute to the broader Canadian culture, what might serve as Canadian cultural self-expression. The problem occurs when certain themes or styles become identified as officially Canadian, that is, promoting a standardized Canadian vision. It has been frequently said that our best Canadian film director, David Cronenberg, seems somehow un-Canadian. His stories of sophisticated people in urban settings confronted with physical horrors don't address the "official" themes of Canadian culture. His films may be about victims, but they are not victims of the cold or of loneliness. They do not endure long and hard trials; rather, they explode in intense and horrific ways. How un-Canadian. Yet he is a director who has lived all his life in Toronto and who has made all his films in Canada. If he is not Canadian, it is because we have an overly rigid expectation of what constitutes a Canadian vision. Organizations like the Canada Council naturally tend to promote works that express a coherent view of ourselves, but this coherence can sometimes become conformity, conformity to an official version of ourselves.

More fundamentally, many people have difficulty accepting the notion that a body of experts can come to valid conclusions about works of art. We can probably all recall moments when a teacher seemed to drone on about the monumental significance of a short story that made us ache with boredom, or the deeper levels of meaning in a poem whose message totally eluded us. It is always right to be skeptical about the experts, but our challenges to authority should also be matched by a willingness to apply the rules of evidence to any work

Some people make an appreciation of the arts a serious commitment.

of art. Just as we must always question the officially proclaimed ideas, we must also discover that some work is simply better than others.

Take the following two sentences, containing roughly the same content, and try to rank them according to merit.

Version 1: Generally speaking, there are a lot more unhappy moments in life than there are happy ones.

Version 2: Happiness was but an occasional episode in a general drama of pain.

As subjectively attached as I am to Version 1 (I wrote it), it must be admitted that while it has a conversational matter-of-fact quality about its grim message, it lacks the complexity and power of Version 2. When we look at Version 2, we notice the precision of the language and the tightness of the structure. Notice how key words are twinned to heighten the contrast: occasional and general, episode and drama, and, most importantly, happiness and pain beginning and ending the sentence. You might also notice that the sounds of the first half of the sentence are softly melancholic, while the second half has a leaden heaviness and finality. No doubt about it, once you examine closely, it is easy to see that in Version 2 the content has found its clearest and most forceful expression.

Let's look at two versions of another grim sentiment.

Version A: Days go by one after the other in a monotonous way. This trivial parade of time ends in death. Life doesn't mean anything; it is just full of noise and anger, ultimately meaningless.

Version B: Tomorrow and tomorrow and tomorrow creep in this petty pace from day to day, lighting the way for fools to dusty death. Life is a tale told by an idiot, full of sound and fury, signifying nothing.

Version B is probably the most famous statement of thoroughgoing pessimism in the English language. It is full of wonderful images, days lighting the passage to ultimate darkness, the ranting idiot's tale, while Version A will never be read anywhere beyond these pages, and even then quickly forgotten.

In literary terms, having the right (write) stuff has its base in the author's ability to create magical effects with language. These effects can be achieved through precise use of words, through an ability to manipulate the sound and rhythm of language, and through an ability to create haunting images.

Look at the following paragraph and notice how it begins in relaxed but precise observation of an ordinary occurrence. Where and how does it turn into something monstrous?

Four men were at the table next to mine. Their collars were open, their ties loose, and their jackets hung on the wall. One man poured dressing on the salad, another tossed the leaves. Another filled the plates and served. One tore bread, another poured wine, another ladled soup. The table was small and square. The men were cramped, but efficient nonetheless, apparently practised at eating here, this way, hunched over food, heads striking to suck at spoons, tear at forks, then pulling back into studious, invincible mastication. Their lower faces slid and chopped; they didn't talk once. All their eyes, like birds on a wire, perched on a horizontal line above the action. Swallowing muscles flickered in jaws and necks. Had I touched a shoulder and asked for the time, there would have been snarling, a flash of teeth.

D. H. Lawrence in his novel, *The Rainbow*, wrote the following description of horses bunching around a woman walking in the fields. The woman has broken off with her fiancé and has subsequently discovered that she is pregnant. She walks the fields in extreme anguish when she confronts a herd of horses.

But the horses had burst before her. In a sort of lightning of knowledge their movement travelled through her, the quiver and strain and thrust of their powerful flanks, as they burst before her and drew on, beyond.

She knew they had not gone, she knew they awaited her still. But she went on over the log bridge that their hoofs had churned and drummed, she went on, knowing things about them. She was aware of their breasts gripped, clenched narrow in a hold that never relaxed, she was aware of their red nostrils flaming with long endurance, and of their haunches, so rounded, so massive, pressing, pressing, pressing to burst the grip upon their breasts, pressing forever till they went mad, running against the walls of time, and never bursting free. Their great haunches were smoothed and darkened with rain. But the darkness and wetness of rain could not put out the hard, urgent, massive fire that was locked within these flanks, never, never.

She went on, drawing near. She was aware of the great flash of hoofs, a bluish, iridescent flash surrounding a hollow of darkness. Large, large seemed the bluish, incandescent flash of the hoof-iron, large as a halo of lightning round the knotted darkness of the flanks. Like circles of lightning came the flash of hoofs from out of the powerful flanks.

Why the horses seem menacing is mysterious, but we're sure that we're seeing them with the eyes of the Ursula, the heroine. Literature can often startle us with this kind of experience, with being inside the head of another (if fictional) person. But it's the *form* of the language that opens the door to this experience.

Michael Herr, in his book *Dispatches*, a chronicle of the Vietnam war, attempts to capture the emotional texture of combat in this paragraph.

Fear and motion, fear and standstill, no preferred cut there, no way even to be clear about which was really worse, the wait or the delivery. Combat spared far more men than it wasted, but everyone suffered the time between contact, especially when they were going out every day looking for it; bad going on foot, terrible in trucks and APC's, awful in helicopters, the worst, travelling so fast toward something so frightening. I can remember times when I went half dead with my fear of the motion, the speed and direction already fixed and pointed one way. It was painful enough just flying "safe" hops between firebases and lz's; if you were ever on a helicopter that had been hit by ground fire your deep, perpetual chopper anxiety was guaranteed. At least actual contact when it was happening would draw long ragged strands of energy out of you, it was juicy, fast and refining, and travelling toward it was hollow, dry, cold and steady, it never let you alone. All you could do was look around at the other people on board and see if they were as scared and numbed out as you were. If it looked like they weren't you thought they were insane, if it looked like they were it made you feel a lot worse.

This is a writer writing at the top of his game, taking the reader on a roller-coaster ride, using his craft to capture the subtle ways terror can grip.

•

There is a deep satisfaction that comes from an appreciation of form. An arrangement of words, images, colours or notes can illuminate a moment, create powerful emotion, and so change our perceptions that we never look at life or art in quite the same way again. Art can be more than form, and to be sure it can be full of ideas, archetypes and moral discriminations. But while it can be more than form, without form it is nothing; it loses its magical hold on us.

Outside of the realm of art, that perfect arrangement is harder to find in human relationships. Many of us find a sense of energy and harmony in nature, and discover a solace in contemplation of the beauties of nature. Perhaps this respect for nature explains our sense of the violation we experience when confronted with massive pollution, and explains why acid rain, the lead in the air, the depletion of ozone, the poisoning of our water, seem obscene. We have become so sensitive to this tampering with natural form that intentional pollution with toxic substances is now considered a criminal and not merely a civil offense. Companies such as Exxon become associated in the public mind with ecological disaster and do so at their peril. The public's tolerance of irresponsible and negligent behaviour on the part of private companies is slowly becoming a thing of the past, and the so-called "green movement" is emerging as a powerful political force.

In Unit IV Tom Olien talked of the search for an underlying principle as the great creative urge of scientists. Toby Fletcher's article in Unit III looks for a new world order to deal with global problems.

> When we transcend sovereign nation thinking, we become citizens of the world. Global interdependence requires new definitions. Our personal and national interests can only be served through a more sophisticated, cooperative and collaborative relationship among nations.

Clearly, this relationship among nations can only be achieved by providing the institutions (the form) which will guarantee enough safety and security for sovereign nations to surrender some portion of their power to a world body.

This global view is evidenced in the way we look far beyond our national borders, the way we appreciate the inter-connectedness of nations. We listen with keen interest to reports from the former Soviet Union hoping for a better life for the average Russian and a more secure future for us all. If we accept the good things of interdependence, however, it is also true that we feel more keenly the tragic disappointment of hopes in China, as the tanks and boots of the army attempt to crush the democratic spirit of the young students. It is an event that takes place far away, yet it touches us because we share the same urge for freedom as the Chinese students—our freedom already won, theirs in the process of a fierce and bloody struggle with a repressive government.

Whenever new ideas clash with an existing form, there is some dislocation, something lost as well as gained. Unit II of this text looked at what happens when the old values are challenged by new technologies and new ideas. People cannot see what is happening to them and vainly try to deny the impact of the change. Some societies can be aware of the process of change in varying degrees, but the task of integrating new forms with old always challenges our best efforts.

Finally, it is in our own lives that form has the greatest significance, as we attempt to find shape and meaning in the daily flow of our existence. The facts, the contents of our lives, are distressingly similar, as a comparative glance at any number of résumés shows. We are born, go to school, make friends, take part-time jobs, go to college and then on to a career. Along the way, we may form romantic attachments, get married, have children, grow older, watch children leave us, retire from our jobs and grow older still. But this sameness doesn't tell the whole story. As the old jazz lyric goes: "It ain't what you do, but how you do it." Some people's lives are tragic, while others with the same observable facts seem heroic. After we bury some people, all we can hear, after our own tears subside, is the sound of their laughter. What makes this life comic and that life pathetic? Clearly, it has something to do with perception, the perception of the individual who lives it as he or she contemplates the moment and discovers the pattern in the flow of daily experience. These moments of perception are often struggled for, but sustain the idea of a conscious life. To be conscious, to understand what is happening to you, and to others, here and now, is a large part of the urgency and energy of human life.

DON'T
DREAM IT
BE IT

THINKING AND WRITING SKILLS

Humanities is concerned with the issues and topics that have preoccupied humankind throughout history. Because of the complexity of the issues, clarity of thought and expression are essential. It is obvious that certain thoughts require high levels of skill in language. The development of these high-level skills is achieved more efficiently when we attempt to grapple with challenging content. It is the purpose of this course to offer such content and to help the student develop the skills necessary to express his or her own thoughts about the content.

The following skills section will help you be more precise in your use of terminology and assist you in performing essential thinking and writing tasks such as summary, comparison and contrast, and evaluation.

Definition of Terms Used in Essay Examinations

Don Holmes

* The seven most often used.

*COMPARE When you are asked to compare, you should examine qualities, or characteristics, in order to discover resemblance. The term *compare* is usually stated as *compare with*, and it implies that you are to emphasize similarities, although differences may be mentioned.

*CONTRAST When you are instructed to contrast, dissimilarities, differences, or unlikenesses of associated things, qualities, events or problems should be stressed.

*CRITICIZE In a criticism you should express your judgment with respect to the correctness or merit of the factors under consideration. You are expected to give the results of your own analysis and to discuss the limitations as well as the good points or contributions of the plan or work in question.

*DEFINE Definitions call for concise, clear, authoritative meanings. In such statements details are not required, but boundaries or limitations of the definition should be briefly cited. You must keep in mind the class to which a thing belongs and whatever differentiates the particular object from all others in the class.

*DESCRIBE In a descriptive answer, you should recount, characterize, sketch, or relate in narrative form.

DIAGRAM For a question which specifies a diagram, you should present a drawing, chart, plan, or graphic representation in your answer. Generally the student is also expected to label the diagram and in some cases to add a brief explanation or description.

*DISCUSS The term *discuss*, which appears often in essay questions, directs you to examine, analyze carefully, and present considerations pro and con regarding the problems or items involved. This type of question calls for a complete and detailed answer.

ENUMERATE The word *enumerate* specifies a list or outline form of reply. In such questions, you should recount, one by one, in concise form, the points required.

EVALUATE In an evaluation question, you are expected to present a careful appraisal of the problem, stressing both advantages and limitations. Evaluation implies authoritative and, to a lesser degree, personal appraisal of both contributions and limitations.

EXPLAIN In explanatory answers, it is imperative that you clarify, elucidate, and interpret the material you present. In such an answer, it is best to state the "how" or "why," reconcile any differences in opinion or experimental results, and where possible, state causes. The aim is to make plain the conditions which give rise to whatever you are examining.

ILLUSTRATE A question which asks you to illustrate usually requires you to explain or clarify your answer to the problem by presenting a figure, picture, or concrete example.

INTERPRET An interpretation question is similar to one requiring explanation. You are expected to translate, exemplify, solve, or comment upon the subject and usually to give your judgment or reaction to the problem.

JUSTIFY When you are instructed to justify your answer, you must prove or show grounds for decisions. In such an answer, evidence should be presented in convincing form.

*LIST Listing is similar to enumeration. You are expected in such questions to present an itemized series or a tabulation. Such answers should always be given in concise form.

OUTLINE An outlined answer is organized description. You should give main points and essential supplementary materials, omitting minor details, and present the information in a systematic arrangement or classification.

PROVE A question which requires proof is one which demands confirmation or verification. In such discussions, you should establish something with certainty by evaluating and citing experimental evidence or by logical reasoning.

RELATE In a question which asks you to show the relationship or to *relate,* your answer would emphasize connections and associations in descriptive form.

REVIEW A review specifies a critical examination. You should analyze and comment briefly in organized sequence upon the major points of the problem.

STATE In questions which direct you to specify, give, state, or present, you are called upon to express the high points in brief, clear narrative form. Details, and usually illustrations or examples, may be omitted.

SUMMARIZE When you are asked to summarize or present a summary, you should give in condensed form the main points or facts. All details, illustrations, and elaborations are to be omitted.

TRACE When a question asks you to trace a course of events, you are to give a description of progress, historical sequence, or development from the point of origin. Such narratives may call for probing or for deductions.

ANALYZE To analyze means to find the main ideas and show how they are related and why they are important.

COMMENT ON To comment on a problem or topic means to discuss, criticize, or explain its meaning as completely as possible.

Reading *Humanities*

Barbara Ritchie

You're probably wondering about the title of this article. Why is there a section on reading? You know how to read; you've been doing it since you were six or seven. So what's so special about reading the *Humanities* text?

Well, as you have no doubt discovered by now, reading a college text is very different from the reading you did in high school or the reading you do when you are relaxing with a favourite novel or the sports page. The articles in your *Humanities* text (and in virtually all your other college courses) are more challenging, more factually dense, and yes, more difficult than the kinds of articles you have probably encountered before. If you are like the majority of students, you will benefit by using specific study reading strategies to improve your comprehension and retention skills.

Keep in mind that the selections in your *Humanities* text cover a wide range of topics and are written in a variety of styles. Naturally you will be more interested in some than others, and just as naturally you will probably find you have little or no difficulty comprehending those articles that deal with topics you are interested in and already know something about. For example, students interested in relationships will enjoy Wendy O'Brien-Ewara's article on "The Gender Dance" while those whose interest is of a more scientific or technological bent will no doubt be intrigued with "Acid Raid" by Michael Badyk. We think the selections in the *Humanities* text are of high interest and, for the most part, are highly readable. However, we would like to present some strategies you can use to make your reading more effective and efficient.

Before you begin your first *Humanities* reading assignment, take a few minutes to preview the entire text. This will give you a sense of the purpose and organization not only of the text, but of the course. By glancing at the table of contents, you will see that the Appendix of the *Humanities* text is devoted to the skills you will need to demonstrate in order to be successful in the course. This is a good section to refer to before you write a test or an essay since it not only provides definitions of terms commonly used in testing situations, but it also includes specific examples of how to set up essay-type questions.

Further perusal of the table of contents will show you that the *Humanities* text is divided into five units and each unit is subdivided into two issues. Flipping through the pages at random will also aid you in your endeavour to get a general sense of the organization of the text—you will note, for example, that some of the articles are followed by questions helpful to you in your studying.

Once you have previewed the text, you are ready to begin your first reading assignment. When you are reading for studying purposes (and basically most of the reading you do in college is of this kind: reading you will be tested on), it is often helpful to approach the assignment with specific steps to take *before you read, while you are reading,* and *after you have completed your reading.*

BEFORE YOU READ

You would not attempt to run a marathon or play a championship game of tennis without first warming up your body; if you were a good enough athlete you might be able to complete these tasks, but it stands to reason you would not be as effective at either if you did not properly prepare your body for the task at hand. In the same way, it is necessary to warm up your brain for the equally challenging mental task of reading. Just as the athlete's warm-up makes him or her a more effective competitor, so your mental warm-up will make you a more effective reader and student. Here's what you do before you read.

Preview the chapter.

BEFORE YOU READ

Read the title, asking yourself specific questions about the title.

Read the introductory paragraph.

Read the last paragraph or summary.

Read the questions that follow.

(a) **Read the title, asking yourself specific questions about the title.** What does the article seem to be about? What do you already know about the topic? Based on the title and what you already know about the topic, what kind of predictions can you make about the article you are about to read?

(b) **Read the introductory paragraph.** The main idea of the article is often found in the introductory paragraph.

(c) **Read the last paragraph or summary.** The concluding paragraph often reiterates the main points and the conclusions.

(d) **Read the questions that follow.**

WHILE YOU READ

WHILE YOU READ

Make sure your study environment is conducive to studying.

Take an active part in the reading process.

Mark significant ideas and details.

Ask questions as you read.

Have you ever finished reading an assigned chapter in a textbook and found that at the end of the chapter you had not understood one word of what was written? Or have you ever found yourself in the middle of an assigned chapter and realized that although you have been "reading" the text, in fact, you have been thinking about your part-time job or your date for Saturday night or any other of a hundred things more interesting to you at that particular moment than the textbook?

Most of us have been in these situations. Sometimes what we are reading has too many unfamiliar words for us to make much sense of the content without spending half our time looking up meanings in the dictionary. At other times, we are not really concentrating on our reading and we let ourselves be distracted. The problem, however, is that the reading must be completed and understood and hence, we must reread the chapter. Inefficient reading wastes valuable time.

In order to make the time you spend reading your *Humanities* text (or any college text) as effective as possible you must learn to concentrate on your reading and to become actively involved in it. Here are some suggestions on how to do just that.

Make sure your study environment is conducive to studying. Despite what many students claim, it is impossible to read effectively in a noisy environment. This means you turn off the stereo and the television while you are reading.

Take an active part in the reading process. This means developing strategies to help you make sure you understand what you are reading and to help you concentrate on the material at hand. For example, you could do the following.

> **(a) Mark significant ideas and details.** The important word here is *significant*. Don't mark everything you read! After all, the purpose of marking is to set off important points so that you can come back to them later when you are studying. Marking most of the text won't be much help to you if you want to scan the text quickly for the salient points before a quiz. How do you know what to mark? Well, the following list should give you some idea of what to underline or highlight when you are reading:

> > **i.** *Main ideas in paragraphs.*

> > **ii.** *Vocabulary words* that are unfamiliar to you so that you can look them up later.

> > **iii.** *Definitions and examples.*

iv. *Signal words*—words that signal the direction of the writer's thought. Such words are commonly used by writers to indicate emphasis, illustration, cause and effect, comparison and contrast, sequencing and conclusions.

Here are a few examples of **signal words**. (Your Communications instructor may refer to these words as *transition words* and give you a more complete list.)

Words which signal **EMPHASIS**
>   the main value
>   should be noted
>   the primary concern

Words which signal **ILLUSTRATION**
>   for example
>   for instance
>   to illustrate

Words which signal **CAUSE AND EFFECT**
>   therefore
>   as a result
>   thus

Words which signal **COMPARISON**
>   in the same way
>   like
>   similarly

Words which signal **CONTRAST**
>   however
>   in contrast
>   on the other hand

Words which signal **SEQUENCING**
>   first of all
>   next
>   then

Words which signal **CONCLUSIONS**
>   finally
>   in conclusion
>   last of all

(b) Ask questions as you read. Since reading is an act of communication, in order to ensure that you understand everything the writer is trying to tell you, approach the assigned article with specific questions in mind. For example, you could ask yourself the following questions as you read

AFTER YOU READ
Recite to yourself the important points in the article immediately after you have finished reading it.

   i. What is the main purpose of the article? (to inform, to instruct, to analyze, to criticize, to entertain?)

   ii. What is the main idea of each paragraph, section, or complete article?

   iii. What specific details (examples, statistics, facts) does the author use to develop his main ideas?

   iv. What conclusions can I draw from this article?

AFTER YOU READ

In order to ensure that you have fully comprehended your assigned article, it is imperative that you recite to yourself the important points in the article immediately after you have finished reading it. A written paraphrase of a short article or a summary of a lengthy article are good indicators of how well you have understood the assigned reading.

* * *

We think you will find the selections in the *Humanities* text interesting as well as informative. The preceding strategies will be especially helpful if you come across an article that you find a little more challenging than the others, but the basic premise that you should read your college texts actively applies to all the selections. And remember, if there is something in the text that you don't understand even after applying the strategies, ask your instructor for help. After all, that's what he or she is there for.

Writing a Summary

Linda Smithies

sum·ma·ry *n* : a condensed statement—
adj brief; concise

Summarizing is something we do all the time without really being aware of it. After watching a good movie or television show, a friend may ask, "What was it about?" Generally we answer with details about the plot, the main characters, the special effects, and so on. But most of us will probably embellish these objective details with our own subjective impressions, too—which actor or actress we thought was the most convincing, which special effects were the most spectacular, which part of the plot didn't make sense, and so on. These embellishments certainly add spice to our conversation, but they probably reveal as much about us, particularly our thoughts and feelings, as they do about the movie or show.

However, when you are asked to summarize, either in writing or orally, an article in this book or one of the *Humanities* lectures, you should make sure you don't include these thoughts and impressions. These will become important later when it comes time to evaluate what you have read or heard, but you can't evaluate until you know the content well, so doing a summary is the best way to get started.

What you must do, though, is identify the main points of the article or lecture. But, sometimes finding the main points can be a daunting task, especially when they are mixed in with lots of minor points, such as examples, case studies, colourful language, repetition, and comparisons. In fact, most good writers or lecturers strive to use lots of these minor points to make the main points more interesting and less abstract or theoretical. So your job of separating the main points from the minor ones can be a difficult one.

To help you accomplish this task, ask yourself a few questions when reading an article or listening to a lecture:

1. What is the specific *topic* or *issue* under discussion? Just like the rest of us in our everyday conversations, writers and lecturers often get side-tracked and may ramble on about

concepts that are very interesting, but not really on the main point. By constantly reminding yourself about the topic or issue under discussion, you will be better able to separate the "relevant" from the "ramble."

2. What is the *main purpose* of the article or lecture? Is the writer or lecturer trying to persuade us to see the issue or topic from his or her point of view? Give us the historical background? Provide us with detailed statistical or factual information to increase our knowledge about the topic or issue? Often, writers and lecturers will address all these questions, but generally there is one all-important purpose which has guided their selection of material to talk or write about. Since knowing this all-important purpose helps you to select the main points, listen carefully to a lecturer's opening comments and read carefully the introductions to the articles—these are the places where you will find "statements of purpose."

3. What *clues* has the lecturer or writer provided to help you separate the main points from the not-so-important points. Phrases like "First of all...," "We must consider as well...," "Furthermore...," "What is also important..." tell us the writer or lecturer is moving from one main point to another. In contrast, phrases like "For example..." and "Take the case of..." tell us that we are now going to read or hear an embellishment of the main point, not the main point itself.

4. Finally, once you feel you have found all the main points, *review your notes*. Fill in any gaps you may have missed the first time through, eliminate any repetition or irrelevant information, and make sure you know the definitions of all the words and concepts. Once you know the content and can summarize it effectively, you are ready for the next stage—evaluation.

Comparison and Contrast

Clive Cockerton

This course, like many other courses, will frequently ask you to compare and contrast two or more thinkers, issues and situations. When you are asked to compare and contrast, you are being asked to do more than just *describe* two things. You are being asked to do the work of finding the most significant points of similarity and difference. It is a complex task involving both analysis in detail (breaking up whatever is being compared into smaller parts) and synthesis (bringing the parts together in the new light shed by your comparison).

Many people, when asked to compare, for example, Freud and Skinner, would launch into an essay that would list everything about Freud followed by everything about Skinner and would look something like this:

Introductory Paragraph:
Topic Identified

Part A: Freud

Part B: Skinner

While this essay format can *describe* the ideas of the two men in a very sophisticated way, it doesn't really bring them together and compare them on the basis of some element (their attitude to the question of free will, for instance). A much better format would look like the diagram below.

INTRODUCTORY PARAGRAPH:
Identify topic. Name elements of comparison: fundamental views of human nature, therapeutic strategies, free will.

PART A: Fundamental Views of Human Nature

PART B: Therapeutic Strategies

PART C: Free Will

PART D: Conclusion

Theories of Human Personality

ELEMENTS	FREUD	SKINNER	MY CONCLUSION
View of human nature	We are largely unconscious of the interplay of powerful urges (eros and thanatos). Psyche divided into three areas: id, ego, superego.	We are extremely flexible beings whose behaviours are controlled and shaped by the environment and the effect of rewards and punishments.	
Therapeutic strategies	Talking with analyst. Attempts to make patients conscious of the forces that motivate them.	Behaviour modification. Change the behaviour by changing the consequences.	
Free will	No free will	No free will	

It should be clear from this format that the elements (the fundamental views of human nature, therapeutic strategies, and free will) are the main organizing elements of your comparison and must be carefully chosen to make an effective comparison.

Of course, we use this comparison technique outside of school all the time, whenever we need to make a choice, whether it be what car to buy or in which restaurant to have dinner. In both cases, we look for the most significant elements. In the instance of the car, the first step is to analyze the decision into its elements—such as cost, technological innovation, space, comfort, and safety. There may be many more elements but usually there are only one or two dominant ones such as cost and safety upon which we naturally concentrate most of our time. Similarly, the example of restaurants yields a number of factors such as cost, quality of food, decor and service. Again, there are priorities. Although decor and service may form a minor part of our decision, most often the choice will be made based on value and quality. When comparing thinkers and their ideas we analyze or break down the subject into elements as well. This is a critical phase and many writers like to use a grid, such as that above, so that they can chart their comparison in a more graphic way. As well you may wish to include space for your conclusion or decision on the relative merits of the competing theories.

As in the case of cars and restaurants, you may quickly decide that one or two elements are dominant with the others playing supporting but minor roles. You may wish to group all the minor elements into one paragraph, and plan to spend at least one paragraph on each of the major elements. It is useful to think about the rhetorical structures that can be helpful in comparison. Such structures might include:

1. *While* Freud emphasizes X, Skinner, *on the other hand,* suggests Y.

2. *Although* Freud and Skinner disagree about A, there seems to be some common ground on the subject of B.

In many cases, your consideration of the elements will lead you to decide that a particular thinker has an advantage in his explanation of the various elements, and you may wish to provide the reader with a sense of where you stand on the issue and which thinker you support.

When you have read the first selection in Unit Three, you might like to try filling out the following grid on the views of human nature of Hobbes, Locke, Marx, and Mill. Be sure to come to your own conclusion on each element. Ask yourself if there are any important elements of comparison left out of this grid. After completing the grid, think about how you would turn the elements into paragraphs.

COMPARISON AND CONTRAST

When you are asked to compare and contrast, you are being asked to do more than just *describe* two things. You are being asked to do the work of finding the most significant points of similarity and difference.

Theories of Human Nature

THINKERS Elements	HOBBES	LOCKE	MARX	MILL
The nature of the individual				
Relationship of the individual to society				
The role of authority				
Importance of a fair contract				
Self-interest *vs.* altruism				

Evaluation

Wayson Choy

"What's my life worth?" "What do I mean when I say 'I want to be happy'?" "What can I do about changing my life?"

These are questions every intelligent person comes to ask. There are, of course, no easy answers. However, in the *Humanities* course, the same questions are raised in challenging ways—and you are asked to take on the adventure of coming to some possible conclusions. You are asked to *evaluate* the knowledge presented to you in your readings, in the lectures and in the give-and-take of the seminar classes.

You are asked to *evaluate* ideas, theories, concepts, and feelings—to begin to understand how to take information and discover the differences between opinion and knowledge. If you're fortunate, you may also discover the differences between knowledge and wisdom, feelings and insights.

For example, most people assume that "one opinion is as good as another." In fact, most opinions are not to be trusted, however sincere the opinion-maker may be.

Naturally, if our life does not depend on the opinion, we may simply ignore it or politely nod our head. But, if your life depended on the opinion, "It's hot outside!" — because your rare blood disease will kill you at any temperature over 30 degrees—you would probably need to evaluate that opinion. You would depend, not on the opinion, "It's hot outside!"—but more wisely on the statement, "The official Canada Weather Thermometer Report reads 25 degrees Celsius…"

People's lives have actually depended upon these opinions:

"The bottom line is that you can't fight City Hall!"

"Russia is the Evil Empire."

"Only homosexuals get AIDS. That's God's punishment."

"That grenade is not defective."

"John knows a scientist who says smoking is harmless."

"Tell you the truth, all you need is money to be happy."

"You can't do anything about poor single mothers."

"If you fail this test, you're just stupid."

"People should have the right to carry guns."

"Any one gets raped, they asked for it!"

"You just have to work hard to succeed in life."

"Foreigners shouldn't take work away from Canadians."

"Women should stay home; it's more natural."

"A man should always stand and fight!"

Imagine accepting all of these opinions as if they were true; as if, indeed, we need only hear them and nod our heads and live our lives accordingly. Many people do just that regardless of how disturbed they may be when they hear the words spoken.

The process of education begins with that feeling of being disturbed: Education of any personal worth is often a process of disturbance—first, disturbance; then, evaluation.

You will hear startling things, discover that your world may be more complex than you ever realized. You will test modern social and psychological theories, use new ideas and new language to begin to understand your own life. You will refer to authorities, artists, writers, facts and figures, make judgments, use logic in your debate, think in new ways, and—perhaps reluctantly at first—you may even throw out some ideas you thought were true. There will be fresh ways to test your most sacred ideas, and, if you work hard, you will learn how to communicate your new insights more clearly to others.

You will begin to *evaluate*. It is, finally, your own life that you will evaluate.

EXERCISE

Take any *one* of the opinions above that disturbs you, and explain why you think it is "only an opinion" and *not* knowledge. Begin by defining what you mean by "opinion" and "knowledge." Finally, discuss the steps which would help you logically challenge that particular opinion—and perhaps change the mind of those who believe the opinion to be true.

Tips on Writing an Essay Exam in *Humanities*

R. Chris Coleman

ere is an actual question taken from a previous essay exam in Humanities. The answer had to be a minimum of 250 words and was worth 70 points. Fifty percent (35 points) was given for content and 50% for how well the sentences communicated ideas. How would you go about answering this question?

QUESTION:
How does ONE of the five theories of personality explain human nature? For instance, why are we frequently in conflict with ourselves? How does our personality develop? Can we change our basic personality behaviour? Explain.

In answering an essay type question, it's important not to make the task any more difficult than it is already. Your instructor wants you to show *(a)* that you took notes during lectures, *(b)* that you read the assigned sections in the text, *(c)* that you understood and remember what was said, and *(d)* that you appreciate its relevance and significance.

Also, it is especially important to realize you are not expected to explore just your own thoughts, feelings and opinions. In the example above, for instance, it would be a mistake to write something like this:

In my opinion, our basic personality is already formed at birth as a result of our past-life experiences before we were born.

While some people may believe this theory, it is not one of the five theories of personality dealt with directly in the Humanities course material.

On an essay exam, you are expected to recall as much as you can of the course material. So, of course, it's a major advantage to know the material well before you write.

One of the challenges in writing an essay exam is that time is limited. Because of the lack of time to rewrite, planning and preparing become more important than usual.

One helpful tip is, *before you start actually composing your essay*, jot down in point form everything you can think of related to the question. Don't worry yet whether or not you will include every point in your final answer. Just make the list as long as you can. Having such a list helps you organize your material and keeps you on topic.

To illustrate, suppose in answering the question above that you chose to explain the psychoanalytic school of personality theory. Somewhere in your list of points you would include these points, though probably not in this order:

USEFUL TIP ~

Before you start actually composing your essay, jot down in point form everything you can think of related to the question.

SIGMUND FREUD (turn of century)
3 Aspects Of Personality:
1) **ID** = unconscious
        - *eros* = instinct for life
        - *thanatos* = death wish
        - child-like

2) **EGO** = awareness of self
        - thinks, deals with, reacts
        - mediates between id & superego
        - adult

3) **SUPEREGO** = conscience, shoulds
        - *socialization* = internalize values
        - parental
(etc.)

Of course, to be complete for the above question, your actual list would be much longer.

Your list might even include a quotation or two that you've memorized during study for the exam. Including memorized passages in an essay-type answer is fine, providing you fully understand what they mean and can explain them in your own words. Here's a quotation that would be useful in formulating a line of argument for the answer to the above question:

"Human personality emerges ... by the interactive functions between *ego*, *superego*, and *id*." (*Humanities*, p.8-9).

Once your list is more or less complete, you are ready to *organize* the material. Usually the question itself not only will tell you what your instructor expects, but also will hint at how you should arrange the material.

Generally speaking, key words in the question like "**DEFINE, SUMMA-RIZE, COMPARE, CONTRAST, EVALUATE**" are cues as to how your instructor expects you to organize your answer. The introductory sections in your Humanities text show you how to organize material for each of these types of answers. In the example we're working on, there are two key words, very closely related: "*explain* and *how*". You must explain how human personality emerges and develops, according to Freudian psychoanalytic theory.

Any essay is basically an *argument*. First you make a definite statement, called a **THESIS STATEMENT**. Then you *support* or back up your thesis statement using specific points taken directly from the course material. Try to show, prove or demonstrate that there is sufficient evidence to support your thesis statement.

For many questions on *Humanities* exams, there is no single, absolutely right answer—just those answers that are adequately supported with specific points, and those answers which, unfortunately, are not. Therefore, it is advisable to use as much material from the text and lectures as you can.

In organizing your answer, you might find it helpful to construct an outline. Some people actually jot their outline down on paper. Others, to save time, merely keep their outline in their heads. It doesn't really matter, as long as you proceed according to some definite plan or strategy.

Don't make the mistake of just starting to write hoping something positive will magically happen.

For the question above, your outline might look something like this:

1. Thesis statement; Define 3 parts of personality:
   id, ego, superego.
2. Explain how they interact with each other.
3. Why we are frequently in conflict with ourselves.
4. How our personality develops.
5. How we can change.

Notice how similar the outline is to the question itself? It should be. Otherwise you may not be covering everything the question is asking for.

The average sentence in college level writing is about 15–20 words. Therefore, if you plan to write a short paragraph for each of the 5 points on your outline, with each paragraph containing 3–5 sentences, you should have no trouble meeting the requirement of a minimum of 250 words: (5 paragraphs) X (4 sentences) X (15 words) = 300 words. Of course, this is a very rough guide.

With your list of points and your outline complete, you are ready to start composing your answer. One difference between an essay exam

USEFUL TIP ~

Usually the question itself not only will tell you what your instructor expects, but will also hint at how you should arrange the material.

and a regular essay is that you already know that your audience is your own instructor. So imagine your instructor sitting directly opposite you, and proceed to talk to that person on paper the way you would if you were face to face.

Do not try to impress your instructor by using "big" words. On the other hand, you should avoid street language as well. Use precise vocabulary. *Write to express what you mean, clearly.*

Another difference between an essay exam and a normal essay is that you are not expected to write a striking introduction, or a thoughtful conclusion. Simply start with your thesis statement. Very often the wording of your thesis statement will be quite similar to the question itself. For example, using the quotation you memorized, you might write something like this as a thesis statement:

> Sigmund Freud, who originated psychoanalytic theory at the turn of the century, suggested that "human personality emerges by the interactive functions between ego, superego, and id." (26 words)

The next step is to define terms. Compose sentences incorporating the points you jotted down on your list of points. *Try to be concise by combining as many specific points as you can into each sentence you write without being verbose.* It would be ridiculous to write something like this:

> In my opinion at this point in time it seems like what Freud was saying was that the id is the same as what we in this day and age in our society call the unconscious. *(36 words)*

Although this sentence is 36 words long, it would get only one or two marks for content. In fact, it might even lose a mark or two because it communicates the ideas so poorly. Think about it this way. If somebody were to write just seven such sentences, although they would be well over the 250-word minimum, their mark for content would be only 14 out of 35, or 40%.

A much better sentence might look something like this:

> The id or unconscious, the most important aspect of personality, contains eros and thanatos, two instincts that govern all behaviour. *(20 words)*

This sentence is only twenty words long, yet it contains about seven valid points.

> The id or unconscious *(point)* the most important *(point)* aspect of personality *(point)* contains eros *(point)* and thanatos *(point)*, two instincts *(point)* that govern all behaviour *(point)*.

Now, if you could write 20 sentences, with each sentence containing only two valid points, you would have 40 points, well over the 35 points

USEFUL TIP ~

Don't make the mistake of just starting to write hoping something positive will magically happen.

USEFUL TIP ~

Compose sentences incorporating the points you jotted down on your list of points. Try to be concise by combining as many specific points as you can into each sentence you write without being verbose.

USEFUL TIP ~

Try to give yourself
enough time at the
end of the exam to
read your answer over
a couple of times.
Read first for your
ideas. Then read to
correct grammar,
spelling and
punctuation.

offered for content for this question. Of course, not all instructors will mark answers exactly this way, but this can be a useful guide for constructing your answers.

The next sentence in your answer might define eros and thanatos:

Eros is our drive for life, sex and pleasure, while thanatos is for death, aggression, hostility and destruction. (18 words)

Notice that there are more points included in this sentence than appeared on the original list of points. Obviously, it's a good idea to incorporate more points if they occur to you as you're writing.

Following these three sentences might come a sentence defining ego, then another defining superego. Then you would have a five sentence paragraph defining the parts of personality according to psychoanalytic theory.

In the next paragraph, you might discuss how these parts interact with each other and what happens if one part gets repressed or has too much expression. This paragraph would naturally lead into a third paragraph that explains why we are frequently in conflict with ourselves. And so on.

As you go, you might want to give examples from your personal experience to illustrate your points. This is often a good idea, providing you have enough room to include all the course material as well, and providing your illustrations are very brief and concise:

For example, when I want a donut, my id says, "Go for it!"; my superego says, "Don't. You're on a diet!"; and my adult ego says, "Let's have carrot sticks instead."

Often you can be more persuasive if you consider opposing views. Anticipate what someone might say, or already has said, to argue against you. Then show why you think your argument is more logical, consistent, justified or valid. In answering the question above, it might be useful to mention the other three theories of personality. In no more than a sentence for each, you might indicate how each differs from the theory you have chosen to explain more fully.

Some final tips. Although you will be trying to write fast, be careful not to write so quickly that your writing becomes illegible.

Also, try to give yourself enough time at the end of the exam to read your answer over a couple of times. Read first for your ideas. Then read to correct grammar, spelling and punctuation.

Good luck.

Acknowledgements

Photography and Illustrations

cover, ii : Musée de Marmottan, Paris, France.

x, 28, 33, 46, 51, 58, 60, 69, 100, 103, 105, 114, 125, 169, 200, 207, 230, 279, 284 : Dick Hemingway.

2, 160, 178 : Gary Gellert.

5, 12, 19, 140, 163 : *The Cartoon Connection* by William Hewison, Elm Tree Books/Hamish Hamilton Ltd.

7, 10, 13, 35, 135, 193 : The Bettmann Archive.

21 : Radio Times Hulton Picture Library, London.

24 : U.S. Congress Office of Technology Assessment, "Mapping Our Genes—The Genome Project: How Big, How Fast?" (Washington, D.C.: US Government Printing Office, April 1988).

40, 74 : Ontario Women's Directorate, Toronto, Ontario.

42 : Canadian Labour Congress.

71, 195, 219 : Universal Press Syndicate, Kansas City, Missouri.

79, 80, 96 : Statistics Canada, Ottawa.

128 : Prints and photographs Collection, Moorland-Spingarn Research Centre, Howard University, Washington, D.C.

130, 145, 149 : Time/Life

153 : Charles Moore, *Black Star*.

171, 221 : Canada Wide Feature Service Ltd.

176–77 : *Colors Magazine* (No. 4, Spring-Summer, 1993, pp. 52-55).

180 : Royal Library, Windsor Castle.

190 : National Portrait Library, London.

214 : Scott Willis, *San Jose Mercury News*.

213 : *Brick: A Literary Journal*, Number 45, Winter 1993.

225 : Canapress Photo Services.

228 : Caspar D. Fiedrich, *On a Sailing Ship*, c 1818–19, oil on canvas, Hermitage Museum.

233 : British Museum, London.

234 : Georges Seurat (1859-91, France), *Sunday Afternoon on Island of La Grande Jatte, 1883-84*, oil on canvas.

237 : Edvard Munch (1863-1944, Norway), *The Scream, 1885*, lithograph. National Museum, Oslo, Norway.

243 : Thomas Dannenberg, Toronto.

251 : Paul Strand (1890–1976), *Young Boy, 1951*. Paul Strand Archive, Millerton, NY. Reproduced by permission.

257 : Jean Marc Desrochers, reprinted with permission of PEN Canada.

268 : Vincent Van Gogh (1853-90, Netherlands), *Self Portrait, 1886-87*.

273 : Edward Hopper (1882-1967, USA), *Nighthawks, 1942*, oil/canvas. ©Art Institute of Chicago.

Text

24: *Mapping the Code: The Human Genome Project and the Choices of Modern Science* by Joel Davis, © Joel Davis; reprinted by permission of John Wiley & Sons, Inc., 1990.

25: "Behavioral Genetics: A Lack of Progress Report," *Scientific American*, June 1993.

55: "Family Values—The Bargain Breaks," *The Economist*, December 26, 1993.

68: "Do Men Speak Another Langauge," by Penney Kome, *Homemaker's Magazine*, October 1985. Reprinted with permission of Penney Kome.

75: "Notes of a Black Canadian" by Adrienne Shadd. Reprinted with permission of Adrienne Shadd from *Seeing Ourselves* by Carl James, Sheridan College, 1989.

82–90: "Multiculturalism—The Cultural Mix [excerpts]. Reprinted with permission from Carl James, *Seeing Ourselves*, Sheridan College, 1989.

95: "Human Rights: Employment Application Forms and Interviews," Ontario Human Rights Commission.

97: "Sex, Statistics and Wages," Reprinted with permission of the *Globe & Mail*, January 21, 1993.

98: "Are Women's Salaries Behind Men's?," Reprinted from the *Globe & Mail*, with permission from Nancy Riche.

118: "Know Your Rights," Ontario Human Rights Commission.

158: "The Unknown Citizen," from *Collected Shorter Poems by W.H. Auden*, edited by Edward Mendelson; copyright 1940, renewed 1968, by W.H. Auden; reprinted by permission of Random House, Inc.

216: "Towards a Green Future," reprinted with permission from *Brick: A Literary Journal*, Number 45, Winter 1993.

250: Excerpt from "On Photography" by Susan Sontag; copyright © 1973, 1974, 1977 by Susan Sontag; reprinted by permission of Farrar, Straus and Giroux, Inc.

259: "Appetizer," by Robert H. Abel; reprinted from *Ghost Traps* with permission of the University of Georgia Press.

PRINTED IN CANADA